SHELLAC
~AND~
SWING!

SHELLAC
~AND~
SWING!

~

A SOCIAL HISTORY OF
THE GRAMOPHONE
IN BRITAIN

~

BRUCE LINDSAY

FONTHILL

To Julie, Sam and Alex,
for sticking with me as I delved into the often-esoteric world of
the gramophone. To Emile Berliner, for starting it all.

Fonthill Media Language Policy

Fonthill Media publishes in the international English language market. One language edition
is published worldwide. As there are minor differences in spelling and presentation, especially
with regard to American English and British English, a policy is necessary to define which form
of English to use. The Fonthill Policy is to use the form of English native to the author. Bruce
Lindsay was born and educated in Great Britain; therefore, British English has been adopted in
this publication.

Fonthill Media Limited
Fonthill Media LLC
www.fonthillmedia.com
office@fonthillmedia.com

First published in the United Kingdom and the United States of America 2020

British Library Cataloguing in Publication Data:
A catalogue record for this book is available from the British Library

Copyright © Bruce Lindsay 2020

ISBN 978-1-78155-760-0

Typeset in 10pt on 13pt Sabon
Printed and bound in England

Acknowledgements

I contacted many people while writing this book and almost without exception they responded with help, support or advice. I have tried as much as possible to take on board the sage advice I was given and I have incorporated numerous insights gained from interviews into the text.

Dave Guttridge (a.k.a. DJ78) and Professor Steve Baker deserve particular thanks for being with me from the start, freely giving me their thoughts and insights, usually in some of Norwich's finest coffee houses. A big 'Thank You' goes to Mike and Liz Delf, first-generation rock 'n' roll fans, for their stories and their Dansette. I would also like to thank the following people, whose contributions helped me to make sense of what turned out to be a far more complicated story than I first imagined: Paul Buck, Greg Butler, Garth Cartwright, Catherine Clarke, Michael Cumella, Tony Cleary, Phil Dravec-Delf, Lewis Durham, Jenny Hammerton (of the Shellac Sisters), Francesco Martinelli, Courtney Pine CBE, Christopher Proudfoot, Karla Richards (a.k.a. Karla Chameleon), Joel Schlemowitz, Peter Wilson (a.k.a. Duke Special), Lucy Wright PhD. My thanks also go to the staff at the Accademia Nazionale del Jazz, Siena; Kate O'Brien and colleagues at the BBC Written Archive; Future Radio; the staff of the History of Advertising Trust; Graeme Clarke and colleagues at Erddig, Bethan Partridge and colleagues at Felbrigg Hall and Helen Taylor, House Steward at Polesden Lacey (all properties in the care of the National Trust); Gemma Layton and Daniel Brine at the Norfolk and Norwich Festival; the staff of the Norfolk Record Office; Radio Norfolk; the volunteers at the RAF Oulton Museum at Blickling; and Jay Slater and the team at Fonthill Media.

As always, if there are any mistakes or inaccuracies to be found in the text, the fault lies with me alone, however much I wish that this was not the case.

CONTENTS

Introduction

At some time in the middle of 1963, using money from a now-forgotten source, I bought my first record: it was a 45-rpm, 7-inch, vinyl disc featuring Elvis Presley performing 'Devil in Disguise' (on the RCA label). Mum and Dad were not interested in Mr Presley's style of popular music, but they let me play my new disc on the family radiogram. This great big brute of an object—a shiny, dark wood lump of furniture—sat in the front room, facing the window that looked out onto the glories of Bath Street.

The front room was special. It spent most of its time empty of life, reserved for receiving guests at weekends. Even on those occasions, the radiogram went unused, so it might remain mute for months on end; the wireless Dad made provided music in the kitchen, and the little black-and-white TV brought entertainment to the living room. The radiogram was big, but it was not treasured; it cannot have been because Mum and Dad allowed me to play it unsupervised. As long as I touched nothing else (the room held a few trinkets and gewgaws, a clock, antimacassars on the sofa and armchairs), I could operate the record player and listen to Elvis for as long as I wanted. This was how it began.

As the months and years passed and we left the Bath Street terrace behind, Elvis was joined by the Beatles, the Hollies, and Pink Floyd. By the time I left home a decade later, singles had given way to LPs, and the LP had taken second place to the white-hot technology of the tape cassette. The format did not really matter. Music was the important thing, and it still is.

Shellac and Swing! is not the story of vinyl, singles, albums, or—Heaven forbid—cassettes. It is the story of the records that came before and the machines that played them: the 78-rpm discs and the gramophone. In particular, it is the story of how these relatively humble objects became part of British society, influencing and being influenced by it, in turn, for over half a century. My first memory of these venerable old records is a destructive one. Scrambling through the attic of our house, I clambered over piles of dust-covered shellac and heard (and felt) the discs crack under the pressure of my skinny knees. Who knows how many of these discs I managed to destroy? I certainly cannot remember and I never told my parents, so they never got the chance to count them. I feel a bit guilty about such wanton vandalism these days. *Shellac and Swing!* is my attempt to make amends, a celebration of the ways in which gramophones and 78s changed life in Britain forever.

PROLOGUE

Monsieur Scott has a Great Idea

Édouard-Léon Scott de Martinville decided to record the human voice. With commendable restraint, Scott described his decision calmly, objectively, and without hyperbole; the thought had occurred to him 'of fixing on a sensitive stratum the trace of the motion of the air during song or speech.'[1]

Scott was in his mid-thirties, based in Paris, and aware of the many new discoveries and inventions that science was bringing to the world. Photography could fix forever a pictorial image of a moment in time, so why could the same not be done for sound? In the next few years, Scott developed a machine for recording sound, named it the phonautograph, and used it to make a series of permanent records, which he called phonautograms. On 27 January 1857, confident in his achievement, he presented the *Académie des Sciences de l'Institut de France* with the details of his work.

On one of his earliest phonautograms, Scott recorded a guitar, and a few years later he captured the sound of a cornet; however, for the most part, he made recordings of human voices—the voice of a young girl, a deep voice, voices at a distance, voices holding a certain pitch, speaking voices, and singing voices all found their way onto one of his tracings before he felt confident enough to leave his sealed envelope with the Académie.[2] He achieved all of this with an instrument inspired by the anatomy of the human ear, using animal membranes as diaphragms and a boar's bristle as a stylus. He attached the 'sensitive stratum' to a cylinder, which he rotated by hand.

Thirty years later, when Emile Berliner announced his own machine for recording sound, he acknowledged the debt he owed to Scott and described the Frenchman's method: he covered a cylinder with paper, smoked it over a flame, and attached a stylus to the centre of a diaphragm, which, under the influence of words spoken into a large barrel-like mouthpiece, 'would trace sound vibrations upon the smoky surface.'[3] A wiggly line, traced on a piece of smoky paper, captured the human voice for eternity.

Once captured, what was to become of this sound? Scott was clear about his intention. After recording, the paper would be carefully removed from the cylinder and flattened out. Once this had been done, any interested party could look at, marvel at, and scientifically study the wiggly line. Sound would be studied visually, not aurally, by eye rather than by ear. It would be seen but not heard. Was this really such a great idea?

Posterity should give thanks to the scientists, engineers, businessmen, and artists who followed Scott. They took his phonautograph and, eventually, turned it into the gramophone. They took his phonautograms and turned them into gramophone records. They created a revolution in home entertainment, changing the way we listen to and understand sound. They enabled a previously ephemeral activity to be captured in the moment and preserved forever. They changed the way we furnished our homes, enjoyed ourselves on picnics, joined in with our favourite songs, and listened to politicians and cultural leaders. They gave entrepreneurs new ways to make their fortunes and to separate the rest of us from our money. They offered us new ways to express our patriotism and new ways to promote propaganda. They absolved us from the responsibility of listening to untalented family and friends at intimate soirees and allowed us instead to hear the greatest artists in the world in the comfort of our own homes. They offered new ways for the sporting gentleman to enjoy some of his more private pleasures and turned singers and instrumentalists into world-renowned and fabulously wealthy superstars.

After a few decades, the discoveries and inventions made by other scientists, inventors, and artists would advance Scott's great idea beyond its modest beginnings and impact the lives of millions of people across the world. Britain, at first resistant to the charms of recorded sound, would embrace the idea and become a world leader in the art and science of the gramophone record. From the ballrooms of stately homes to the cramped front rooms of artisans' cottages, from the furthest corners of the British Empire to the muddy trenches of the Western Front, from Antarctica to the English Channel, and from E. F. Benson's humour to the murderous plots of Agatha Christie, gramophones would become part and parcel of everyday life.

On the Record: 'Au Clair de la Lune', Anonymous (Scott phonautogram, 9 April 1860)

Scott de Martinville may never have intended his phonautograms to be heard, but he failed to recognise that the scientific curiosity that drove him to record them in the first place would eventually drive others to develop the technology that would render his recordings listenable.

In 2008, the First Sounds organisation began its attempts to recover the sound from one of Scott's black and smoky recordings.[4] Since then, it has successfully reproduced the sounds from a series of these phonautograms, including the popular French song familiar to British children for decades: 'Au Clair de la Lune'. Scott recorded 'Au Clair de la Lune' on a few occasions; this version from 9 April 1860 is, at the time of writing, the earliest recording from which the audio has been retrieved and enables us to hear a voice from 160 years ago.

The recording lasts barely twenty seconds, just enough time for the vocalist to begin the second line. The vocalist may well be Scott himself; even with modern technology, the voice is hard to hear and not obviously male or female. The words are unclear, but it is undeniably a human voice (though not one that appears to have much of a talent for singing). One line of a folk song, barely audible, sung with little enthusiasm and even less ability was an inauspicious start for the record industry, but it was a start, nonetheless.

The Old Familiar Voice

Édouard-Léon Scott de Martinville never wanted to be a music business mogul. His intention was always to create a visual representation of sound in order to enable the detailed scientific study of the human voice. He hoped for the day when 'the musical phrase, escaped from the singer's lips, will be written by itself ... on a docile paper and leave an imperishable trace of those fugitive melodies', but he showed no interest in profiting financially from turning those imperishable traces into a commercial product.[1] Instead, he carried on with his experiments with little publicity and barely any interest from the outside world. He left the development of a reliable recording and reproducing machine to other innovators.

The Slow Rise of the Talking Machines

The British scientific establishment first heard about the phonautograph at the 1859 meeting of the British Association.[2] Prince Albert, the Prince Consort, attended the meeting in Aberdeen while leading scientists and engineers presented papers on up-to-the-minute discoveries and developments, from the exciting to the eccentric. In the physiology section, Professor MacDonald gave a paper regarding a female greyhound which had never given birth yet was able to suckle a kitten. In the zoology and botany section, Reverend W. S. Symond gave a talk 'On different Pebbles found in the Stomach of a Cow'. *Abbé* Moigno was particularly busy; the fifty-five-year-old French Catholic priest gave papers on Newton's method of resolving equations and on a portable apparatus for analysing light, took part in the discussion of Sir David Brewster's paper on double refraction, and gave details of a process for preserving milk. He also presented a paper titled 'On the phonautograph, for registering simple and compound sounds.' The paper failed to cause a stir within Britain's scientific community and it would be almost twenty years before another recording device emerged. This time, it would reproduce as well as record sound, but even this advance would garner little enthusiasm among the British public.

Charles Cros, another French inventor, sent his own paper to the *Académie des Sciences* on 30 April 1877, detailing his method of recording and reproducing audible phenomena.[3] Cros's machine, the paleophone, would make a spiral tracing on a surface blackened by flame in response to sound and would then retrace the mark, reproducing the recorded sound. He explained his theory clearly but failed to produce a model of his intended device, never mind a working prototype; his paper stayed in its envelope until December, when it was read to the Académie's members at an open session.[4] The eight-month gap gave someone else the chance to grab the glory. Across the Atlantic, an entrepreneurial, partially deaf, thirty-one-year-old inventor produced a working model of his own creation.

At his base in Menlo Park, Thomas Alva Edison was working on improvements to the recently invented telephone when he began to think about a talking machine. By the early winter of 1877, Edison had produced a working prototype, which recorded sound onto tin foil wrapped around a cylinder. Edison spent some time considering names for his invention; acoustophone, liquphone, didaskophone, brontophone, bittako-phone, and many others made the list, but he decided on phonograph.[5] The audio revolution could have arrived, but it did not. Bored, frustrated, or lacking development funds, Edison soon moved on to a new project: the electric light.

In the early 1880s, Gardiner G. Hubbard, an early patron of the telephone, reinvigorated research into sound reproduction by the simple expedient of providing money for experiments.[6] Alexander Graham Bell, Chichester A. Bell (Alexander's cousin), and Charles Sumner Tainter set to work. Chichester Bell and Tainter soon designed their own machine, replacing foil with beeswax and changing the recording process from Edison's indenting method to an engraving method, which dug wax out of the cylinder to form a 'hill and dale' groove. Bell and Tainter received a US patent for their new machine, which they named the graphophone. Edison noted the upstart new invention and returned to the fray: perhaps there was money to be made from the phonograph after all.

Edison confidently predicted the phonograph's impact on modern life, giving numerous examples including the recording of court proceedings, audiobooks for blind or sick people 'or even … the lady or gentleman whose eyes and hands may be otherwise employed', educating children in spelling or elocution, letter-writing in the form of notes to be typed up by a third party, and recordings to be sent through the mail.[7] Edison suggested two more functions of equal, if contrasting, importance. The machine would record the voice of a dying family member, preserving their last words for posterity.

It would also act as an alarm clock that could tell the time, call its owner to lunch, and—in a rare show of rather naughty Edisonian humour—'send your lover home at ten,' a time- and potentially marriage-saving idea, if only your husband or wife could be guaranteed to stay out of the house until ten minutes past ten.

Edison predicted that music, too, would find a home on the phonograph cylinder, although his ambitions in this regard were rather limited. The phonograph could reproduce music with such power and clarity that 'a friend may in a morning-call sing us a song which shall delight an evening company'—charming but hardly the global industry that recorded music would become.

Architect and writer Philip G. Hubert enthusiastically supported the phonograph.[8] Mr Hubert had personally heard a phonograph recording of Dickens's *Nicholas Nickleby*; sound reproduction was so clear that fewer than one word in twenty was lost—a ringing endorsement of the instrument's quality. Operation required skill and technical understanding—the 'office boy or typewriter girl' could not be trusted with such a delicate instrument—but even so, Hubert predicted that wax cylinders would be reproduced in their thousands, that a novel could be recorded on a single cylinder and sold for a few cents and that operas from Vienna, plays from London, and Congressional debates would all be accessible on wax cylinder. Indeed, thought Hubert, books and stories need never be produced on paper; why not simply send them straight to wax? Newspapers, too, could be published on cylinders, with music critics able to include examples of the performance they critiqued. Hubert foresaw a brave new world of audio transmission, but he was already behind the times.

The Phonograph Arrives in Britain and an Argument Ensues

The people of Britain did not hold their collective breath in expectation of this brave new world. *The Times* first mentioned Edison's invention in a report on a lecture about the telephone from a Professor Barrett, who referred to Edison's 'talking phonograph' and proposed that an understanding of the waveforms of articulate speech would enable science to reproduce speech artificially; for him, a talking machine was an electronic device for the creation of human-like sounds rather than for the recording of actual human sounds, what might be called a synthesiser. *The Times* felt it necessary to explain how a 'talking phonograph' operated, given that readers would doubtless have no personal experience of the machine, but the following week, it devoted an entire article to Edison's invention, asserting that it would be a scientific marvel.

Soon after, the machine was the subject of the sort of argument beloved of correspondents to *The Times*, an argument about the derivation and correct spelling of 'phonograph'. 'Pedagogus', 'Nuper Etonensis', and Mr E. Walford MA joined in, debating whether the word should be 'phonegraph', expressing disgust at the 'barbarous termination—graph' and drawing on esoteric Greek philosophy to justify their propositions.[9] As with many debates in the letters pages of broadsheet newspapers, no one took any notice.

When the first phonographs arrived in Britain, people engaged with the instruments in different ways. Mr Garner of Brighton added a chapter on the phonograph to his book on constructing a telephone, 'by which failure is impossible.' At a London dinner party, Mr Preece of Her Majesty's Telegraph Department demonstrated a phonograph to guests, including the Duke of Argyll, Mr and Mrs William Gladstone, and Anthony Trollope. Public demonstrations were organised at the Crystal Palace by the authority of the London Stereoscopic and Photographic Company; one formed part of the Clematis Show in May 1878, alongside Goldings Ventriloquial Entertainment, Living Marionettes, seals in a newly arranged pond, and (presumably) clematises.[10] The sporting world followed suit when Mr Adrian's two-year-old colt, Phonograph, ran his first race at Newmarket. The horse came last.[11]

When Edison made improvements to the phonograph at the end of the 1880s, the British press was more enthusiastic. The new instrument was about the size of a sewing machine, used wax cylinders (cutting a groove that was described poetically as a 'delicate and ridgy trace'), and was notable for its exquisite workmanship.[12] George Gouraud (a retired US Army colonel, a veteran of the American Civil War, and holder of the Congressional Medal of Honor) acted as Edison's agent in Europe. Gouraud, whose father was French, envisaged a great future for the phonograph and enthusiastically promoted it. He travelled to England in 1887 with a strategy for gaining the attention of society by recording some of its leading figures.

Gouraud interviewed well-known men and women from European social, cultural, and political life, recording these interviews on cylinder. Over two decades, he succeeded in recording figures including actors Henry Irving and Sarah Bernhardt, the composer Sir Arthur Sullivan, William Gladstone, Florence Nightingale, and Otto von Bismarck.[13] Colonel Gouraud was an unashamed admirer of the phonograph and its inventor; when the Gouraud family moved to England, they took up residence in a house called 'Little Menlo'.[14] When he received the first of Edison's improved phonographs from the Menlo Park factory in New Jersey, he immediately wrote to *The Times*. The machine arrived with a selection of cylinders (which Gouraud called 'phonograms') containing music, poetry, and a message from Edison himself. Gouraud informed readers that he had dictated his letter onto a cylinder, from which a family member transcribed it.

Gouraud insisted that this machine was 'perfected' but was unwilling to offer a public demonstration. One journalist noted that sound was poor, heard clearly only when it was 'conducted into the ears of the listeners by tubes.' However, the writer was optimistic that a great future awaited the instrument; covert surveillance was high on the list of potential uses, for if a phonograph could be hidden successfully then it would be 'a terror to evil doers, and a source of joy to novelists as an entirely new source of startling disclosures and of unexpected *dénouments*.'[15]

A fresh delivery of a phonograph and cylinders gave Gouraud the confidence to go ahead, inviting selected guests to Little Menlo for his demonstration.[16] The new phonograph was the first to be fitted with an amplifying horn, removing the need for listeners to use hearing tubes, and it would reproduce sound with 'marvellous fidelity'. Mrs Alice Shaw, an American performer known as *La Belle Siffleuse* (a more romantic title than its English equivalent, 'the beautiful whistler'), was prevailed upon to whistle into the machine. Played back, her whistling was reproduced with impressive accuracy and proved to be far louder than the music and song on the pre-recorded cylinders. At the British Association meeting a month later, demonstrations of the phonograph and the graphophone proved to be the hit of the weekend with crowds 'besieging' the room to judge the merits of each machine.[17] Colonel Gouraud carried on spreading the word through demonstrations and lectures, including a Boxing Day demonstration at Olympia, featuring *La Belle Siffleuse*.[18] Meanwhile, the London Stereoscopic and Photographic Company, holders of Edison's original British patent, began advertising phonographs for sale and offered home demonstrations for the exorbitant fee of 3 guineas.[19]

Of course, talking machines were not replacing silence. Nineteenth-century Britain was filled with the sounds of factories and mills, of traders crying out their wares in the streets and markets, of children playing in the fields, and of birds singing in the skies. There was plenty of entertainment on offer, too, from amateur musicians and singers at home to professional performers in the music halls and theatres, tirelessly singing, playing instruments, and telling jokes. Phonographs were slowly muscling in on this lively soundscape when the next great talking machine appeared, this time emerging from the inventive mind of a German émigré to the United States.

Berliner's Gramophone Appears

Emile Berliner was born in Hamburg in 1851. Originally named Emil, he added the final 'e' because he thought it looked better.[20] He moved to the USA in 1870, worked in a Washington dry goods store then moved to New York, taking on odd jobs and studying at the Cooper Institute. Berliner became intrigued by the telephone, which he saw demonstrated in Washington in 1876. Within a few years, he patented an improved transmitter, sold his patent to the Bell Telephone Company, and joined it as a research worker. He stayed with the company for a few years before going independent in 1884 to pursue his new interest in the talking machine.[21]

On 8 November 1887, Berliner was awarded a US patent for 'certain new and useful Improvements in Gramophones'—an odd phrase, suggesting that gramophones already existed. *The Electrical World* published the story of Berliner's new sound-reproducing equipment.[22] Illustrations showed a gramophone with a face mask—looking scarily like the mask used to administer anaesthetic—to be used for the recording process and, waiting to be fitted, a small horn to project the sound. Another illustration showed a section of a gramophone record; the flat disc, with its spiral groove moving from its outer edge to its centre, is instantly recognisable. A few days later, Edwin A. Houston spoke to the American Philosophical Society about Berliner's machine, offering a concise summary of those 'new and useful improvements'.[23] They were mainly in the recording process, said Houston. The gramophone recorded onto a flat glass disc, covered in printer's ink and soot from a coal oil lamp. The stylus made a groove in the sooty ink, which was parallel to the surface rather than at right angles to it. It was on such seemingly simple, even mundane, developments that a new industry would be forged.

Berliner made a detailed public announcement, with a practical demonstration, at the Franklin Institute in Philadelphia the following May. Berliner confessed that he had initially been unaware of Charles Cros's work, but Berliner was an honourable man and he wanted to give credit where it was due, declaring that Cros was the first to develop a means of reproducing recorded speech. His declaration was both admirable and expedient. Cros gained his rightful place in the invention of talking machines, Berliner avoided the possibility of legal action by the Frenchman and Edison's status as the inventor of sound recording was subtly questioned. Berliner intended his gramophone to be used for the production and sale of 'recitations, songs, and instrumental solos or orchestral pieces of every variety'. He predicted that every city would contain at least one recording machine and related equipment (including a piano) available to everyone who wanted to make a recording. A large funnel (or 'acousticon') would concentrate sound and send it to the recording stylus: 'Persons desirous of having their voice "taken" will step before the funnel, and, upon a given signal, sing or speak, or they may perform upon an instrument.'[24] After the session, the customer would leave with as many copies of the recording on discs as they wished.

Berliner foresaw a time when the best performers would make an excellent living from recordings. 'Prominent singers, speakers, or performers, may derive an income from royalties on the sale of their phonautograms,' he wrote, going on to predict that people would soon be collecting recordings and spending evenings listening to their favourite artists. Berliner did not envisage an entire future of entertainment; the voices of the dead would speak through the gramophone, just as Edison suggested they would speak through the phonograph. The voices of dead relatives and friends would join those of the great men and women, famous actors, and notable singers, their utterances captured for eternity. Berliner referred to 'tone pictures', which would condense a lifetime onto a few discs: 'five minutes of the child's prattle, five of the boy's exultations, five of the man's reflections, and five of the feeble utterances from the death-bed.' It would be, he claimed, like holding communion with immortality.[25]

Berliner demonstrated his new talking machine to the Franklin Institute by playing a selection of phonautograms. There were no recordings of great men, no croaky death rattles, and no recitations by leading poets. Berliner selected half a dozen popular songs: 'Home, Sweet Home', 'Tar's Farewell', 'A Wandering Minstrel I', 'Yankee Doodle', 'Baby Mine', and 'Nancy Lee'.[26]

News of Berliner's gramophone reached Britain a few weeks after the publication of the article in *The Electrical World*. The gramophone, said the 'Scientific and Industrial Notes' column of the *Manchester Times*, would offer strong competition to the phonograph. The *Leeds Mercury* placed the gramophone in the context of work by Scott, Cros, and Edison. The first mention of Berliner's machine in *The Times* was brief, noting only that Edison's phonograph was now improved by the graphophone and Berliner's 'grammophone [*sic*.]'. In the 'Scientific Notes' section of *The Graphic*, T. C. H. reported on the gramophone as a rival to the phonograph but warned that the gramophone's 'sound-record,' which T. C. H. noted as being made of a zinc plate, 'cannot very readily be sent away by post.'[27]

The Globe claims the notable achievement of being the first British publication to use the gramophone to insult a leading politician. On the same day that the *Leeds Mercury*'s article appeared, one of *The Globe*'s commentators bemoaned the 'want of originality' shown by those responsible for naming the talking machines: 'Surely a more imaginative and appropriate name for a talking-machine would be the "Gladstone".'[28]

The *Aberdeen Weekly Journal* was more enthusiastic and light-hearted, noting that while the gramophone would do everything that the phonograph could do, it would do so at a substantially lower price—just a couple of guineas compared to the phonograph's likely cost of at least 25 guineas. This was quite a prospect:

The gramophone will reproduce your voice, to be taken down later on in evidence against you; and, if you are musically inclined, 'Yankee Doodle,' as played by a band in the States some months ago, will be given on this side of the Atlantic, without any apparent symptoms of sea-sickness during transit.[29]

Parkins and Gotto, Court Stationers and purveyors of fine travelling bags, offered gramophones for sale in London at Christmas 1891. The Oxford Street store advertised the 'Gramophone or Talking Machine' as 'an apparatus for reproducing the human voice or other sounds as often as desired'. Although it was solid brass and cost 42 shillings, it was advertised as a toy—a seasonal gift for a child, albeit a child from a comfortably well-off family.[30] In Ireland, the gramophone created a sensation in Belfast's Bank Buildings, where it could be heard and purchased along with a selection of 'plates' of recitations, songs, instrumental solos, and orchestral pieces. It was 'the rage of the season as a Xmas present.'[31]

Parkins and Gotto took some of their advertising copy from a Berliner Gramophone Company leaflet.[32] A young girl, aged perhaps ten or twelve, is pictured on the cover. She sits at a table, operating the gramophone herself, though she is far from thrilled with the cutting-edge technology. She sits unsmiling, looking bored and perhaps even a little anxious. The gramophone horn points away from her as if the volume of sound will damage her ears should she get too close. The machine may be simple to operate, but it requires constant attention. She must rotate the turntable by hand, at a steady speed, if she is to hear any sound at all; stop for just a second and the pleasure ends. None of this looks like fun. If the illustration has a positive message, it is about ease of use. Here, the photograph seems to suggest, is a machine that even a child can control, a machine that can be easily accommodated in the smallest house or apartment. Beneath the photo was a brief explanation of what the machine did. 'The GRAMOPHONE is an apparatus for making permanent records of the human voice or other sounds, including music of all kinds and for reproducing the same at any time thereafter as often as desired.' The gramophone would reproduce the voice in its natural quality, projecting sounds at such a volume that they could be heard clearly even in a large room. Parents concerned about their offspring and the machine were reassured: 'As the reproducing machine has no gearing or other intricate mechanism, even children can operate it without risk of derangement'—a comforting statement, although it is not clear whether it was the child or the machine that might become deranged.

Bored, anxious, or deranged children could be dealt with, but hand-cranked turntables were a problem. A motor that drove the turntable without the need for constant attention was a vital improvement, but not one for which Berliner could take credit. In 1896, Berliner approached Eldridge Reeves Johnson, an engineer from New Jersey, to see if he could develop an efficient clockwork motor. Johnson's motor was soon fitted to Berliner's gramophones.[33] Previous motors proved unreliable or underpowered, but Johnson's enabled the turntable to revolve with a consistent speed and, just as importantly for commercial purposes, it meant that the listener could wind up the motor, set the turntable in motion, and relax as the disc played rather than having to provide constant motive power personally. Johnson's clockwork motor was the final stage in the development of a reliable, commercially viable instrument. The gramophone was now a machine to revolutionise home entertainment.

One innovative busker saw the potential of the gramophone even before the clockwork motor arrived. When Daniel Moore fell into rent arrears, his landlord took his gramophone in part-payment of his debt. Moore went to the Enfield Petty Sessions in an attempt to get his property back and had to explain to the puzzled magistrate that a gramophone was a type of talking machine. He needed it to help pay off his arrears, claiming that he could earn ten shillings with it on a Saturday night, probably by playing the machine on street corners or giving impromptu performances in Enfield's pubs. The magistrate was unmoved; Moore's gramophone remained with his landlord.[34]

The Beetles Make Records

At first glance, the gramophone disc is a rather simple object. Eighty years after it first appeared, the Welsh rock band, Man, would succinctly sum it up in the title of their second album: *2 Ozs of Plastic with a Hole in the Middle*.[35] At the time, the description was immediately recognisable to every music lover, not just to fans of Welsh psychedelic rock; however, for most of its existence, the disc was not 2 ounces in weight and it was not made of plastic. The hole in the middle does seem to have been around from the start, however.

Berliner made his first discs, available in 1890, to fit the products of German toy manufacturers Kämmer und Reinhardt: 3-inch discs for a talking doll and 5-inch discs for small, hand-cranked gramophones.[36] Berliner's first commercially available clockwork gramophone used 7-inch discs—a useful size but still limited in playing time. The first 10-inch discs arrived in 1901, followed a couple of years later by 12-inch discs. Seemingly random 'in-between' sizes—such as German company Odeon's 10.75-inch Orange Label discs—were also available, but the 10-inch and 12-inch discs became the industry standard for the next fifty years.

In his early experiments, Berliner made discs from metal or glass.[37] For commercial use, he tried celluloid and rubber-based compounds.[38] Eventually, he settled on the compound most usually associated with the gramophone record—shellac. This is a resin secreted by female lac beetles, native to India and other parts of Asia. It is produced in different colours depending on the species of tree in which the lac beetle lives, and it is still used as a wood-finishing product and in food production (it even has its own E-number—E904). Berliner's choice was a boon to the British Empire; India was the main exporter of the resin, and by the late 1930s, around half the shellac produced was being used for gramophone record production.[39] In fact, the beetle produced just one constituent of the material; around one-third of a so-called shellac disc is actually shellac, with most of the rest composed of pulverised rock or mineral filler, with some cotton fibres and a small amount of carbon black to give the disc its usual colour.[40] The precise mix of materials was a compromise to give the best combination of good-quality sound, long-term survival of the disc, weight, and consistency of reproduction.

The groove on Berliner's gramophone record starts at the outer edge of the disc and moves towards its centre. Therefore, the needle must do the same, beginning at the outer edge of the disc and being drawn by the groove towards the middle. This, too, would be the industry standard, although the Paris-based Pathé produced discs using the 'hill-and-dale' groove and started the groove in the centre of the disc, so that it progressed to the outer edge as the recording played. In France, this was initially a successful approach, but eventually, Pathé changed to lateral cut grooves that moved from the outside to the middle.[41]

By 1903, the gramophone record was established as a black disc, 10 or 12 inches in diameter, with a hole in its centre so that it could be fixed to the spindle on the player and a groove that drew the stylus from the outer edge to the centre. It lacked one final refinement; the groove was only cut on one side of the disc. It would take a year or two more before someone had the bright idea of recording sound onto both sides of the record.

The Gramophone Company—Britain's First Gramophone Company

In 1897, an East European nobleman sailed to England and landed at Whitby, taking care to stay out of the Yorkshire sun. His name was Count Dracula; his story, as written by Irish journalist Bram Stoker, was the first major work of literature from the British Isles to feature a talking machine. Two lead characters, Dr Seward and Lucy Westenra, owned phonographs and Dr Seward made regular use of his instrument to record his personal diary. Dr Seward's use of the phonograph marked him out as a modern man—a man of science—as opposed to the ancient Count Dracula. Mina Harker knows what a phonograph is, but until she spies Seward's machine on his table, she has never seen one; when the doctor lays his hands on the machine Mina becomes 'quite excited over it' and asks to hear it play something. Unfortunately, the serious-minded Seward uses it only to record his diary; there is no chance of a jaunty reel or a seductive ballad and the moment passes. In an act of anger, occasioned perhaps by frustration at not owning such a fine instrument himself, or by a Luddite objection to modern technology, Dracula destroys Seward's cylinders by casting them into a fire.[42]

Another migrant arrived in Britain in 1897, this time from the west. William Barry Owen was thirty-seven years old and experienced in the American talking machine industry, most notably as general manager of the National Gramophone Company. He aimed to establish the gramophone in Britain and to expand the business into Europe on Berliner's behalf. Trading at first from his base in the Hotel Cecil on the Strand, he planned to import gramophones bought from the National Gramophone Company, giving Berliner a royalty on each one he sold. Owen found a business partner in Edmund Trevor Lloyd Williams, a London lawyer. They formed the Gramophone Company as a partnership, with offices near the Strand at 31 Maiden Lane, then established it as a limited company in 1899. Despite their links with Berliner, Owen and Williams did not have an easy time, and barely a year after the Gramophone Company's formation, it took on a new name to reflect its expansion into a new field of business: Gramophone and Typewriter Ltd. The decision to expand into typewriter sales was perhaps an indication of panic or of a lack of faith in the future of the gramophone. The typewriter in question was the Lambert typewriter, which was not a success.[43] By the early 1900s, production had ceased in the US and the UK; the gramophone would prove to be the longer-lasting instrument, and in 1907, Owen's company abandoned the typewriter market and started trading as the Gramophone Company Ltd.[44]

When Owen arrived in the UK, the Edison-Bell Consolidated Phonograph Company Ltd, based in Charing Cross Road, was selling a variety of cylinder recordings from many entertaining (and not-so-entertaining) genres at 2s 6d each.[45] The new Edison-Bell phonograph ('For commercial use and home amusement') cost £6 6s and was beginning to find a market. Edison-Bell offered recordings by marching bands and orchestras, solo recordings on numerous instruments (including the flute, 'clarionet,' banjo, and bagpipes), sentimental and comic songs, whistling solos, and recitations. There were selections by 'serious' composers such as Mozart and Richard Wagner, but for the most part the music was light opera, religious pieces, and popular tunes.[46] For the patriotic or the politically minded customer, there were cylinders featuring William Gladstone and, following Gladstone's death, tributes to the late Prime Minister from Lords Rosebery and Salisbury and A. J. Balfour. These worthy politicians were named in the catalogue, but the musicians, comics, and singers who appeared on the vast majority of the company's cylinders remained anonymous.

For a few years, as the Gramophone Company built its business, the cylinder trade continued to flourish. In May 1903, the first issue of *Talking*

Machine News appeared—its full title was *Talking Machine News and Record Exchange: A Monthly Journal devoted to the Interests of Users and Makers of Phonographs, Automatic Machines, and Scientific Inventions*. Although it acknowledged all types of talking machines, in its early years, the journal emphasised phonographs and cylinders, concentrating especially on the technological side of the business rather than on the artists and performers. The first issue revealed the eclectic tastes of King Edward VII; among the cylinders (rather than discs) taken by him on the royal yacht during a visit to Portugal were various light classical compositions, violin solos, the descriptive 'Departure of a Troop Ship', popular songs including 'Lily of Laguna', and five recordings of sketches featuring the popular Irish character of Casey.[47]

As patents expired, more and more firms entered the phonograph market and prices for instruments and recordings fell; instruments could cost as little as £1.[48] The Russell Hunting Record Company (originally the Sterling Record Company) arrived in 1904, becoming a major producer of cylinders for the British market; it may have sold 1 million cylinders in its first year.[49] Hunting was an American performer who would become known in Britain for the Casey series of comedy records as well as his recording and production. In 1896, Hunting had been charged with making obscene cylinder recordings—a trip across the Atlantic may have seemed like a smart move after his conviction.[50]

A combination of low prices and favourite tunes made cylinders popular with working-class customers, but they, in turn, were vulnerable to economic downturns. By 1908, a depression was hitting the luxury goods market hard. Both cylinder and disc markets were affected, but the cylinder trade was especially badly hit. Cylinders were more popular with working families, who were struggling against low wages and falling employment rates, so cylinder companies dropped their prices and profit margins fell as a result.[51] The Gramophone Company's persistence, technological developments, and marketing strategy slowly began to pay off. Discs played for longer than cylinders (around three minutes for discs, just two minutes for cylinders) and were easier to store. Both formats were fragile, but many people felt that discs sounded better. The phonograph's ability to record as well as reproduce may have enabled it to be commercially profitable as a business dictation machine, but the public never saw this facility as important. The Gramophone Company's disc catalogues soon outstripped cylinder catalogues in choice and artistic quality. In June 1908, the Gramophone Company opened its first British record pressing plant, at Hayes in Middlesex.[52] By the 1913–14 financial year, disc sales in Britain reached 3,867,406.[53]

The Columbia Graphophone Company would prove to be the Gramophone Company's chief competitor. Smaller companies also entered the market, selling discs and machines, often at lower prices than the larger firms. These lower prices appealed to poorer households which, in previous years, might have been seen as the ideal market for the cylinder business. Businesses still used phonographs as dictation machines, but for home entertainment phonographs were no longer the instruments of choice. Berliner's gramophone was triumphant.

Emile Berliner Bows Out

Emile Berliner stepped away from the gramophone business before the instrument's final victory could be claimed. His early work and commercial partnerships ensured that he lived the rest of his long life in financial security; when he died on 3 August 1929 at seventy-nine years of age, he left an estate worth $1,527,573. The bulk of his fortune went to his widow and four children but he left his house and $100,000 to the Bureau of Health Education.[54] He gave some indication of his attitude to life and money in a handwritten note regarding his funeral, which he wrote the year before his death:

> When I go I do not want an expensive funeral. Elaborate funerals are almost a criminal waste of money. The kind advertised for $125 plus extra autos is ample. I have always admired the plain pine coffins of old with a black cloth thrown over. A long bar handle on each side could be added. I should like Alice [his daughter] to play the first part of the Moonlight Sonata and at the close maybe Josephine [his daughter-in-law] will play Chopin's funeral march. Give some money to some poor mothers with babies and bury me about sunset … I am grateful for having lived in the United States and I say to my children and grandchildren that peace of mind is what they should strive for.[55]

Berliner's wishes were granted. He was buried in a simple ceremony at sunset, Alice and Josephine performed the requested pieces.[56] No gramophone records were played at his funeral.

On the Record: 'My Old Dutch', Albert Chevalier (Gramophone Company, 1899)

In the early days of the British gramophone industry, music hall stars made some of the most popular discs and were a mainstay of record company catalogues. Albert Chevalier was already a star when he made his initial recordings for the Gramophone Company as the first artist to sign a royalty-based contract with the firm. His full name was Albert Onésime Britannicus

Gwathveoyd Louis Chevalier.[57] He was born in London's Notting Hill in
1861, the son of a language teacher named Jean Onésime Chevalier, and
became known as the 'coster's laureate' because of his songs about working-
class cockneys, performed in his version of a cockney accent.[58]

'My Old Dutch' is Chevalier's most famous song (he wrote the lyrics, with
music by Charles Ingle, a pseudonym for his brother Auguste). 'Dutch' is
probably Cockney rhyming slang for wife (Duchess of Fife) or mate (Dutch
plate); on at least one version of the sheet music, the song is referred to as a
'Cockney Song'. It is a sentimental number, which Chevalier sings in character
as an elderly Londoner who is still in love with his 'pal' of many years.

The Gramophone Company's 1899 catalogue gave Chevalier's first
recordings the full marketing hype:

> Mr. Albert Chevalier has long been a favourite with the Public, and the
> popularity of such songs as 'My Old Dutch' and 'The Future Mrs. 'Awkins'
> will live long and ultimately be handed down to posterity. Our records
> of these and other selections will give posterity a chance of hearing them
> sung as the Composer intended, whereas without these records this Artist's
> rendering of them would be lost.[59]

The song gained some notable cover versions, including one by comedian Peter
Sellars. The tune is simple, the chorus has a singalong quality, and even 120
years after the song appeared on record, many people can sing one particular
line—'We've been together now for forty years and it don't seem a day too
much'—even if they might be hard-pressed to identify the song. Legend has it
that when the Beatles received their OBEs, the Queen asked them how long
they had been together, to which Ringo Starr and Paul McCartney replied by
singing 'We've been together now for forty years'. Posterity may not always
treat the music hall with respect, but 'My Old Dutch' does seem to have
stuck around.

From Bum Artists to William Gladstone

The Gramophone Company owed much of its eventual success to the company's extensive roster of artists. Although America supplied plenty of recordings, it was clear to William Barry Owen that patriotic British record buyers might spend even more money if artists from their homeland were represented on record. Britain needed its own recording industry. Frederick William Gaisberg, a young American protege of Emile Berliner, would be the man to create it.

How to Make Records

Fred Gaisberg worked with Emile Berliner in the United States, learning the art of sound recording and becoming a trusted recording engineer. In the early summer of 1898, Berliner decided to take additional action to support the Gramophone Company's presence in Britain and sent the twenty-five-year-old Gaisberg to London, to establish Britain's first recording studio. Gaisberg arrived in Liverpool in July 1898 and travelled south to meet his new boss, William Barry Owen.[1]

The young recording engineer set up his studio at the Gramophone Company's London premises and started recording on 8 August. His London recording sessions featured singers, comics, quartets, and solo instrumentalists from Britain and the USA.[2] He often found the experience frustrating—Gaisberg was at home in a recording studio, but for performers used to playing to an audience the process of recording was unfamiliar. Comic vocalist George Mozart arrived for his first session with a large trunk. When Gaisberg entered the studio to begin the session, he found Mozart in full costume and make-up, apparently unaware that the results of the day's work would be heard but not seen.[3]

Gaisberg soon embarked on recording trips across Britain, mainland Europe, and beyond. He was an enthusiast for sound recording and for the pleasures of good food, good booze, and conversation, but he was unimpressed by much of the 'talent' on offer in the British Isles and vented his frustration in his diary.[4] Scotland disappointed him. He declared that male singers in Glasgow 'would be run out of town in Italy.' He found few talented singers in Belfast and a recording session in the city produced 'more bum artists'. Dublin was no better; he thought the singers were conceited and untalented. Mainland Europe proved a more fruitful source of high-culture artists. In April 1899, Gaisberg was in Paris, recording opera singers and the actress Sarah Bernhardt. By mid-May, he was in Leipzig; by early June, he was in Budapest; and in mid-August, he was recording in Madrid. Return trips to the Continent were just as fruitful; in the spring of 1902 alone, he recorded Enrico Caruso, bass singer Pol Plançon, sopranos Emma Calvé and Suzanne Adams, and the baritones Anton van Rooy, Maurice Renaud, and Antonio Scotti. Caruso became the first major international recording artist. Gaisberg first heard Caruso in March 1902, in a leading role in *Germania* at La Scala in Milan.[5] The following month, Gaisberg recorded him at the Hotel Milan in the city; the resulting discs appeared on the Gramophone and Typewriter Company's Red Label later that year.[6] The Gramophone Company's roster of high-culture artists was unchallenged in the British market. According to Owen, the roster cost the company a lot of money but gave it a standing far above any of its competitors'.[7]

Gaisberg produced records that stayed on the Gramophone Company's lists for many years, a testament to his ability as an engineer. Mechanical recording was a difficult process to master. Standard orchestral instruments (such as the double bass and piano) proved difficult to record and loud instruments (such as trumpets) could easily overwhelm the softer sounds of clarinets or harps, making it hard, if not impossible, to record large ensembles with any clarity. Recordings were made directly onto a master disc with no way of editing out mistakes or mixing together the best bits of different takes. Records made during the mechanical era were 'one-take' recordings. Sound recording might have been a scientific endeavour, but there was an art to making good-quality discs.

In early recording studios, pianos stood on raised platforms so that they projected directly into the recording horn; the Gramophone Company acknowledged that 'One of our greatest difficulties up till the present time has been to get a satisfactory Piano record.'[8] Other musicians sat or stood uncomfortably close to each other in unusual combinations or were forced to spread throughout the room to ensure that their instruments could all be picked up by the equipment. It was a strange experience for musicians used to playing in clubs or concert halls. Despite these problems, large bands and orchestras did make records. Military and brass bands were popular; brass instruments recorded relatively easily, and the use of tubas or sousaphones as bass instruments was more successful acoustically than the use of double basses.

When the Gramophone Company signed the opera singer Dame Nellie Melba, it found an artist who was enthusiastic about and skilled at self-promotion. She would prove invaluable to the company's marketing strategy, even though she became one of the most expensive artists on its roster. Melba was happy to talk to the press, willing to lend her name to appropriately upmarket products, and keen to promote the company as long as she promoted her own career in the process. If Harold Begbie's description of one of Nellie Melba's recording sessions is to be believed, the studios she used were homely and domestic and recording sessions went without a hitch.[9] The room in which Begbie observed Melba's recording session was carpeted and decorated with palms and a table set with decanter and glasses. The amplifying horn (which he refers to as a trumpet) projected through a partition of wood and frosted glass 'as though somebody from the other side were pursing his lips for a shrill blast.' Next to the amplifying trumpet a piano sat 'dizzy, on a tall, rough, wooden stand.' There was no room for an orchestra; this intimate setting could cope with no more than three or four performers. For this session, the pianists Herman Bemberg (the composer of three of the seven songs to be recorded) and Landon Ronald took it in turns to accompany Melba and the violinist Jan Kubelik. Each recording began a second or two after an electric bell sounded from behind the frosted glass. The pianist climbed into a high seat in front of the piano, Melba and Kubelik stood side by side close to the amplifying horn, the singer's mouth just a few inches from the opening. Around three minutes later, the recording was complete and everything could be made ready for the next one. If there were any hitches, if Melba forgot her words or Kubelik fluffed a phrase, if more than one attempt was needed to produce a usable master disc, Begbie decided to keep mum.

W. H. Berry, a comedian and singer who recorded for Columbia, was happier to discuss the problems of recording. He found the process of recording comic songs especially challenging without the atmosphere created by a theatre audience and explained how the acoustic recording equipment required him to shout, rather than sing, 'in a voice more in keeping with a gentleman who sells coals, than a highly respectable and harmless humourist.'[10]

High Culture, Low Culture and Everything In-between: Content Creation

Music dominated the British gramophone industry from its beginning. The Gramophone Company's earliest catalogues featured music and song from around the world—sacred songs, hymns, opera, patriotic songs, classical compositions, popular tunes, and folk tunes sung by soloists, duos, and quartets in English, French, Welsh, Urdu, Hebrew, and Arabic. They were played on pianos, cellos, violins, banjos, trombones, and cornets by orchestras, bagpipers, and military bands. Comic songs and sketches also sold well. Music hall stars such as Gus Elen, Dan Leno, and Harry Randall joined artists from the USA to provide the Gramophone Company with an extensive choice of humorous discs. Russell Hunting appeared on seventeen recordings as his well-known Irish character, Casey, telling tales of 'Casey Bathing', 'Casey at the Dentist', and 'Casey selling his Health Restorer'. If potential customers were unaware of Casey's origins, the catalogue helpfully explained that the name was 'looked upon as typical of a particular class of Irishmen, dealt with in these records.'[11] Columbia could boast of George Robey ('The Prime Minister of Mirth'), Harry Tate, Raymond Hitchcock, and Mark Sheridan.[12]

Zonophone (originally an independent label from the USA, but purchased by the Gramophone Company in 1903) was a good source of budget records featuring music hall stars.[13] Around 20 per cent of Zonophone's roster was recorded by comics or spoken-word artists. Music hall stars Florrie Forde and Harry Champion recorded extensively for the label, the great Marie Lloyd appeared on three discs, and Harry Lauder—the Scots comedian billed in the catalogue as the highest paid entertainer in the world—was on eighteen records. The label seemed unimpressed by these great entertainers, making the bold, if erroneous, claim that 'The biggest "scoop" to date in the history of the Talking Machine Trade is without a shadow of a doubt the engagement, *exclusively for Zonophones* [their emphasis], of the Band of H. M. Royal Irish Fusiliers.'[14]

Lovers of the theatre could buy discs featuring scenes from famous plays. The Gramophone Company offered Charles Wyndham reciting a speech as the famous eighteenth-century actor David Garrick, or Cyril Maude and Winifred Emery enacting a scene from *The Little Minister*. Bransby Williams performed dramatic recitals for Columbia (some with musical accompaniment), including scenes from Dickens.[15] These recordings, alongside opera and classical music, helped the gramophone companies to promote their machines as instruments of high culture, but they were never bestsellers. Fans of the gramophone were, from the start, fans of low culture as well as high, and many of them favoured music hall and low comedy. After all, why offer seventeen different records of Hunting's supposedly hilarious Casey skits if no one was buying them?

High-culture artists were expensive but gave the industry respectability and signalled its intention to be a serious contributor to the arts, so it continued to pay them well and to allocate large sums of money to their marketing budgets. Dame Nellie Melba's first Gramophone Company discs appeared on a special Melba label, packaged in lavishly produced sleeves with an image of the great singer and a facsimile of her autograph; they were priced at 1 guinea each—more than the weekly wage of an agricultural worker. The company sold 2,000 copies of her records in one month alone, but once royalties and advertising costs were taken into account it made a loss of £391 on those discs. Sydney Dixon, the company's manager, claimed that the advertising budget for Melba records was £4,000 in just three months.[16] Celebrity records such as these were really no more than high-class advertising, with sales never matching those of the stars of music hall, the brass bands, and the military bands. At their peak, in 1907–8, celebrity records achieved sales of 64,671 in the Gramophone Company's total annual sale of 1,995,463 records; low-cost Zonophone discs accounted for 75 per cent of that total. Harry Lauder and Florrie Forde were the company's big sellers, not Caruso or Melba.[17]

Berliner had been extraordinarily prescient in predicting high levels of royalties for some artists, but others made do with less rewarding arrangements. The Gramophone Company's first royalty deal, in 1898, was with Albert Chevalier (the popular singer and composer of 'My Old Dutch'), who received an advance of £15 plus a royalty of 1 shilling for every twelve records sold. Other—ultimately more famous and successful—artists began their recording careers with much smaller rewards. Harry Lauder claimed that one of his first recording contracts paid just £5 for a six-song session, with no further payments. Once an artist became popular and their disc sales increased, a company might pay them an annual retainer as well as recording fees, but this fell well short of the royalties earned by international opera stars. Florrie Forde, a top-selling Gramophone Company artist, earned a total of £1,133 in retaining fees and recording fees in the decade from 1904. In the same period, Caruso and Melba were each earning up to £6,000 per year in royalties from British sales alone.[18]

Stars of the West End, culturally somewhere between the classical and music hall worlds, embraced the recording industry. Performers like musical comedy star Gertie Millar and Isabel Jay, a leading light in musical comedy and Gilbert and Sullivan operettas, drew large crowds to London theatres, but seldom toured the provinces. Their recordings of some of their best-known songs helped to spread the word about their latest shows, as well as providing them with useful additional income.

Two Sides for Less Than Twice the Price: Tempting the Customer

By 1903, the Gramophone and Typewriter Ltd catalogue offered thousands of discs, all recorded on one side only.[19] In most cases, the second side was left blank but the company did find a use for this spare area of shellac—as a home for its name and its trademark, the Recording Angel. On its 7-inch records, the 'blank' side featured the Recording Angel at its centre, roughly the same diameter as the paper label that adorned the grooved side, with the work GRAMOPHONE repeated twice around the outside in large, upper-case text.[20] It is a surprisingly attractive image, but it does make one wonder why no one thought to cut a recorded groove onto that side instead.

When recording on both sides of a disc finally began, the innovation was not an immediate success. The Odeon label produced its first double-sided discs in 1904 and was criticised for giving customers a second recording that they had not asked for and may well not have wanted. Some record companies produced two-sided discs with different artists on each side, sometimes from completely different musical genres, often rotating at different speeds. Gradually, the idea of a double-sided disc featuring the same performers on both sides and rotating at the same speed took hold, but it took time. As late as November 1908, *Talking Machine News* declared that the position was not yet clear, although it backed the double-sided disc to emerge victorious.[21] Two sides did not necessarily mean that consumers paid twice the price; a relatively unknown act might make a double-sided disc that retailed for less than a single-sided release by a more famous artist.

Descriptive discs—'documentary' records of great and not-so-great events—held a small place in the market before the Great War. Zonophone's brief list featured 'A Naval Disaster' coupled with 'Departure of a Troop Ship', 'A Lancashire Crowd's Welcome to the King and Queen (Parts 1 and 2)', and 'Football Match, No. 1, Newcastle United *v.* Manchester City' coupled with 'Football Match, No. 2, Manchester City *v.* Newcastle United'.[22] Although these records might at first seem like on-the-spot recordings, it is clear that they were not. Neither Fred Gaisberg nor any of his fellow recording engineers were likely to be on hand at the time of a naval disaster and if recording equipment was present at a football match, which three or four minutes of the game would be committed to disc? Listening to the few examples that survive, it is obvious that these discs were studio recordings, attempting to capture the flavour of the live event rather than to record things as they happened; what is harder to decide is just how seriously the listeners took these recordings.

'A Naval Disaster' is a particularly risible attempt at recreating the drama of a sinking ship. Most of it is a 'stiff upper-lip' dialogue between two 'officers' as they face almost certain doom, underpinned by the sound of thunder and a swanee whistle interpretation of a howling gale. The disc ends with a stirring duo rendition of 'Sons of the Brave' as the last of the crew leaves the ship. Thankfully, there is no loss of life; the captain does not go down with his ship, choosing to take the final place on the lifeboat instead of drowning. 'Departure of a Troop Ship' is a jollier record, full of shouts and cheers as the unnamed vessel sails away to the accompaniment of a band playing 'Soldiers of the King', 'The British Grenadiers', and 'God Save the King'. It is easy for the world-weary twenty-first-century listener to dismiss these records as amateurish attempts at drama, but for listeners in the 1900s, these records were a new experience. Early cinema audiences apparently screamed in terror as an on-screen train rushed at top speed towards them, so early gramophone listeners may have treated these descriptive discs seriously—not as recordings of actual events, but as dramatic recreations worth listening to with a straight face.

As the number of discs on offer rocketed, this embarrassment of entertainment riches needed one thing—customers. The gramophone might have been the best things since sliced bread (in fact, it predated commercially available sliced bread by almost forty years), but it did not sell itself. Unlike bread, the gramophone was not a necessity. Even when prices dropped to the point where gramophones and discs became affordable to most of the population, they were still forced to compete for customers. The record-producing companies developed strategies to ensure that everyone was aware of the new entertainment medium.

The Gramophone Company led the way with stylish and lavishly illustrated catalogues. The 1899 catalogue was 101 pages long, dwarfing Edison-Bell's twenty-six-page publication.[23] Many of the recordings listed were imported from the USA or made by American artists when they travelled to Britain to perform in music hall—the Georgia Glee Singers, the American Comedy Four and banjo duo Mays and Hunter among them—but the catalogue noted that an increasing number of records were from British acts (thanks partly to Gaisberg's enthusiastic work). Photographs of great landmarks from Britain and Empire—such as the Forth Bridge, Holyrood Palace, and the Dublin Custom House—adorned many pages. The intention was clear: the gramophone and its discs were a part of the British way of life, part of the global Empire. It was a patriotic Briton's duty to build a collection. More importantly for the eager customer, the artists were named and described, with many having their photographs included. Customers seeking to purchase a recording of Maurice Farkoa singing his famous 'Laughing Song' could find it listed beneath a photograph of the artist and alongside a selection of his other recordings in English and French. Fans of American performer Burt Shepard could view his photo while choosing from seventy-five of his 'talking records', comic songs, and popular ditties. Female artists were well represented, including singers such as Ellen Beach-Yaw and the impressionist Cissie Loftus, whose records included one on which she impersonated another Gramophone Company vocalist, Eugene Stratton. The haughty looking but fashionably dressed Mr G. H. Snazelle contributed talking records, classical songs and sacred songs; legend has it that Mr Snazelle's on-stage style was the origin of the term 'snazzy'.[24] Even the stern-faced men of the Rhondda Royal Glee Society were shown in a photograph, which made the group's association with glee seem rather unlikely, although Gaisberg was impressed by the musical ability of this choir of 'hardy colliers ... [all] swarthy and of a small frame.'[25]

Caruso, Melba, Marie Lloyd, and Harry Lauder were big stars. Minor artists were far less expensive to hire but needed to be carefully promoted to the public. Photographs did much to demystify the artists, while pen portraits were equally useful. A photograph of Mr Scott Skinner revealed him to be a balding, moustachioed, middle-aged Scot with an enormous sporran but gave nothing away regarding his artistry. A description helped to clarify matters; he was 'a marvellous specimen of a left-handed violinist' with a characteristically Scottish repertoire.[26] Fred Gaisberg recorded Skinner during a trip to Scotland in 1899, but despite Skinner's reputation as the country's champion fiddle player, Gaisberg was not impressed by the man, who he described as 'a queer character and very conceited.'[27] Strange and unusual instruments required explanation. The Gramophone Company felt that the instrument favoured by the Musical Avolos ('the world's foremost xylophone ensemble') was such an instrument and enlightened readers with this simple description: the xylophone is 'made solely of pieces of wood of different lengths and thicknesses which are supported at either end by crossway pieces which are padded, and it is played with little wooden hammers'.[28]

The Gramophone Company also offered an extensive range of recordings from across Europe, the far corners of the British Empire, and beyond. Customers were encouraged to buy recordings from India because 'they must be of especial interest to all loyal Englishmen, as being representative of our large Eastern possessions.' Wales, Scotland, and Ireland all received their own sections of the catalogue, and pages were reserved for German and French artists, recorded in London. International conflict offered a marketing opportunity. When the Russo-Japanese War broke out in February 1904, the Gramophone and Typewriter Ltd issued a supplementary catalogue of Russian and Japanese national anthems, war songs, and military marches. After all, any patriotic Briton with an interest in world affairs beyond the bounds of Empire would surely be interested in hearing the music of these two warring powers, a culturally authentic collection representing 'with absolute truth the national characteristics of the patriotic music of the two nations'.[29]

Past conflicts also had their uses. On Trafalgar Day 1905, the Gramophone Company placed a large advertisement in *The Times*.[30] A gramophone sat atop Nelson's Column (the Admiral was nowhere to be seen), the words 'ENGLAND EXPECTS EVERY MAN THIS DAY TO DO HIS DUTY' blasted from the horn, and the names of the company's greatest recording artists covered the height of the column. The advertisement called on readers' patriotism, conjured up a nostalgia for great figures of the past, and emphasised that the gramophone now had the ability to be everywhere, bringing home comforts to 'the men who watch the outposts of our Empire'. The advertisement promoted the £11 Monarch Senior gramophone, 'an influence of high order in the spread of civilisation'. When civilisation's spread seemed to end with the outbreak of the Great War, the industry would make commercial use out of that conflict as well.

Catalogues were informative, but there were other opportunities to add to the customer's knowledge. The Gramophone Company's first discs, supplied by Berliner, provided basic information—song title, artist's name, catalogue number, sometimes a facsimile artist's signature—inscribed directly onto the surface of the central space. Paper discs, glued to the central space, followed within a year and offered scope for colourful designs and more detailed information. These simple paper discs soon transformed into something more informative as their carefully constructed designs became instantly recognisable—the 'record label'.

Once established in the public mind, the record label could signal many things to consumers; the likely content to be found on discs marketed under the label, the quality of the discs, and the diameter of the discs could all be quickly communicated. So, too, could the likely cost of each disc. Some labels were marketed as high quality in terms of production and performers and would command a high price. Others were targeted at mass markets, produced with quantity rather than quality in mind, and consequently sold much more cheaply.

The Gramophone and Typewriter Ltd's Red Label collection—10-inch discs retailing at 10 shillings each—featured leading opera singers, including Caruso. The company's Monarch Records label featured a more varied, if less famous, range of artists, including military bands, orchestras, singers, and comics on 12-inch discs for 7s 6d each. When the company acquired the Zonophone label, it used it as an outlet for cheaper discs. Many of the artists were relatively unknown, but big names also appeared on the label, which rapidly became popular. In 1913, the Gramophone Company and Columbia both established budget labels—the Gramophone Company's Cinch and Columbia's Phoenix. The intention was to compete directly with the cheapest labels on the market, especially German imports, using old recordings from their back catalogues as well as new releases. Discs on both labels cost just 1s 1d. A distinctive label design was important. Winner Records, which first appeared in 1912, were recognisable from the images of racehorses that adorned their labels. Russell Records featured stylised Union flags.[31] Label designs gave some indication of the target market; according to one rather snobbish music historian, Winner records were crude-looking and poor-sounding discs aimed 'purely towards the fancy of the masses'.[32]

Columbia, the Gramophone Company's major competitor by the start of the Great War, favoured eight different labels, the single-sided 12-inch Pink

Label Grand Opera discs being the most expensive at 12s 6d.[33] The 10-inch
Dark Blue label discs featured military bands, colliery bands, selections from
musical theatre and revues, and Albert W. Ketelbey's 'Famous "Tangled
Tunes"' ('a melodious medley of multitudinous musical movements'). The
dominance of the Gramophone Company and Columbia failed to dampen the
enthusiasm of entrepreneurs who fancied their chances in the world of disc
production. Around 300 record labels were available in the UK from 1898
to 1926.[34] Giants like Columbia were in the minority; some labels such as
Neophone existed for only a year or two, while other labels were produced
and sold by a single retailer (for example, the Portland label, sold by Curry's),
and others existed to record the work of a single artist (the Waverley label
from Glasgow produced twelve discs, all by accordionist William Hannah).

Record labels soon came to signify as much about the purchaser as they did
about the product. A large collection of the Gramophone and Typewriter Ltd's
Red Label records or Columbia's Pink Label discs signified a taste for high
culture and the deep pockets necessary to support it. A complete collection
of Melba's 1-guinea discs suggested even deeper pockets. A home filled with
Pathé's quirky discs with their in-to-out grooves (and the specialist instrument
needed to play them) suggested an individualist, even an eccentric, or perhaps
an early adopter of disc technology who chose the losing side. Owners of
Betamax video recorders, eight-track cartridge players, or minidiscs will
know the feeling.

Record sleeves were another source of information. The first discs were
sold in plain paper sleeves (sometimes called envelopes), which offered a small
degree of protection against dust or sticky fingers but gave no practical help
to the enquiring mind of the record collector. Local record retailers produced
sleeves advertising their stores and perhaps some of their range of talking
machines. Some of them included space in which to note details of a disc's
title, artist, and playing speed—a piece of information that was especially
important to the first generation of disc collectors. E. Roberts of Garratt Lane,
London, advertised their services as repairers, their easy payment scheme, and
the products of HMV on one side of a record sleeve, leaving the other side free
to advertise another company's products. One company to take advantage of
this was the Songster Needle Company, whose advertisements offered a series
of 'Gramophone Hints'.

When the record companies recorded longer compositions requiring four
or more discs, a more complex packaging system developed. Sleeves were
packaged together in sturdier front and back covers, giving the appearance of
a book or a collection of family photographs. The 'record album' was born,
the term persisting well after such multi-disc packages disappeared to be
replaced by long-playing discs. Collectors could also buy empty albums and
use them to keep individual discs, perhaps by the same artist, safe and secure.

Persuading the wealthiest customers to pay for expensive instruments or discs needed advertising that appealed to their love of the high arts, to their desire to be seen as cultured and to their snobbery. Nellie Melba's expensive Melba label recordings proved to be an ideal vehicle for such a campaign; the Gramophone Company proudly declared that copies of those discs were sent to European royal families, to major country houses, and to the homes of the most important musicians and musical critics. Buying Melba's discs could clearly put you on a par with the crowned heads of Europe, or at least on equal footing with the local gentry (although 'sent to' is not the same as 'enjoyed by'). The Gramophone and Typewriter Ltd upped the stakes with other celebrity endorsements, declaring that during December 1904 it had supplied Melba's records, plus Melba model gramophones (at £15 each), to Queen Alexandra, King Carlos of Portugal, King Alfonso of Spain, and King George of Greece. Few prospective purchasers could fail to be impressed by this royal quartet, but for anyone still doubting the gramophone's status as the latest high-culture object, there was one more international celebrity to call on—the Pope owned a gramophone. The Gramophone and Typewriter Ltd gleefully announced the Pope's latest acquisition, which the company gave him along with a selection of recordings of Gregorian chants. Advertisements reproduced a letter from his secretary, Cardinal Merry Del Val, thanking the company for the gift to His Holiness and congratulating it on the faithful reproductions of the chants.[35]

The Wonder of the Age

The British public became more and more aware of the gramophone and with the press proclaiming it as the wonder of the age, they were eager to hear the machine for themselves. For most people, early machines were too expensive to own, so entrepreneurs soon followed the example of Daniel Moore and gave public demonstrations. Allen and Sons of Shrewsbury advertised their availability to give such demonstrations across Shropshire, although their insistence on attributing the gramophone's invention to Thomas Edison may have caused potential customers to question their expertise.[36]

The inmates of Exeter City Workhouse enjoyed Mr Marriott's gramophone concert, which he gave free of charge in July 1898. The charitable gentleman played discs of bands, singers, and trombone and banjo soloists. The inmates received one record with 'especial pleasure' and demanded it be played more than once—a recording made in Washington, D.C., on the declaration of America's war with Spain (which took place the previous April). The disc included a band playing 'Yankee Doodle' and a cry of 'three cheers for George Washington'.[37] It is an unusual and unexplained choice, and the record does not seem to have survived. The war did make another contribution to gramophone history, though. On 20 April 1898, Berliner recorded William 'Buffalo Bill' Cody making a pro-war speech and urging President McKinley to use force against Spain, possibly the first use of the gramophone as a propaganda tool.[38]

The Royal Albert Hall hosted one of the grandest gramophone demonstrations just in time for Christmas 1908. The finest artists on the Gramophone and Typewriter's roster appeared, not in person but on record. Enrico Caruso, Marie Hall, Adelina Patti, and Nellie Melba all performed for the invitation-only audience through the medium of the auxeto gramophone or auxetophone (a mechanical amplifier operated by compressed air and designed especially for performances in large venues).[39] Madame Tussauds Wax Museum made regular use of an auxetophone, giving daily concerts of recordings from Caruso, Melba, Patti, 'and other wonderful records.'[40]

How to Buy a Record, Where to Buy a Record

The gramophone industry faced one last hurdle: how to build a retail network so that the public could buy their discs with the minimum of fuss and inconvenience. The industry developed two solutions: selling records by mail order and retailing through a network of shops.

Mail order offered customers the chance to choose any discs from a catalogue and have them posted direct to their home or office; a postcard sent to the record company would bring a catalogue by return of post, usually with an order form attached. For many people, especially those living away from the cities and larger towns, this was the easiest option, but it was not without risk. Shellac records were fragile and could arrive broken and unplayable, or the chosen discs might not be available. Record companies considered the possible problems and offered solutions. Edison-Bell declared that 'We should esteem it a favour if Customers, when ordering Records, would name a few extra ones as "second choice"'. If the records—first or second choices—broke in transit, the loss was the purchaser's: 'Owing to the great risk of damage by transit it is impossible for the Company to exchange Records which have been chosen or delivered to order'.[41] Other companies took a more customer-friendly approach. Pathé offered allowances for broken records, based on their selling price: 9*d* for a 3*s* disc rising to 1*s* 10*d* for a 7*s* 6*d* disc.[42] The broken disc had to be returned to the company along with an order worth at least the original selling price of the broken disc. The allowances may seem rather low, but the company did not differentiate between discs broken by the postal worker and those broken by the purchaser, nor did it appear to put a time limit on such returns.

Customers could order by post with confidence, but what about buying on the high street? At first, the gramophone industry sold discs and instruments through existing shops, whether or not the retailers had any experience of musical instruments or furniture. In Knightsbridge, Harrods sold records in its piano department. In Norwich, piano-dealer Saul Salkind moved into record retail, becoming the city's 'Best house for high-class Talking Machines' and proudly advertising its stock of 'GENUINE GRAMOPHONES' from the Gramophone Company.[43] Photographic shops like Cardiff's Photo Supplies moved into the new technology. Bicycle shops often stocked gramophones and discs, perhaps because owners were used to selling round objects, perhaps to help them deal with seasonal variations in bicycle sales. Specialist shops soon appeared—Wilcox Record Supply on Oxford Street; J. B. Cramer and Co. of Moorgate Street, which sold piano rolls and records together; or Charles Powell of Fairford, a 'Gramophone specialist and phonograph dealer' with a stock of 'all kinds of records'.

Some of these shops were in business for decades, sometimes becoming well-known brands: Levy's of Whitechapel and Millers of Cambridge, for example.[44] Levy's started out selling bicycle parts and sewing machines, then became an early retailer of cylinders and 78s. It would eventually establish its own record label: Levaphone. Spillers Records of Cardiff, established in 1894 to sell phonographs and cylinders, also moved into gramophone and disc sales, proudly displaying Amberol cylinders, phonographs, discs, and disc-playing machines in its window alongside the slogan 'Expert repairer. All Makes of Phonographs and disc machines repaired on the premises'. The shop is still operating today and claims to be the oldest record shop in the world.[45]

Imhof's of New Oxford Street claimed a central role in the British gramophone market. It was one of the oldest gramophone and record retailers in the country, established in 1845 by Daniel Imhof to sell musical instruments of his own invention, including the mysterious Orchestrion, a large, clockwork-driven device. Fifty years after Berliner invented the gramophone, Imhof's laid claim to a series of firsts: the first dealers in the country to sell gramophones (in 1896), the first official His Master's Voice dealer, producers of the first seamless metal horn (used by the Gramophone Company), the first company to produce non-metallic needles (they were made from bamboo), the development of the Stentophone (the 'First public address type of gramophone operated by compressed air' in 1916), and the invention of the Panatrope ('the first home electrical reproducer of records, and immediate forerunner of the radiogramophone', in 1925).[46] The claims may not stand up to close scrutiny—Parkins and Gotto sold toy gramophones in 1891, and the auxetophone operated by compressed air in 1906—but the shop was definitely an important part of the trade from the beginning.

The network of retailers expanded rapidly. When the 1-guinea Melba discs appeared in 1904, over 120 shops stocked them, from London to Cork and from Ayr to Penzance.[47] These shops included Harrods and all were high-end retailers whose customers could afford 1 guinea for a disc. At the bottom end of the market, shops served customers with far less free cash, so 1-guinea Melba records would not feature on their shelves. H. G. Wells's fictional Grubb and Smallways epitomised this end of the trade—a bicycle business that 'struggled along with a flavour of romantic insecurity in a small, dissolute-looking shop in the High Street,' selling obscure makes of bicycle and cheap gramophones.[48] Small and dissolute such shops may have been, but they helped to ensure that gramophones and records were readily obtainable across Britain, even in small market towns and villages. The Gramophone Company targeted its Zonophone records at these shops (bicycle dealers, sports shops, hardware retailers), even though many of them would sell records and instruments for only part of the year, focusing on their core products when warmer weather appeared.[49]

Angels, Cherubs, and a Small but Devoted Dog

As competition grew, the trademark offered a way of establishing a brand identity through an easily recognisable visual image. Edison's chosen trademark was obvious and uninspired: the signature of Thomas Alva Edison.[50] Columbia showed little more imagination, choosing a pair of musical notes with the words 'Magic Notes' written underneath. Zonophone used a circle within which the word 'Zonophone' was printed twice, from left to right and from top to bottom; later, it added 'The Twin', a pair of demure cherubs hiding their modesties behind a banner, to advertise the label of the same name.[51] Pathé chose the rooster, which still serves the company in the twenty-first century.[52] One company would produce a truly memorable and long-lasting trademark, forever associated with gramophone records. The Gramophone Company's 1899 list of records was titled simply 'Gramophone Record Catalogue'. The company had sole use of the term 'gramophone', so there was no need to identify itself further. Inside the catalogue was a painting of a terrier staring down the horn of a gramophone, underscored with the words 'His Master's Voice'. When the competition arrived, the little dog would prove to be invaluable.

The Gramophone Company's first trademark was the 'Recording Angel', an androgynous young child reclining on a large disc and apparently tracing a groove with an oversized quill.[53] The picture was used, often alongside the His Master's Voice image, until around 1910 when the company lost control of the word 'gramophone'. The company's December 1908 catalogue featured a painting of a highly stylised angel—tall, slender, and female, clad in a long, white, gown and holding a gramophone as she hovered over a snow-covered street.

The Recording Angel was charming, but Nipper seemed tailor-made for the Gramophone Company. Nipper the terrier—attentive, curious, a little puzzled, and maybe a touch melancholy—presented an endearing picture of the loyal pet. The gramophone, with its large horn directing sound straight at Nipper's head, was the latest thing in entertainment technology, a modern instrument carrying on an ancient relationship between man and animal. The picture made it clear that the gramophone could soon be as normal a part of British home life as the presence of a faithful dog. Decades later, when the clockwork gramophone with its ungainly horn was no longer representative of cutting-edge sound systems, the image would still register with the British public.

Nipper moved in the best circles. On the cover of the Gramophone Company's 1907 catalogue, he is seated next to a Monarch gramophone, surrounded by the ladies and gentlemen of the hunt who are enjoying a drink and musical entertainment after a hard day of chasing foxes. The cover of the 1909 catalogue showed Nipper at a musical *soiree*, the guest of honour, seated between a man and woman in full evening dress and in front of a large and impressive gramophone.[54] Yet who was Nipper's master? Why was the dog sitting at the gramophone rather than lying at his master's feet? Was his master's voice one of the voices of the dead, the sound of a beloved but deceased human? Or was the terrier's master an international singing star, leaving a record to comfort Nipper while he travelled the world to perform in the great theatres of Russia, Italy, or the USA? Maybe Nipper belonged to Mr Snazelle, or the great Caruso (in whose native Italy, Nipper listened to '*La Voce del Padrone*'), or Harry Lauder. Whatever the story of Nipper and his master's voice may have been, the Gramophone Company kept one key part of the tale secret: Nipper was really listening to a cylinder.

The terrier belonged to artist Francis James Barraud's brother, Mark. After Mark's death, Francis looked after the dog and was amused by his reaction to the sound of the phonograph. Nipper died in 1895 and Barraud painted the picture as a memorial to the animal. The original version featured Nipper listening to a recording on a cylinder, the sound emanating from a dark coloured horn. A little while later, Barraud painted a new version, featuring a gold coloured horn and a gramophone. The Gramophone Company bought this painting and the copyright and gave it the title of 'His Master's Voice'.[55]

As the market for instruments and discs grew, the gramophone became a common sight in Britain's homes—at least, in those that could afford the prices. As Britain's gramophone-owning population expanded, so, too, did the range of instruments and discs available. Discerning disc collectors were learning a new vocabulary—soundboxes, tone arms, record labels, and horns. Famous artists were happy to record their best-loved songs and sketches. Up-and-coming performers longed for the chance to record. The gramophone was poised to lead new trends, not just to follow.

On the Record: '*Questa o Quella*', Enrico Caruso (Gramophone and Typewriter Company Red Label, 1902)

Enrico Caruso's decision to become a recording artist was crucial for the record industry and for other 'high-culture' singers. Many major performers, especially from the worlds of opera and classical music, were wary of making recordings in the early years of the talking machine industry, concerned that poor quality records would reflect badly on their talents, or that the primitive recording techniques would prove damaging to their voices. Once Caruso was making records, his fellow artists felt more comfortable in following suit. Caruso's contract ensured that he received generous royalties and his presence on the Gramophone Company's roster enhanced the company's reputation.

'*Questa o Quella*', from Verdi's *Rigoletto*, was one of Caruso's first recordings for the Gramophone Company, at the Grand Hotel in Milan on 11 April 1902. Caruso's voice is strong, but he sounds relaxed, displaying a remarkable clarity for a record made over 115 years ago; heard on modern headphones, he is easily capable of inflicting tympanic membrane damage if the volume is too high. On this recording, Caruso is accompanied by Salvatore Cottone's jaunty and uncomplicated piano playing, which has also recorded clearly despite the difficulties associated with piano recordings (Fred Gaisberg knew what he was doing). The results are technically and artistically impressive, although we do not know how many attempts it took to achieve this performance.

'*Questa o Quella*' appeared in the Red Label catalogue as one of ten songs recorded by Caruso and composed by Verdi, Donizetti, Puccini, and others. Caruso would go on to record different versions of '*Questa o Quella*', and no doubt, each one has its supporters. The 1902 recording may not be the finest, but in terms of the gramophone's place in high culture, it is crucial.

3

Parlours, Pubs, and Parliament: The Gramophone Moves In

As Gaisberg and his fellow pioneers created extensive catalogues of records, the industry tackled some pressing commercial issues. Would potential customers find the gramophone too complicated to operate, too expensive, or too ugly to display in a stylish lounge or sitting room? Would the middle-class households of Manchester or Edinburgh be willing to spend money on a gramophone if it failed to offer the entertainments they desired? Could gramophones appeal to the mass market of working-class families? Most importantly, could they be produced cheaply enough to be affordable to those families? The industry needed to resolve all of these questions if it was going to maximise the gramophone's potential.

Disrupting the Décor

The gramophone was a stranger in the home, a new type of furniture.[1] It needed visual appeal to be welcomed into the parlour, an ability to blend in with the fashionable décor of the day. It might well be making a statement about its owner's taste and wealth, but it had to make this statement in ways that enhanced its owner's reputation among friends and family. A gramophone that was considered too ugly or obstructive was likely to be hidden away and not be used—a lost commercial opportunity for the record company and a bad investment for its owner. In the small living rooms of the working class or lower middle class, space was a problem; the gramophone and its horn needed a sufficiently large room to avoid being a constant obstruction always at risk of being knocked over or damaged.

The Gramophone Company's 1898 Trademark instrument was typical of the first commercially available machines—a table-top model with a brass horn that pivoted precariously on a metal arm fixed to its base.[2] One accidental nudge and the horn was likely to spin, tip, and crash. Yet these instruments needed to be accessible, to be clearly heard. A quiet evening alone with one's record collection might pose little difficulty as the listener could select a suitable spot to sit down, but a dinner party or a musical soirée could be a disaster if some guests heard almost nothing while others found their ears assailed by too high a volume of sound.

The gramophone's primary function was to play records, but it could have other uses. For many, it was an object to display proudly.[3] A gramophone signified wealth, style, or culture—especially worth doing if friends and neighbours did not yet own one. It could serve as a conversation piece, the shock of the new occasioning discussion before it became commonplace. Instruments with flat-topped lids could be used as an impromptu storage space for books, magazines, or vases of flowers—not necessarily a good idea practically or aesthetically.[4] Top of the range instruments were made of the finest materials, as is to be expected of an object suitable for the finest British homes. The Gramophone Company's £25 Monarch gramophone of 1904 was one such object. It sat on top of a wooden pedestal of the same width and depth—a tall and thin item of furniture with the appearance of a skinny police box. Its horn was so large that it required a metal support, fixed to the side of the pedestal, to keep it from toppling over.[5] It was an impressive item of furniture, a statement piece that not only declared the owner's love of the talking machine but also their up-to-the-minute style and their financial status.

With annual wages in 1900 averaging just over £40, the Monarch was far too expensive for most households.[6] For the wealthiest, more expensive instruments soon emerged. The Grand ('... the highest perfection which the Gramophone has yet reached ...') cost £52 10s 0d, making the Monarch look like a bargain.[7] Smaller free-standing machines and table-top models soon entered the market; these were easier to fit into the living rooms of the terraced villas of the middle-class. Monarch table-top models were designed to fit on any table, but they still needed a metal support for their amplifying horns and still cost between £8 8s and £16.[8] Cheaper machines became widely available from the early 1900s, opening ownership to a wider cross-section of the British population and causing something of a price war. The Gramophone and Typewriter Ltd introduced the Style No. 3 in 1903, for £3 3s. In early 1904, the company reduced its price to 42 shillings, then on 1 November, it reduced it again to 30 shillings—a price reduction of over 50 per cent in less than two years.[9] With careful economies, even some working-class families could afford a gramophone.

Smaller manufacturers and sellers entered the market, with offers that made ownership even easier. G. W. Robey of Coventry sold the Robeyphone ('world-famed' and 'hand-painted in six charming tints') on credit with a down payment of just 7s 6d.[10] The Graves Gramophone (not a model dedicated to replaying the voices of the dead, but one sold by Sheffield retailers, J. G. Graves Ltd) had a self-supporting external horn, making it suitable for smaller rooms. More importantly for the less wealthy enthusiast, it retailed at £2 10s and was available on easy terms at just 5 shillings with order. It is unlikely that the Robeyphone or the Graves Gramophone were market leaders in sound quality, but they were affordable for many.

Amplifying horns were a nuisance, taking up space and at constant risk of being damaged. They were ugly, too. Nipper stared attentively at a gramophone horn, but he was just a dog and people were unlikely to be so intrigued. Another feature of the horn gave concern for a different reason—it was decidedly phallic; even the name was suggestive of sexual activity. The solution to the horn problem (its size, symbolism, and fragility) was simple: internalise the amplifying mechanism. The Gramophone Grand was the Gramophone Company's first model with an internal horn.[11] A sumptuous instrument, in the Sheraton style and made of mahogany, it was 4 feet high and 2 feet wide with storage space for 120 discs. Below the turntable, at the front of the instrument, was the internal horn—a box with a square opening hidden behind two doors that could be partially opened or closed to create a primitive volume control, with more nuanced control achieved by stuffing a sponge or rolled-up sock into the box. The phallic symbolism of the external horn was no longer a problem, and the new symbolism of an opening hidden behind two flap-like doors could be ignored. The external horn would still be produced for some years, but its heyday was over.

Internal amplification was aesthetically pleasing, made it easier to position the gramophone safely, and greatly reduced the risk of damage, but acoustically, it was a backward step when compared to the external horn, giving poorer sound quality. Compton Mackenzie, editor of *The Gramophone,* was one authority who railed against 'the abominable distortion of sound' created by internal amplification. He recognised, however, that aesthetic decisions could trump audio-based ones. The external horn, he wrote, 'offended against gentility. People were ashamed of the gramophone and wanted it not to look like a gramophone.'[12] Mackenzie maintained his decorum by refusing to expand on how this part of the instrument offended against gentility; if the offence was as widespread as he suggests, then there was no need to explain.

Fakes, Frauds, and Counterfeits

Expensive instruments, a rising market, and a greater understanding of the technology among smaller manufacturers meant that the criminal classes became interested in the gramophone. Record piracy (the unauthorised copying and distribution of records, without payments to the artists or the original producers of the recording) is as old as the record industry.[13] Edison had to deal with pirates, as did Berliner. British law offered no protection; copyright law did not apply to recorded music until the 1911 Copyright Act.[14] Even when legal protection was available, piracy continued, often using the most basic strategy.

Pirates with the appropriate technology could press their own records by creating a new master disc from a copy of a legitimate disc. These pirated discs almost certainly provided poor-quality recordings, but they sold cheaply and customers would be willing to put up with second-rate sound if it came at a low enough price, much like the car-boot DVDs of more recent times. This was the preferred method of American pirates, notably Albert T. Armstrong's American Vitaphone records that were pirated from Victor and Columbia.[15] It is unclear how widespread this approach was in Britain, but the Gramophone Company's Russian business was badly hit by pirate discs. Eventually, the company called on Chaliapin, the bass singer, to use his influence with the Russian Secret Police to put pressure on the pirates.[16]

In Britain, piracy took on a more prosaic form. Buy up bankrupt, fire- or water-damaged, or otherwise cheap discs, replace the original paper label with your own (or simply paste yours onto the original one), and you had a 'new' disc that could be sold to the public without the effort of arranging recording sessions or royalty agreements. Northampton dealer F. P. Wykes sold records on his Blue Seal label, which he pasted onto Pioneer and Coliseum records. The exceedingly rare Pilot Records sported handwritten labels stuck over the products of labels such as Zonophone, Winner, and Imperial.[17]

British record piracy seems to have been carried out on a fairly small scale, occasioning little concern beyond the owners of legitimate record companies. By contrast, the Gramophone Company actively pursued the producers of counterfeit disc players and parts. As the official British representative of Berliner's American company, it claimed the exclusive right to use the term 'Gramophone' and did its best to ensure that this was the case. In its catalogues, the company gave a loud and clear warning:

THE WORD GRAMOPHONE IS NOT A GENERIC TERM. GRAMOPHONE DESCRIBES THE INSTRUMENTS MADE BY THE GRAMOPHONE & TYPEWRITER LTD. THERE ARE MANY KINDS OF TALKING MACHINES. THERE IS ONLY ONE GRAMOPHONE.[18]

It took Charles Howell to court over his manufacture and sale of a Melba soundbox, claiming that Mr Howell was suggesting that his soundbox was connected to or supported by the company and the singer, despite having no connection with either party.[19] A few months later, the company was acting against its former agent, Granville Hawley Edgerton Cooke, accusing

Cooke of selling an instrument as a 'gramophone' when only the horn was a product of the company.[20]

In 1910, the High Court heard the Gramophone Company's application to use 'gramophone' as a trademark.[21] Mr Justice Parker gave an admirably succinct history of the gramophone as an object, the recording process, the gramophone business in Britain, and the use of the word 'gramophone' in technical and general discourse, noting that to the British public, the word described a talking machine that used discs rather than an instrument produced only by the Gramophone Company. Accordingly, he dismissed the company's application, leaving the way open for companies like Graves of Sheffield to call their machines 'gramophones' without fear of litigation. Luckily, His Master's Voice was already a well-known trademark, and little Nipper was the most recognisable dog in the country. Within weeks, advertisements were emphasising His Master's Voice rather than the Gramophone Company; other gramophones were available (although the advertisements did not offer this information) but 'THE Gramophone Company' was the one with the famous trademark.[22]

Sounding Good

There was plenty to criticise about the mechanical gramophone and its recordings—limited sonic range, an inability to record large orchestras or stringed bass instruments effectively, the necessity for singers to focus on vocal power rather than subtlety, surface noise on the discs, and the tendency for discs and needles to wear out relatively quickly. Despite these issues, many writers were surprisingly uncritical of the recordings. The record companies claimed that their discs reproduced sound so precisely as to be indistinguishable from a live performance; supposedly 'independent' experts felt the same way. When Harold Begbie reported on Nellie Melba's recording session, he described what he heard in glowing terms: 'how is it that these scratches across a metal disc can give back to us, not only the words, but the very tone and intimate reality of the singer's voice?' Melba, never one to shy away from self-promotion, told Begbie that her record was a fine representation of her voice and personality. Other artists were just as willing to extol the virtues of this new instrument. Adelina Patti found the Monarch gramophone to be a remarkable instrument that 'reproduces the human voice to such a fine point.' Listening to discs by Caruso and others in her South Wales home, it sounded to Madame Patti as if 'those artistes were actually singing in my saloons'. For Edward Lloyd, the gramophone of 1904 was so good that he felt confident in committing his own voice to disc, 'content that future generations shall judge my voice by the Gramophone.'[23]

Some listeners were more critical. Gramophone concerts, designed to promote the instruments through public performances, showed how the instrument was improving but highlighted its remaining faults. A concert at St James's Hall persuaded one reviewer that the gramophone was getting better, but it was far from perfect. Each disc still opened with crackling noises, 'less like cats upon the housetop than it used to be', but still unpleasant.[24] Six months later, a *Times* correspondent reported on a demonstration of an improved model, held at the Savoy Hotel in the Strand, where 'the temerarious gramophone challenged comparison with the living voices of two famous singers'.[25] Clara Butt and Kennerley Rumford sang live, then the audience listened to the same performers on record. The instrument performed well, but on disc, Madame Butt's voice gained a faint nasal tinge and a tightening in the higher register. The orchestral accompaniments on other discs suggested a 'wheezy harmonium'. Clearly, there was still much to be done before the gramophone could accurately reproduce the sound of a live performance, but the reporter was happy to declare that it was a 'wonderful' instrument 'in the mere fact of its singing at all'.

Demonstrations in the concert halls of the great cities were impressive, but the rest of Britain needed to hear the best of the gramophones, too. The Gramophone and Typewriter Company Ltd was again at the forefront, with a mobile demonstration unit that took its instruments to the farthest corners of the country. The unit was, in fact, no more than a motor car with a gramophone fixed to its bonnet, which travelled the island of Ireland on a promotional tour. No such unit would be complete without Nipper, so a stuffed black and white terrier was duly acquired and attached to the car in Nipper's famous posture.

Columbia was not to be outdone by Nipper's Irish tour. In Belfast, the company placed a graphophone with a 56-inch copper horn on the fourth floor of the Scottish Provident building and played selected discs to an enthusiastic public gathered in the street below. One evening, as a ball to honour the Lord Lieutenant of Ireland took place elsewhere in the city, the graphophone played popular songs and tunes for four hours to a crowd of 5,000.[26]

New Roles for the Gramophone

The early twentieth century was a time of active social movements, and the gramophone proved to be a useful tool in their activities. The Salvation Army was quick off the mark, deciding as early as 1898 that the talking machine could help to bring the voice of its leader, General Booth, to the masses and keen to try out the gramophone on an extensive scale.[27] The Salvation Army Staff Band recorded five discs for the Gramophone and Typewriter Ltd while

General Booth appeared on two discs for Columbia (in effect, competing against his own musicians), giving four stirring speeches, including 'Please Sir, Save Me', 'Vividly picturing a touching Shipwreck incident'.[28]

In a bid to offer alternative entertainments to the drinking public, the Temperance Legislation League opened a centre in Middlesbrough. Among the cards, chess sets, and dominoes provided for the entry fee of 1*d* was a gramophone, set playing at various times of the day to provide a musical accompaniment to the games. The League's District Secretary, F. W. Walker, was proud of the centre's success but was sniffy about the gramophone's role; the instrument may have added interest, but 'one cannot call it joy'.[29] In London, Sir J. G. Tollemache Sinclair offered to donate gramophones and records to the Boards of Guardians 'to cheer, control and brighten the lives of those who take refuge in the workhouse'. Most of the guardians gratefully accepted the offer, sure of the benefits to the poverty-stricken citizens under their care, but the Hampstead Board turned it down, afraid that this 'vulgar instrument' would weaken the purpose of the workhouse as a deterrent to the workshy. *Talking Machine World* was scathing in its criticism, referring to the guardians as tyrants, asking 'Could there be a greater display of ignorance and lack of broadmindedness than is here displayed?'[30]

The Gramophone and Typewriter Company found another way to reach the hearts and minds of its British customers and make some profit along the way—the health of the nation's children. What better way to encourage healthy exercise than through the creation of a dedicated musical accompaniment? Who better to provide that accompaniment than the Gramophone and Typewriter Company? The Scholastic Gramophone appeared in 1904, along with manual for teachers and a set of nine records of music from the band of the Coldstream Guards, selected as suitable for children's drill exercises. The package of gramophone, stand, manual, and discs cost £9—a small price to pay for a strong future generation of labourers, factory hands, domestic servants, soldiers, mothers, and Gramophone Company customers.[31]

The gramophone soon found its way into political life. Joseph Heap was a pioneer of its use, sending a gramophone around the rural parts of the Blackpool constituency during the 1900 by-election with a recording of his address to voters. He was apologetic about his strategy, regretting that the 'rushing of the election' made it necessary.[32] The strategy failed, and in a two-horse race Mr Heap came second, but he would not be the last politician to record his election messages. The political big guns were happy to use the new technology to their benefit; some of the biggest guns took to the gramophone to spread the word about the 1909 budget. The Budget League hired six instruments to be used in the halls of villages and small towns across the country. Herbert Asquith (the Liberal Prime Minister), David Lloyd-George, and Winston Churchill travelled to the Gramophone Company offices to make their recordings (the equipment was too heavy to transport to Downing Street). Sir Henry Norman demonstrated the discs to journalists in Parliament, stressing that 'care will be taken to ensure that the meetings are solely political, and that the instruments are not used as a form of entertainment'.[33]

The leaders of the movement for women's suffrage seemed to have made little use of the gramophone. A recording of Christabel Pankhurst's speech on suffrage for women, made by the Gramophone Company in 1909, perhaps explains why recordings by the Pankhursts and other women leaders were not more common. Her speech is uninspiring and hesitant; of course, the all-male record company managers may have deliberately kept this new form of communication away from female activists, and in fairness to Miss Pankhurst, she made the recording just hours after being released from Holloway prison.[34] The Municipal Reform Party was more ambitious, hiring 350 gramophones to spread its word in the London streets. The word was not universally well-received. Edward Gardner, an analytical chemist, grew angry 'in a political sense' at the message emanating from one instrument and threw a vial of nitric acid into the horn.[35]

Thomas Sloan, MP for Belfast South, has the honour of the first recorded appearance of the word 'gramophone' in *Hansard*. Speaking in support of the Sale of Intoxicating Liquors on Saturdays (Ireland) Bill, Sloan spoke of publicans whose bars and gin palaces were 'now made interesting and pleasant with phonographs and gramophones'.[36] It was over four years before *Hansard* once again recorded the use of the word, coincidentally in another debate about Irish politics. This time, the honour went to John Mooney, MP for Newry, when he referred to another MP as 'the gramophone of some clerk in a back office in Dublin'.[37] The thinly veiled insult, the suggestion that a fellow MP was simply acting as a mouthpiece for a third party, would reappear in succeeding decades.

How could future generations be served by the gramophone? Once again, the Gramophone Company had an idea that combined high ideals with a spot of free publicity, and Dame Nellie Melba was part of it. In 1907, the company recorded a series of single-sided discs featuring Dame Nellie, Caruso, and others, placing them in two sealed containers beneath the Paris Opera, ordering that the containers would remain sealed for 100 years; this instruction was duly adhered to. The Bibliothèque Nationale de France made the recordings available in 2009 after removing them from the asbestos in which they had been placed for protection.[38] Fourteen years after the recordings, Melba was dismissive of the affair. She referred to it as 'another dumb compliment.'[39]

England, Sweet England

The Gramophone Company may have been quick off the mark in recording the musical traditions of Empire, but the traditions of England took longer to appear on disc, arriving well after opera, orchestral music, Scottish bagpipers, and Welsh choirs. By 1900, collectors and musicologists such as Cecil Sharp, Lucy Broadwood, and Percy Grainger were actively seeking out the traditional songs of England, but they were concerned with academic study rather than a commercial product. As performance researcher Lucy Wright puts it, this revival of interest in English traditional music and song was 'a pedagogical project—it was about collecting the material and teaching it to a whole new set of people with the idea of finding a national music that would help to define English identity.' The singers were not viewed as artists by these collectors, according to Wright, but as 'living storehouses of memory' whose songs were tidied up, made a little more appropriate for middle-class mores (with all traces of sex or innuendo removed), and repackaged as choral numbers.[40]

Due to the practical problems associated with transporting a phonograph across rural England, many collectors preferred to use paper and pencil rather than one of the new-fangled talking machines, although Grainger did start to use a phonograph in 1906.[41] Then, in 1908, Joseph Taylor, a seventy-four-year-old steward from Saxby All Saints in Lincolnshire, travelled to London and recorded on disc for the Gramophone Company. The session did not result in royalties or even a one-off fee; the company gave Taylor a set of his records and a gramophone to play them.[42] The recordings were commercial failures.

Grainger, who knew Taylor having already recorded his singing on cylinders, was pleased that the singing of a genuine folk singer was being made available to the public.[43] He had been surprised on his forays into rural England to find that folk singers, usually poor agricultural workers, were already familiar with the phonograph and gramophone from local pubs and elsewhere. They were happy to perform for Grainger and seldom nervous about doing so, even if they found the act of singing directly into an amplifying horn rather odd; Taylor described it as 'like singin' with a muzzle on'. Although Taylor gained some local fame in the two years before his death in an accident with a horse and trap, folk music recordings by authentic singers and musicians were no more than a specialist interest, lacking the potential for profit or the cachet of high culture (although the Gramophone Company may have viewed Taylor's records as assisting Grainger and Sharp's educational aims). Some of Taylor's younger contemporaries, such as Norfolk's Harry Cox and Sam Larner, would eventually record dozens of songs but not until the folk revivals of the 1950s and '60s that brought much greater fame to singers such as Ewan MacColl, Martin Carthy, and Shirley Collins.[44]

Other artforms and artists attempted to employ the gramophone with mixed results. The Norwich Musical Festival made use of 'gramophone effects' in its production of Luigi Mancinelli's 'St Agnes', but the effects failed to add interest to what one critic called a lacklustre performance of an undistinguished composition.[45] Magic was more entertaining. At Cecil Lyle's conjuring show, his illusion with a gramophone proved to be the best of the evening.[46] Mr Lyle set the instrument in motion, playing a march. He draped a cloth over the machine, muffling the music, then removed the cloth, no doubt with a dramatic flourish. The gramophone vanished. A theatre's effects specialist would soon be able to draw on a range of sound effect discs, able to reproduce a howling wind, a motor car engine, thunderstorms, the singing of troops on the march, and the cries of an angry mob. The gramophone could provide music for the interval or 'God Save The Queen' for the end of the night's entertainment, removing the need to employ a local pianist or organist and ensuring a consistently high-quality performance of these important pieces of music.[47]

The gramophone began to make regular, if fleeting, appearances in fiction, adding colour to a scene or detail to a character. Grubb and Smallways, bicycle and gramophone record dealers, appeared in H. G. Wells's 1908 novel *The War in The Air*. In Wells's *Marriage*, Trafford gives a gramophone to his betrothed, along with discs of Nellie Melba, the Reverend Capel Gumm's preaching, and a comic song that went 'gobble, gobble, gobble'.[48] In P. G. Wodehouse's *Mike*, the titular schoolboy used it to good effect to confuse his housemaster, Mr Wain.[49] John Galsworthy opened his essay *The Inn of Tranquillity* with the sound of a gramophone 'breaking forth into the air, as it were the presiding voice of a high and cosmopolitan mind'.[50] None of these authors explained what the gramophone was or did; fiction, like *Hansard*, was reflecting the fact that the instrument was part of British life.

The gramophone enthusiast could happily enjoy the instrument in the comfort of their own home, but social listening, beyond the immediate family circle, brought like-minded gramophone enthusiasts together to talk about their instruments and their collections. Gramophone societies formalised the activity. The first of them, the Prudential Assurance Company Society, formed in 1904 to discuss the technologies of recording and reproducing sound; music was of secondary interest.[51] The City of London Phonograph and Gramophone Society, formed in 1919, is still active and claims to be the senior recorded music society in the world. According to its president, Christopher Proudfoot, the CLPGS grew out of a number of phonograph and gramophone societies that began forming in the London area around 1911, emerging as a breakaway group due to members' dissatisfaction with the way in which the gramophone was taking precedence over the phonograph in other societies.

The new society was named The London Edison Society, but when members asked Edison to be patron, he agreed only on the condition that they changed the name to London Phonograph Society.

If a gramophone society was too formal, the Gramophone and Typewriter Ltd had the solution. Hotels, restaurants, tea rooms, cigar stores, and other establishments of less repute could purchase an Automatic Penny-in-the-Slot Gramophone for only £10. It was simple to operate and could, the company claimed, generate up to £3 income each week, although at 1*d* per side, this would require 720 sides to achieve. The instructions suggest that the process of playing a disc was somewhat tortuous. Customers who were not in full command of their senses could well have found it problematic, and damage or even destruction must have been an ever-present danger in the more boisterous locales. Playing the Penny-in-the-Slot instrument required a number of steps:

1-Drop Penny into Slot.

2-Place Record selected on turn-table.

3-Fit needle into soundbox (A fresh needle must be used for playing each record).

4-Wind handle to utmost limit. Turntable will then revolve, and by means of the Automatically Controlled Action of the Reproducer the Record will play.

N.B. The Winding Handle cannot be removed. Nor should any attempt be made to remove it.[52]

It seems like a rather complex and joyless process. The jukebox eventually took over the job of filling pubs with recorded music, simplifying the customer's role and bringing plenty of gaudy plastic colour and flashing lights along with a wide selection of popular hits on disc.

A Threat to the National Chest

Most people happily accepted and embraced the gramophone, but there were active detractors. Critics considered that it had no redeeming features, believing it would ruin society, destroy musicianship, and threaten the careers of musicians and music teachers. Its supporters believed that it would expand society's exposure to great music, encourage children to learn an instrument, and offer new resources for teachers and new possibilities for musicians to earn a living. Both sides got it partly correct.

John Philip Sousa, one of the world's most famous composers, went to war against talking machines and piano rolls in a 1906 article for *Appleton's Magazine*, predicting a marked deterioration in American music and musical taste, an interruption in the musical development of the country, and a host of other injuries to music in its artistic manifestations.[53] Instrument sales would fall, teachers would lose their jobs, and singing would cease. 'Then what of the national throat? Will it not weaken? What of the national chest? Will it not shrink?' Amateur musicians would disappear, mothers would no longer soothe their babies to sleep but would leave the job to the talking machine, and so he went on.

Such a decline, Sousa insisted, was further advanced in Britain. Here, he claimed, the problem was due at least in part to a craze for athletics. He wrote of a halcyon time when families clustered around the fire and listened intently as each member contributed a song or a tune played with style and talent, when all was well with the world because everyone understood and loved the art of music—a time that was now under threat. Sousa had an ulterior motive, one he made no bones about revealing: he was worried about his own income and financial future, and those of his fellow composers: 'The composer of the most popular waltz or march of the year must see it seized, reproduced at will … without a penny of remuneration to himself for the use of this original product of his brain.'

In Britain, commentators also raised concerns about the gramophone menace. The Betterment of London Association's Street Noise Abatement Committee saw the gramophone as a nuisance on a par with organs, cornets, and other instruments, played by beggars intent on 'pursuing their nefarious blackmailing tactics'. Barely ten years after its arrival on British shores, the gramophone was another weapon in the armoury of the street musician, busking for money and making 'HIDEOUS AND UNNECESSARY NOISES' to the despair of the honest citizen.[54] In *The Decline of Domestic Music*, 'C. L. G.' was more measured but still negative.[55] Sousa may well have read this article; C. L. G. includes a cartoon that was reproduced in Sousa's article and lays part of the blame for a decline in domestic music-making at the foot of the new breed of public-school girls, 'athletic young amazons' more excited by hockey, cricket, golf, tennis, gymnastics, and cycling than by musical performance. C. L. G. placed the gramophone in company with motoring and the player piano as new threats to amateur musicianship and noted that professional musicians were faced with an increasingly tough working environment as musical 'at homes' fell out of fashion, and foreign musicians were more likely than British ones to be hired for concerts.

The gramophone brought the foreign threat into the home in a different fashion, through discs of recorded music from around the world. In a rare flash of inspiration, Edison-Bell recognised a marketing opportunity in its fight against the gramophone, appealing loudly to its British customers to buy cylinders made by British musicians. 'It is GOOD FISCAL POLICY to support home talent and the products of YOUR OWN COUNTRY', the advertisement shouted, emphasising that Edison-Bell was a 'purely British company'. The clincher for any music lover concerned about the corrupting influence of non-British recordings was that all vocals on the Edison-Bell cylinders were loud, distinct, and with 'No nasality or disagreeable foreign accents'.[56] Edison-Bell's jingoism fell on deaf ears, or perhaps on ears that were too busy enjoying recordings from across the world. The gramophone industry was an international one. Even a cataclysmic pan-European war would not change this situation, and the portable gramophone would play its patriotic part in the conflict.

On the Record: 'Creeping Jane', Joseph Taylor (Gramophone Company, 1908)

Joseph Taylor was the first English folk singer to have a record released commercially. 'Creeping Jane' is one of the songs he recorded for the Gramophone Company, a traditional song with a common theme—horse racing.

Taylor recorded these songs in London, but he was familiar with gramophones from his home village in Lincolnshire, an indication of how the gramophone was now part of everyday life even in some of the poorest and most rural areas of England.

The Gramophone Company may have expected Britons in search of home-grown recording artists to make 'Creeping Jane' a bestseller, but the disc-buying public had other ideas. Taylor's recordings were authentic examples of English culture, but the wrong sort. Taylor was a working man, from an obscure rural county, seventy-four years old, and unknown to all except his local audience of fellow farm-workers and their families. His voice was still strong and clear, able to carry the tune without accompaniment, but he was neither famous nor stylish and his direct, unsyncopated delivery lacked drama until the final bar, when he decided to end by leaping to the top of his vocal register—a bad decision, as his voice cracks in the attempt.

'Creeping Jane' is a cheery enough song, telling of an unfancied racehorse who eventually triumphs, although the final verse reveals that Creeping Jane is now dead as Taylor promises to visit her grave to keep her body from being eaten by the hounds. There is a jolly singalong nonsense lyric at the end of each verse: 'All the day, dee-o, a diddle all the day-do'. However, this parochial tale has none of the glamour of London society and Taylor is no Dan Leno or Maurice Farkoa. Tales of rural Lincolnshire sung by an elderly man with odd ideas about vocal drama offered no challenge to ragtime or grand opera and lacked the aspirational qualities of songs from the West End stage. Even the jolliest of Taylor's repertoire reminded the listener of the poverty of much of rural English life. If the gramophone was part of an exciting new world of entertainment, Taylor was part of an old world that was losing its relevance for the urban-dwelling record buyers and was not yet far enough in the past to evoke any feelings of nostalgia. An elderly folk singer and a thrusting young record company was an uneasy partnership that was doomed to fail in those heady pre-war days.

4

In the Drawing-Room or Nursery, and For Out-of-Doors

On 26 April 1911, William Crooks, Labour MP for Woolwich, rose in the House of Commons and called for a national minimum wage of 30 shillings a week.[1] The poverty-stricken women of Tottenham he claimed were in support of his campaign had no desire to become mothers: 'They prefer gramophones to babies.' His intention was to point out to his honourable friends that gramophones provided entertainment but did not need food or clothes and would not suffer from a lack of homely comforts; a minimum wage for the working man could provide the food and clothes that children needed and once again the women of Tottenham might view motherhood with more optimism.

Even if Tottenham women preferred gramophones, it is unlikely that they would have owned one. Mr Crooks was talking about some of the poorest families in London, living on less than £1 a week; even cheap models cost twice that amount, putting them within the reach of skilled working men, perhaps, but not of the unskilled labourer striving to feed a family of five, six, or more, even at 5 shillings per month on finance. The socialist utopia that Crooks desired would have to wait, but the gramophone industry could live without it.

The industry introduced improvements that would lead to better quality sound, more efficient production methods, and lower costs. Improvements would persuade more people to buy an instrument and join the gramophone family; they might also persuade existing customers to buy a second or even third machine, to replace older models perceived as redundant or outmoded. The automatic brake ensured that the end of a song was not followed by the irritating scratch and screech of the needle going around and around in the run-off groove. The internal horn led to smaller, neater gramophones and a loss of the phallic symbolism that threatened to embarrass the more refined listener. Record pockets in the lids of machines made it easy to store a selection of discs. These improvements meant that the gramophone was even more welcome in the lounges, libraries, and front rooms of the nation, but the act of playing a record still needed a degree of skill.

How to Play a Record

To make the most of the gramophone's capability for sound reproduction, its owner had the important task of learning how to operate the instrument. This was not an art, not something that involved a knowledge of science or a command of technology—nothing like the talent and dedication required to play a real musical instrument—but there was something of a craft involved. Manufacturers deliberately referred to gramophones as 'instruments', attempting to give them something of the status of the violin or the piano as an object to be played. The idea caught on, and 'playing records' became the usual way of describing the various processes involved in getting a disc ready to be enjoyed.

The tasks were not complex, but they were numerous. Owners needed to undertake routine maintenance to keep the machine running smoothly, making regular applications of lubricating oil. Needles had to be changed after playing just a single side of a disc.[2] The clockwork motor needed to be rewound after every side. Once removed from the turntable, a disc needed to be carefully put away in its sleeve to prevent damage. Once the next disc was in place on the turntable, the motor needed to be engaged, the tone arm lifted and moved over the outer edge of the disc, and the needle lowered as carefully as possible onto the surface of the disc. Three or four minutes later, the entire ritual would have to be repeated.

A poor choice of needle could lead to unnecessary damage to discs, as well as negatively impacting on sound quality. The gramophone aficionado had plenty of needle types to choose from. The Yorke family, owners of Erddig in Wales, kept an HMV needle cutter for preparing fibre needles along with a selection of seven different steel needles: half tone, medium tone, loud tone, extra-loud tone, Star Brand Highly-Polished and, as needle technology improved, Embassy Long-Playing Radiogram Needles and Columbia Duragold Semi-Permanent needles (each Duragold needle was guaranteed to play ten records). Setting the needle at the start of the record needed a steady hand and keen eye. Most discs were pressed completely flat, without the raised edge that characterises the LPs and singles of later years and helps to steer the needle to the correct position on the disc, so misjudging the position of the needle could easily result in it missing the disc or falling off the edge, with likely damage to record and needle.[3] The *Diss Express* helpfully informed its lady readers that old needles were excellent for securing the backs of picture and photograph frames.[4]

Setting the correct speed was fraught with the potential for artistic disaster. To cope with slight variations in motor speed and the different speeds at which the recordings had been made, each gramophone was fitted with a speed regulator or governor controlled by a metal switch, usually placed on the top front of the gramophone. By sliding the switch clockwise or anticlockwise, the operator could slow down or speed up the turntable by a few revolutions per minute, matching the instrument's speed with the one recommended on the label or in the catalogue (calling these discs '78s' is anachronistic as speed was not standardised until the 1920s). This was no easy task, even if the records all came from the same company; for example, the Gramophone Company's new releases for November 1907 varied from 76 to 81 rpm. Two-sided discs did not guarantee that each side would play at the same speed, with individual Odeon discs varying between sides by as much as 6 rpm.[5]

The variability of the speed of reproduction could be a useful marketing tool, as slowing a disc down (or speeding it up) deliberately could offer benefits to the avid listener and home entertainer. The Gramophone Company listed a range of discs in its 1908 catalogue of new records as being 'In Perfect Time for Dancing'. Recorded at 80 rpm, they could be played at 76 or even 72 rpm if a slower time was required, perhaps for the older or less skilful dancer, or as fast as 86 rpm if a more energetic turn around the floor was desired. 'Perfect time for dancing' was not the same as 'perfect speed for accurate reproduction', but it had much to recommend it to the host or hostess eager to offer guests an enjoyable evening of dance tunes.

Just how closely did the average gramophone owner follow the advice of the record companies? It is impossible to know with any certainty, but it is likely that the answer is 'not very'. At the top of the market, instruments and records were expensive and bought only by the comparatively wealthy, so these customers might well have stuck to the recommendations, but as prices fell and the market expanded, things may well have altered. Changing needles was a chore, and even though packs of replacement needles were relatively cheap, the small additional cost coupled with the additional effort probably meant that many, if not most, people changed their needles less frequently than recommended. Discs were fragile and would pick up scratches and dust specks however diligently they were played and stored, so a lackadaisical approach to disc care would hasten the disc's inevitable demise. As for ensuring the correct speed, would a music fan eager to move from Beethoven to Mozart, or a comedy aficionado keen to hear Harry Lauder after Marie Lloyd, really spend time ensuring that they were spinning at the correct rpm, and were the speed regulators on these early gramophones accurate anyway, even when used correctly?

The potential for speed variation raises the prospect that different people listening to the same disc played on different gramophones could all inadvertently be listening to what were essentially different songs. In a single suburban street, the Smith family could be enjoying their favourite disc as it revolved at 74 rpm, the Ponsonbys next door could be listening to the same recording at the recommended speed of 77 rpm, while young Mr and Mrs Lampton four doors along might have been cutting a rug to the same disc at 82 rpm. The variations in speed would have been sufficient to create differences between the three reproductions of almost a whole tone; at 78 rpm, a difference of around 4.5 rpm is equal to a semitone in pitch.[6] In essence, the Smiths, Ponsonbys, and Lamptons were playing their discs in three different keys—a difference that was not simply academic but could affect the emotional impact of the music.

The Great Outdoor Entertainer

A truly portable gramophone would appear around 1914, but the idea of the *al fresco* gramophone arrived years before this. If Fred Gaisberg could travel the world with his portable recording equipment, surely a domestic gramophone could be taken outdoors in good weather? Large freestanding gramophones with massive external horns would create major logistical problems if anyone attempted to move them more than a few feet, but smaller models posed less of a problem, especially if they could be dismantled. The Gramophone Company's Style No. 6, produced in 1901, could be broken into a few parts and packed into a case containing felt-lined compartments.[7] Outdoor entertainment was achievable with instruments like this, not only on the terrace but also on a picnic, if the case could be squeezed onto the back of a car. As the summer of 1903 approached, the company looked forward to the gramophone becoming once again 'the king of outdoor entertainers'.[8] Yet the instruments were not truly portable. A genuinely portable instrument needed to be light, easy for one person to carry, contained within its own case, fitted with an internal horn, and ready to use without having to be re-assembled. Such an instrument would not arrive on the British market for another decade. Gramophone manufacturers and retailers did not let such practical problems stop them promoting the gramophone as the perfect instrument for open-air fun, however, and some of Britain's more adventurous citizens provided incontrovertible evidence for the gramophone's portability across the seas and into the far corners of the world.

When Lily Smith entered the unforgiving English Channel and swam from Dover to Ramsgate in a new record time of six hours and seventeen minutes, she sustained herself physically with beef tea, grapes, and rice pudding and mentally with a gramophone on her pilot boat, which played 'exhilarating tunes' as she swam.[9] Miss Smith claimed that while she was swimming she was 'frightfully fond of the cheery notes of "Asleep in The Deep"'.[10] It is an odd song to provide succour to a sea-going swimmer, the lyrics telling of two lovers about to drown. 'Many brave hearts are asleep in the deep, so beware,' it warns. Perhaps Miss Smith was driven by the constant fear of a watery grave.

The even more unwelcoming Antarctic posed a greater challenge, but two of the Empire's greatest explorers showed that this bleak, cold, climate was no barrier to the enjoyment of recorded entertainment. Both Robert Falcon Scott and Ernest Shackleton took gramophones on their Antarctic explorations; one photograph from Shackleton's 1907 expedition shows a group of puzzled penguins listening to a gramophone record.[11] Scott took two HMV Monarch gramophones on his 1910 expedition, along with hundreds of discs, to help keep up the morale of his men.[12] Gramophones could function on rough seas and in frozen wastes, but Miss Smith had a crew of helpers, while Scott and Shackleton could rely on trained men and sturdy ships. For a man or woman hoping for a gramophone that could easily be carried by bus to a party or meeting, the ideal instrument was yet to be produced.

Barnett Samuel and Sons Ltd brought this ideal instrument to market in 1914, when it produced the Decca Dulcephone.[13] The company had an eye on the international market; Wilfred Samuels claimed to have invented Decca as a name that would be pronounced identically in all languages and would be 'easily recognised by illiterates', apparently unaware that Decca (or Deccan) was an area of India (sales of Decca handkerchiefs were advertised regularly in *The Times* in the 1780s).[14] Dulcephone is an even more intriguing name. It sounds as if it was another of Samuel's invented words, perhaps intended to indicate 'sweet sounds', but the term was in use during the 1880s as the trade name of an object 'for moderating the tone of the Piano during practice'.[15]

The Decca Dulcephone was the first genuinely portable gramophone, contained in a 12-inch-wide wooden case with a stout carrying handle and weighing a mere 15 lb (just under 7 kg). It was ready for action as soon as the lid was lifted and the motor wound. Sound travelled from the needle, through the soundbox, and directly along the tone arm to a small horn that faced backwards into the concave metal reflector inside the lid. The horn and reflector combination acted as an amplifier, sending the sound back towards the listeners. Barnett Samuels started selling its new instrument in July 1914 for £2 2s.[16] Only a few weeks later, Europe went to war. The Dulcephone was soon on its way to the front line, as was Driver Wilfred Samuels of the Honourable Artillery Company.

Prices rose during the war years, and by October 1918, the Decca was £7 15s.[17] It was a price worth paying in the eyes of many people, especially if it helped sons, lovers, or husbands at the front to remember their homes and families. The instrument gained such popularity with the British armed forces that it became known as the Trench Decca because of the comfort it brought to troops in these miserable ditches; coincidentally, the officer who helped Wilfred Samuel to gain his commission was Lieutenant Colonel B. F. Trench.[18]

Patriotism, Jingoism, and Romance

The outbreak of hostilities caught HMV by surprise, its list of new discs for that month advertising 'Open Air Records. Play them in the garden! ... Take some on your holiday'. The company moved swiftly to meet the challenge of war on its existing roster and added a six-page 'Patriotic Section' to its November catalogue. Some discs featured military bands, Sir Edward Elgar conducted the 'Pomp and Circumstance March', Clara Butt sang 'Land of Hope and Glory' and 'God Save the King', and the Sullivan Operatic Party joined in with 'A British Tar is a Soaring Soul'. Field Marshal Lord Roberts's 'Speech on National Service' was a call to arms that filled six 10-inch records.[19] In February 1915, the company added Arthur Bourchier's delivery of Lloyd George's Queen's Hall speech on 'The Empire's Honour'—a 'most moving piece of oratory' with 'strictures on German treachery ... as sweeping as they were true-based.'[20] The record struck a suitably patriotic tone, but it was hardly likely to cheer up the troops. Ruby Helder, the 'Lady tenor', was more likely to send a thrill through British hearts as she called on the nation's parents to send their sons to fight with her rendition of 'Call of the Motherland': 'Our foes shall be smitten,/While true sons of Britain,/From the East,/From the West,/Send their bravest and best,/At the call of the Motherland.' Stewart Gardner joined in with 'England's Battle Hymn', as did Ethel Leavey ('Carry On') and George Carvey ('March on to Berlin'). Tucked away near the end of the list, under the heading of New Pantomime and Revue Records, was John McCormack's recording of 'It's A Long, Long, Way to Tipperary', first released in the previous month.

'It's A Long, Long, Way to Tipperary' was one of the first songs to win the nation's hearts during the Great War. Written in 1912, it tells the tale of Paddy, a young Irish lad who comes to London from his home in Tipperary. The streets are paved with gold, but Paddy must return home to ensure that his sweetheart does not marry another man. It is not, on the surface, an obvious choice as the nation's favourite wartime song—it even includes a stereotypical Irish joke about Paddy's cognitive abilities—but there are universal themes in the lyrics. The soldiers, like Paddy, were far from their sweethearts and longing to return home. The sweethearts, families, and friends could readily imagine their loved ones' desire to be back. There was no jingoism, belligerence, or hatred, just a wish for life to be as it was. Pathé sold two versions: the Scots Guards Band playing a 'Humouresque on the Soldiers' Song, It's A Long Way to Tipperary' and the Empire Orchestra's version, played as a march with added vocal effects.[21] Columbia offered five recordings including a short version as part of a Panto Medley with the Scots Guards backing Stanley Kirkby and a version by Miss Lilian Braithwaite supported by a male chorus and the 'British Guards Band'.[22]

'Take Me Back to Dear Old Blighty' was another favourite with the troops. It has its patriotic moments but, like 'Tipperary', its essential message is one of longing to go home. The soldiers are doing their bit, but all they want is to be back, cuddling up with their 'best girls'. Unlike 'Tipperary', this was a song written by A. J. Mills, Fred Godfrey, and Bennett Scott in the midst of the war. According to Godfrey, the three men were walking past London's Oxford music hall one day in 1916 and noticed that the current show was called *Blighty*. Inspired by the title, the men worked on a song, and four hours later, it was written.[23] Other popular songs, such as 'Roses of Picardy', drew on similar emotions—the sadness and sense of loss resulting from absence from home, or time apart from a loved one—emphasising the personal sacrifices being made and the hope that these relationships would soon be rekindled, rather than appealing to patriotism or war fever.

The record companies kept up a steady stream of patriotic recordings in the war's early years. Some spoke of the Empire's great feats of exploration (Ernest Shackleton's 'The Dash for the South Pole', at HMV), while others were more overtly militaristic. Zonophone released Godfrey King's two-sided disc matching the descriptive 'Recruiting' with the patriotic 'England's Honour' and discs telling of the 'Landing of the British Troops in France' (which included the chorus of 'Tipperary') and 'The Landing of the Australian Troops in Egypt'.[24] Columbia released Captain A. E. Rees's 'Infantry Squad Drill' as 'A record of unique interest since by its aid squads of soldiers were actually drilled in Public View in London in Trafalgar Square'.[25]

Such overt displays of patriotic fervour lost popularity as war dragged on, but one more macabre descriptive disc was still to come. In the closing weeks of the war, the British attacked opposition forces in Lille. Shortly afterwards, one of the most extraordinary descriptive discs appeared: 'Gas Shell Bombardment'.[26] The 12-inch disc, costing 6 shillings, was an 'Actual recording of the Gas Shell Bombardment by The Royal Garrison Artillery (9 October 1918), preparatory to the British troops entering Lille … An Historical Record which should be in every home.' At the close of the record, a male voice encouraged the listener to 'Feed the guns with War Bonds and help to win the war', but by the time most people had the chance to buy a copy, the war was already won and HMV declared that all profits would be donated to the King's Fund for the Disabled.

The recording itself is surprisingly devoid of excitement. Only a small detachment of artillery is featured, with just four guns (or mortars) firing in turn, in response to the orders of one man. Each shell fires with a 'pop' followed by a 'wizz' as it flies towards the German lines. Each voice (there are two or three, including the officer or NCO in charge) is calm and unhurried; there is no sound of the shells landing, no sense of their impact on the enemy. It is hard to believe that this really was recorded in the heat of battle, even though *Talking Machine World* described it as a 'Real Blood and Iron War Record'.[27] It is claimed that Will Gaisberg (Fred's brother) recorded the attack and furthermore that he died from being gassed during the process.[28] However, *Talking Machine World* (which described Will Gaisberg as a man of great skill, musical ability, and a 'sunny disposition') gave his cause of death as influenza.[29]

Patriotic discs quickly lost their popularity once the public began to realise how costly the war was going to be. Alfred Clark of the Gramophone Company described the initial trade in patriotic discs as 'brisk' but acknowledged that total sales were never more than 'a drop in the bucket'.[30] Louis Sterling, Columbia's London manager, wrote in April 1918 that demand had plummeted, claiming that the troops wanted popular music and opera while the public called for popular tunes and what Sterling called 'good music ... high-class ballads and the very fine string and orchestra selections'.[31] Such records offered an escape from the stresses of war, a chance to listen to familiar music from a more peaceful time and to forget, however briefly, about the destruction. A recording of a gas attack was something of an anomaly.

Although Britain was tired of the conflict, overtly anti-war recordings failed to appear.[32] The Savoy Quartet's 'I Don't Want to Get Well' offered a subtler anti-war lyric. The singer has been wounded on the front line and is now in a field hospital where he is fed regularly by a 'bee-oo-tiful nurse' he has fallen in love with. He is in no hurry to return to the front and risk his life again. It is a humorous song, but the singer's sentiments were no doubt shared by many soldiers and their loved ones.

Making the Most of the War

The record companies and retailers were eager to associate themselves with the troops, enlisting members of the armed forces in advertising campaigns. Harrods advertised its range of instruments with the catchphrase 'for Drawing Room, Hospital or Dugout'.[33] HMV was one of the first record companies to use members of the armed forces in its advertisements, placing the ever-faithful Nipper at the feet of an archetypal Tommy Atkins.[34] The Decca campaign made the most of the military connection. One of its advertisements, inspired by the poem 'In Arras', was illustrated by a drawing of an army officer walking thoughtfully through the ruined streets of the French town. The poem was based on the experiences of Philip Gibbs, an official war correspondent, who, walking those streets himself, thought he heard a woman singing behind a 'shattered door'. It was not a real singer but a disc played on a Decca portable.[35] The Decca was clearly the gramophone for the man of action. It seems rather curious, then, that these advertisements emphasised that it was 'as easy to carry as a handbag'.

After the war ended, Barnett Samuel reminded customers of the Decca's role in Britain's success, drawing on the supposedly genuine experiences of an unnamed soldier: '"Why, it won the war for us,"—laughingly asserted an Officer whose war-worn "Decca" had excited the curiosity of his friends.' It claimed, too, that the Decca had brought comfort to tens of thousands of soldiers.[36] The venerable Sir Edward Elgar personally attested to the value placed by front-line troops on the instruments and their discs, having sent a selection of Mozart records to a friend serving on the Western Front. The friend's section was bombarded by German artillery and forced to retreat; on reforming, one man returned for the gramophone while another rescued the records. In Elgar's words, 'They preferred to save them to anything else.'[37]

Major Christopher Stone DSO, MC, served on the Western Front with the Royal Fusiliers and wrote of the gramophone's importance a few years later.[38] A Decca portable and half a dozen records arrived at his battalion's reserve billet in January 1917 and immediately altered life in the officers' mess. Music became a routine part of an evening's relaxation, even if the 'evening' did not begin until the officers returned from the front line at 3 or 4 a.m. Stone and his comrades bought new discs when on leave, ordered more for delivery by post, or took up discs left by other battalions as they moved on. They commandeered a large clothes basket to transport the machine and records, which went everywhere with the battalion for the remainder of the war, playing in ruined buildings and tents and eventually entering Germany. It never made it as far as the front line but stayed close by with the officers' personal belongings, ready to offer comfort.

The officers were catholic in their tastes, enjoying Wagner, Beethoven, music hall star George Robey, and 'a jolly bit of restaurant music called "Dandy"'. A disc coupling 'Where My Caravan Has Rested' with 'A Little Love, a Little Kiss' by Elsie and Dorothy Southgate was so popular that it wore out and every officer knew the words of comedian Harry Tate's 'Fortifying the Home' sketch by heart. When the war ended, Stone took the Decca home, eventually raffling it for one shilling a ticket in aid of charity in his village. It had been a vital part of his battalion's life, 'the barely portable hero of a thousand nights'.

Back on the Home Front

The record industry was better prepared for the declaration of peace than it had been for the outbreak of war. As soon as the armistice was declared, the record companies swung into action with a programme of celebratory 'Victory' discs. HMV promoted its dance records, while other companies released triumphant songs and popular airs. The Winner label (part of Edison Bell) released a 'potpourri' of popular tunes, military marches, and national anthems. It also released 'The Likes of They' sung by Charles Tree, a disc dedicated to J. Havelock Wilson, MP and President of the Sailors' and Firemen's Union, with lyrics that echoed 'the Union's threat not to unload or handle any German ships for a number of years'.[39] Sadly, if unsurprisingly, it never quite matched the popularity of 'Roses in Picardy'.

Most gramophones arrived at the front as the personal possessions of individual soldiers, but others may have arrived in a more official capacity. One unbranded gramophone, complete with a large, red-painted horn, was decorated with a carving of the official Royal Flying Corps crest.[40] Some may have been constructed on active service by the soldiers themselves, perhaps drawing on their skills from civilian jobs. A particularly striking instrument, using the parts from a Columbia Grafonola table-top machine, was constructed in a repair park at St Omer sometime during 1918 by a group of RAF-enlisted men. The gramophone was placed in a hand-made case with beautiful and elaborate carvings on the lid and sides by A. M. Crawford, including the crests of the RFC and the RAF.[41]

If anyone should doubt the popularity of the gramophone, the experience of Captain Bigglesworth, the fictional pilot of the RFC/RAF, was clear about its value to morale. In *Biggles in France*, the hero wins a gramophone for his squadron and his comrade, Algy, loyally defends the instrument from an attempt by the losing squadron to steal it. It is obviously a valued object as Captain Bigglesworth declares that 'We'll have a merry evening, with a tune on the jolly old gramophone to wind up with!'[42]

In military and civilian hospitals, the gramophone provided entertainment for the sick and wounded. The entertainment was not confined to listening to records, as tricks could be played. One anonymous nurse told a *Spectator* journalist of night duty shifts in London hospitals, among the 'cockney' patients:

[At dead of night] the gramophone will abruptly burst into raucous music—its mechanism has been released by a contrivance which gives no clue to the crime's perpetrator.... Half an hour after the ward has quieted down, the other gramophone (some wards own two) whirs off into impudent song.[43]

Such practical jokes were an annoyance, noted the journalist, but also a badge of acceptance and popularity as unpopular nurses never had these pranks played upon them. Charles Norton, the comedian, was wounded on service and found himself in a hospital in Rouen listening to his own recording of 'Pros at the Races' on the ward's gramophone. The comic kept his identity as the performer a secret from his fellow patients, but hearing the record brought him great cheer.[44]

Barnett Samuel's advertising campaign made the Great War experiences of the featured soldiers seem like weekend jaunts, enlivened by the portable gramophone. War poet Siegfried Sassoon did not agree. In *Dead Musicians*, written in 1918, he remembered his fallen comrades as he listened to a ragtime tune, but when the disc ended, he realised that his comrades were dead and cried 'For God's sake stop that gramophone'.[45]

Patriotism may have initially been useful in the British market, but across the Atlantic in the then neutral USA, it paid to have a more open approach. Columbia jumped at the marketing opportunity offered by European war. In September 1914, the company took out a full-page advertisement in *Talking Machine World*, proudly stating that 'A Line of Foreign Records, representative of every country in Europe is today strengthening every Columbia dealer in handling the present phenomenal demand for European national music.' Emphasising the company's own neutrality, the advertisement included the coats of arms of as many European nations as could be fitted onto the page.[46] In Britain, Columbia lost many of its workers to the armed forces and other war work. Its pre-war workforce of 291 men in its British record plant dropped to eleven, so the company hired more women to fill the gap, increasing its number of female workers by 40 per cent. By 1917, business was strong; Louis Sterling reported that that year was the company's best ever year for record production. The company made the most of air raids, blackouts, and the lack of public entertainment. People were looking for home-based entertainment and the gramophone industry did its bit to provide it.[47]

Within weeks of the war beginning, the Gramophone Company placed its London headquarters at the disposal of the military, moved its offices to its pressing plant at Hayes, and diverted much of its production capacity to the war effort. This was no altruistic act of patriotism; managing director Alfred Clark claimed that the decision to produce munitions saved the company from bankruptcy as record and instrument sales fell.[48] These munitions (made for British, Belgian, and Russian forces) were vital to the war effort and to the company's survival—the workforce increased from 1,100 at the start of the war to 4,000 in 1918—but they did nothing to advance its gramophone designs or technologies. It seems that they did little for industrial relations either. William Tyson Wilson, Labour MP for Westhoughton, declared that the company was paying its workers at a reduced rate, claiming that the War Office payments were too low to afford to pay standard rates.[49] As the industry returned to normal activity, the influenza epidemic reached Britain. The small Guardsman record company was so badly hit that production dropped sharply and four staff died.[50]

As the industry recovered, it conquered one last frontier as the gramophone took to the air. Even the Decca portable might have been a tight fit in the cockpit of Captain Biggles's Sopwith Camel, but another flying machine offered more space. The airship had space for an instrument and a collection of discs, and its slow and steady pace across the Atlantic meant that entertainment was more of a necessity than a luxury. The British crew of R-34 took a 'collapsible gramophone' across the Atlantic in July 1919, but the unnamed machine broke during the 108-hour journey, possibly because it was 'of British make'. The Columbia Graphophone Company came to the rescue, delivering a portable Grafonola and a large selection of discs to the airship for its return trip.[51] This was clearly a crew of some musical sophistication as most of their chosen discs came from a new genre of music: jazz.

Busking, Training, and Language Learning

Had the war not intervened, it is possible that the Gramophone Company would have produced a portable instrument to rival the Decca, but it would take until 1920 before the company entered the portable market. Other companies made the best of what they had got. In 1917, the Orchestrelle Company was attempting to persuade the British public that Aeolian's Vocalion gramophone was 'The Ideal Gramophone for Outdoor Use'.[52] The 20-guinea Vocalion was a large table-top model, at least 12 inches high with a heavy wooden cabinet, but it did boast an internal horn. The advertisement emphasised ease of use and appealed to all generations. In an *al fresco* illustration, an elderly woman sits in a chair, wrapped in a blanket, to the left of the instrument. A younger man, his left foot heavily bandaged perhaps because of a war wound, sits to the right, while a young woman, possibly the man's sister or sweetheart, is in charge of the gramophone. The Gramophone Company eventually entered the portable gramophone market with the HMV PAAO, a heavy-looking machine with an oak cabinet that sold for £15—far more than the Decca.[53] It may not have been a bargain or a technological breakthrough, but it did give the company a start and would soon be followed by more successful models.

In Parliament, the gramophone continued to provide members of both houses with a handy insult. George Barnes suggested that government ministers were 'mere gramophones, drawling out replies given to them by their permanent officials behind the scenes'.[54] Mr Ian Malcolm, MP for Croydon, was not content with abusing individual members and went one step further, accusing the entire House of Commons of being in 'something like the position of a gramophone, which only registers the decrees of the executive'.[55]

Public lectures were rare during the war years, but they soon returned and embraced the gramophone. Harold Wild made use of the instrument in his talks on the history of orchestral music, in which he played numerous discs to illustrate his themes. The records 'created a great impression in an educational respect'.[56] Gramophone discs were a boon to language learning. HMV offered Professor Ripman's conversational French course on sixteen discs, as well as a Russian language course from Neville Forbes MA. The latter was especially useful, the company claimed, as post-war relations promised an Anglo-Russian trade boom. Two courses of Marconi Official Training Signals promised the chance to learn Morse code and other communication systems.[57] Sir Isaac Pitman and Company's Gramophone Method of Rhythmic Typewriting offered practical instruction for 35 shillings.[58] Only weeks before the outbreak of war, gramophone manufacturers Blum and Co. announced a new approach to language learning, combining textbooks with gramophone records. The system was 'simplified', enabling students to follow words and phrases on disc and repeat them until their pronunciation was correct. French and German were available, and the system was named Linguaphone.[59]

Smaller, lighter, and cheaper than its predecessors, providing comfort to the sick or to the faraway soldier, a new source of education and information, the modern gramophone was recognised by all and integral to daily life across the country. The naysayers still had their complaints, however. The portable instrument brought concerns as it facilitated a new breed of 'street musicians': 'We are not speaking of the bands which walk about with the unemployed, but of far humbler efforts. For instance, a gramophone on a perambulator dragged slowly through back streets'.[60]

In *Ulysses*, James Joyce was scathing about the technology and the idea of the voices of the dead:

Have a gramophone in every grave or keep it in the house. After dinner on a Sunday. Put on poor old greatgrandfather. Kraahraark! Hellohellohello amawfullyglad kraark awfullygladaseeagain hellohello amawf krpthsth.[61]

This was far from a ringing endorsement of the gramophone's abilities, but Joyce's opinion carried little weight with a British public that was looking forward to happier times. Such times were just around the corner, for some at least. A brash and exciting new music would usher them in.

On the Record: 'Take Me Back to Dear Old Blighty', Florrie Forde (Zonophone Records, 1917)

Music hall star Florrie Forde (1875–1940) was born in Australia but spent most of her career in Britain. Already famous at the outset of the Great War, she recorded patriotic songs that became popular with the troops at the front, thanks in part to portable gramophones. Her version of 'Take Me Back to Dear Old Blighty' is probably the best known and best loved of the many renditions of the song.

The instrumental backing is upbeat. A marching rhythm underneath some cheerfully melodic wind instruments sets the mood as Forde enters. She sings clearly, ensuring that every word can be understood; listeners would have no problem singing along after just one or two plays. On stage, one imagines, she would soon have her audience joining in the tale of Dick Dunn (Jack Dunn in other versions) and Mickey O'Shea, stuck in the trenches and longing to be home. In truth, the song paints a rather rosy picture of the soldiers' lives, as if shells and bullets were nothing more than temporary, if noisy, nuisances; 'it is nothing worse than a firework display', sings Forde. After a hard day at the front, these soldiers can look forward to relaxing with a portable gramophone. It is unlikely Florrie was fooling anyone by 1917, when the carnage was all too obvious.

Although it was written in just four hours during one night in 1916, 'Take Me Back to Dear Old Blighty' has proved to be remarkably resilient, its life extending well beyond the Great War. It is a fine example of a music hall singalong with a simple structure and an audience participation chorus, supportive of the troops without descending into anti-German rhetoric. Like 'Tipperary', it is as much about longing for home and romance as it is about fighting a war.

Songs are open to interpretation, for reappraisal with the passage of time. A much later version than Forde's paints a darker picture. Kevin Coyne, the idiosyncratic British singer and songwriter, recorded the song on Dynamite Daze (Virgin Records, 1978). Backed by Zoot Money on piano, Coyne sings just one verse and chorus. It is a passionate performance, his voice full of bitterness and despair. Sixty years after the armistice, there is no pretence at romance or patriotism.

Stick Around for The New Jazz Band

'We'll be over, we're coming over, and we won't come back till it's over, over there.' George M. Cohan's 'Over There' promised that the Yanks would come over and they kept the promise. With the war finished, the Americans were going home, yet the song stayed. Courtland and Jeffries, the banjo-playing Savoy Quartet (with vocals by Joe Wilbur), and the band of the Coldstream Guards released versions on HMV, which subtitled the song as the 'Great American War Song'.[1] Once the war was over, Britain sought entertainments that would look to the future rather than dwelling on the past. The gung-ho patriotism of 'Over There'—a song that promoted America's military prowess, rather than Britain's—was soon outmoded. The gramophone would help to usher in a more optimistic and hedonistic time, bringing America's new musical craze to Britain, a craze that would have such an impact on entertainment, fashion, dance, and art that it would give the next few years its distinctive name: the Jazz Age.

Syncopation, Swing, and Style: Britain Goes Jazzing

Jazz challenged the orthodoxy of the recording studio. The Original Dixieland Jazz Band (ODJB) was the first jazz band to make a recording, and not even the American recording industry was prepared for the challenges of this raucous new music. According to cornetist and bandleader Nick LaRocca, the band's first session for Columbia in early 1917 ended with the musicians being ordered out of the studio after recording just two tunes. The band was too loud, the noise reverberated around the room, the studio director retreated to his office and closed the door, and a group of carpenters working in the studio added to the mayhem by throwing their tools around. The recordings—'Darktown Strutters' Ball' and 'Back Home in Indiana'—were shelved away.[2]

The band moved to the Victor Talking Machine Company, HMV's American cousin, and successfully recorded 'Livery Stable Blues' and 'Dixieland Jass Band One-Step' thanks to the engineer's willingness to experiment. LaRocca stood about 20 feet away from the recording horn. Drummer Anthony Sbarbaro sat 5 feet further back but was not allowed to use his bass drum during recording as the equipment could not cope with its sound. Trombonist Eddie Edwards stood 12–15 feet from the horn while clarinettist Larry Shields was just 5 feet in front of it. Pianist Henry Ragas sat closest of all to the horn.

Despite sound engineer Charles Souey's best efforts, the band needed to alter their usual performing style. LaRocca was used to counting his fellow musicians in by stamping his foot, but the Victor team refused to allow foot stamping, so the band watched the studio's red light, counted to two after it came on and then started playing. The effort proved worthwhile as the disc, released in March 1917, eventually sold over 1 million copies. The band arrived in Britain on 1 April 1919, playing its first date at the London Hippodrome on 7 April, under two months after pianist Ragas died of influenza. The audience included many American troops and the band received a standing ovation.[3] Jazz had officially arrived in Britain.

It all sounds lovely, but the story ignores the role of black musicians and ensembles. When the USA entered the Great War, over 2,000,000 American troops crossed the Atlantic. Among them were the bands of the African-American regiments, most notably Lieutenant James Reese Europe's Hell Fighters, part of the African-American 369th US Infantry. Europe was credited by *Talking Machine World* as 'the one man who made jazz music the favorite music of the day.'[4] Although these military bands did not perform in Britain, some British forces personnel would have heard them play, helping to set the scene for the arrival of the ODJB.[5]

Will Marion Cook's Southern Syncopated Orchestra did arrive in Britain at about the same time as the ODJB and played concerts across the country, including a season at London's Philharmonic Hall.[6] The African-American band's music was described as 'Southern folk songs', and a review of a Coliseum show spoke enthusiastically of the band's melodies, of the drummer's 'lightning dexterity', the singers' joyous harmonies, the SSO's talent for syncopation, and its ability to switch from syncopated rhythms 'to the darkie folk-songs and melodies that will live long after jazz and ragtime'.[7] We will have to take the reviewer's word for it as there is no evidence that they ever set foot in a studio.

Music with 'jazz' in its title appeared in Britain months before the ODJB and the SSO set foot on these shores. 'Stick Around for the New Jazz Band' by Courtland and Jeffries appeared in December 1918. The song offered a few odd orchestral effects and was, HMV promised, 'a most amusing number'. The Mayfair Orchestra's 'When I Hear that Jazz Band Play' appeared in

February 1919. By September 1919, HMV's roster listed eleven discs of 'jazz', including 'Balloons and Kisses' and 'The Jazz Nightmare' from the Mayfair Orchestra, 'The Jazz Band' (two versions, by Elsie Janis and by the Savoy Quartet), and Janis's version of 'The Darktown Strutters' Ball'.[8] The Savoy Quartet and Janis discs came from a revue, *Hullo America!*, which ran for 358 performances at London's Palace Theatre from 25 September 1918.[9] Sailors on the transatlantic route could have brought copies of the ODJB's records back to Britain before the official British release of any 'jazz' record (as we saw in Chapter 4, the crew of airship R-34 brought jazz records home in the summer of 1919).

The day after the ODJB played its first British engagement, Horatio Bottomley MP spoke of 'Jazz bands' during a debate on the Housing and Town Planning Bill, and so gained the first mention of jazz in *Hansard*.[10] Just a few months later, Dr Donald Murray informed his Commons colleagues that the Minister of Labour, Sir Robert Horne, had just 'jazzed into the Lobby'; it is hard to imagine what such a move entailed, but the phrase is memorable.[11]

Record companies eager to cash in on the jazz craze gave little consideration to the accuracy of their descriptions or to the claims and counterclaims about who invented what. Initially, this may have been because they did not understand this new music; later, it may have been a more cynical ploy. The same applies to British musicians; simply adding the word 'jazz' to a title or lyric did not make a jazz tune, but before the ODJB's discs were available, the vast majority of the listening public had no benchmark to guide them. HMV's keenness to enter the jazz market showed itself in an almost charmingly disingenuous fashion. Before the ODJB arrived in London, the company marketed a few so-called jazz discs, stretching the definition way past breaking point. Waltzes, foxtrots, two-steps, and one-steps were all included; most excitingly, all were played by the Coldstream Guards Band.[12] Soon after, HMV released a seven-page catalogue of dance music discs, 'All Suitable for Jazzing'.[13] Genuine jazz artists were notable by their absence, but the catalogue was endorsed by the internationally famous dancer Irene Castle, who claimed to find the discs 'remarkable for their accuracy of time and fidelity of rhythm'. A second endorsement came from the less well-known Henri De Bray, 'The Original Exponent of the Tickle-Toe', who commended the discs for 'Society Dancing'.[14]

Any link between the Coldstream Guards and 'jazzing' was soon forgotten once HMV released the ODJB's discs, but other artists kept up the connection. Florrie Forde invited her fans to 'Heigho, Jazz it with Me'. Jack Pleasants, a music hall comic from Bradford, was happy to admit 'I Went a Jazzing'. The Manhattan Jazz Band went even further, claiming that 'Everybody's Jazzing Now'.[15] The idea of jazzing lent itself to the double entendre. In Pleasants's song, credited to Robert Weston and Bert Lee, 'jazzing' is clearly a form of dance, for the most part, but it is also a euphemism for another recreational activity.

A growing number of music lovers and musicians were keen to hear the authentic sound of jazz. Records were vital, as historian Francesco Martinelli notes, because sheet music could not communicate the tempo and timbre variations used by the innovative players of this new music. Even when radio arrived in the mid-1920s, records remained crucial; in order to learn or transcribe melodies, solos, and arrangements, musicians needed to hear each piece repeatedly.[16]

Authentic jazz or not, dance music provided the soundtrack for dancing, parties, and social gatherings across Britain. The top British bands sold hundreds of thousands of discs, gathering fans across the country and filling dance halls in every town they visited. Gramophone records gave people the chance to hear the bands whenever they wished, allowing them to become familiar with some of a band's tunes before seeing them for the first time, or enabling them to revisit a few of its songs as a means of remembering the dance or concert appearances they had enjoyed. The gramophone enabled dance music fans to share a musical experience even though they were hundreds of miles apart—a shared musical experience that did not rely on concert performances or amateur interpretations of sheet music (although it did rely on each gramophone's speed being set correctly). There were plenty of dance halls and nightclubs in Britain by the end of the 1920s; as many as 11,000 opened during the first half of the decade.[17] These venues employed bands large and small, giving customers the chance to dance to the latest tunes, played by bands of varying quality, but this was no guarantee that a favourite tune would be played by a top band. To hear a particular tune played by a particular band, for most people, most of the time, meant putting on a gramophone record.

Gramophones brought music to smaller social gatherings, when a band would have been out of the question for reasons of finances or space. William Patrick Roberts's 1923 painting, *The Dance Club (The Jazz Party)*, is a colourful and energetic interpretation of one such event. In a small, windowless room, a group of about twenty dancers is squeezed together, each couple pushing and being pushed by their neighbours. In the bottom right, a group of four men play cards. On their table sits a horned gramophone, the music emanating from it seemingly so powerful that it forces the dancers towards the far end of the room.

How could these people talk to each other above the din, assuming they wanted to? Harold Acton, the historian and poet, claimed that the clipped and terse private language of the aesthetes, artists, and wealthy party animals known as the Bright Young People evolved specifically to carry over the noise of loud gramophone records.[18] The gramophone played its own role in the development of language by introducing American slang to the people of Britain, often relating to sex, drugs, or other nefarious and non-British activities.[19] Jazz and blues records from the USA were gaining followers among the fashionable young set familiar to Harold Acton and among other inquisitive music fans across the country. Their titles alone brought new words and phrases into the conversation. Duke Ellington's 'Hop Head', Slim and Slam's 'Flat Foot Floogie', Mildred Bailey's 'Rock It for Me', and Lattimore's Connie's Inn Orchestra's 'Reefer Man' all helped to introduce or popularise slang terms among those in the know.[20]

What was played on these gramophones could be an important indicator of taste, good or bad. In Evelyn Waugh's 1928 novel *Decline and Fall*, the quiet of the day is broken by a young woman's gramophone playing Gilbert and Sullivan in her 'little pink boudoir'. Both the choice of record and décor are, according to writer and critic D. J. Taylor, 'aesthetic marker flags, in which characters betray their inadequacy through the second-rateness of their cultural tastes'.[21] Take that, Gilbert and Sullivan.

Soon, Britain's favourite discs were dance music discs, whatever level of cultural taste they may have signalled to snobs such as Waugh. In the 1930 *Merchandising Survey of Great Britain*, almost a third of respondents (29.3 per cent) said that dance records were their favourite music discs, compared to 23.1 per cent who favoured 'vocal' records and 16.1 per cent who preferred opera. Humorous records came in below opera at 15.5 per cent, while 'serious' music was top of the list for just 0.4 per cent of respondents.[22] The survey's classification system was open to interpretation. Dance records included jazz, 'vocal' records could have included dance tunes with vocal refrain as well as popular songs from musical revues, and exactly how 'serious' music had to be to make it into that category was not clear.

The record companies routinely described records in terms of the dances they were suitable to accompany. The ODJB's 'Bluin' the Blues' was a foxtrot, and 'At the Jazz Band Ball' was a one-step.[23] One-steps and waltzes were popular, but the foxtrot was the dance most of these discs were suited to—'the ubiquitous fox-trot' in Vocalion's words.[24] In the Jazz Age, dances were slaves to fashion, liable to fade from popularity as quickly as they arrived. When the Savoy Orpheans recorded 'The Charleston' for HMV early in 1925, it introduced a new rhythm to Britain's dance-crazy youth.[25] The dances were especially popular among the bohemian artistic and literary community; Ezra Pound, the London-based American poet and critic, was fond of 'kicking up fantastic heels in a highly personal Charleston'.[26]

Top dance bands made records with surprising regularity. Jack Hylton, one of Britain's most popular bandleaders, offers a striking example. Between 28 May 1921 and 6 March 1940, Hylton recorded around 2,200 sides with eleven different bands. He made the vast majority of these recordings with the Jack Hylton Orchestra, but he also recorded as a member of the Embassy Dance Orchestra, the Queen's Dance Orchestra, and the Ariel Dance Orchestra as well as leading bands such as the Jack Hylton Jazz Band, Jack Hylton's Brighter London Band, and Jack Hylton's Kit-Cat Band. He recorded in HMV's Hayes facility, London's Kingsway Hall, New Gallery Cinema, Friends Meeting House, and Madame Tussaud's Cinema, and in Berlin, Milan, Glasgow, and Paris. His recordings appeared on HMV, Zonophone, Decca, Mayfair, Panachord, and Electrola.[27] For Hylton fans, there was a constant stream of new releases to be collected, if they could afford to buy them all.

As the dance music craze boomed, the Gramophone Company decided to set up its own retail outlet. Of course, Britain's leading gramophone and record company could not make do with a little provincial store or a shop in a suburban back street; a great company demanded a prestigious and centrally located position. On Wednesday 20 July 1921, the company opened the His Master's Voice gramophone house at 363–367 Oxford Street in the centre of London.[28] To call it a 'record store' is to damn with faint praise. This was a large and stylish emporium, a shrine to the gramophone and its place in British culture that would be impossible to miss even in the hustle and bustle of Oxford Street. The building was decorated in ivory and gold, with a 1,500-square foot illuminated sign featuring Nipper on its frontage. Inside, every room was soundproof (achieved by using thousands of yards of felt), and numerous audition rooms were at the service of customers who wished to hear before buying. The ground floor was divided into two sections—one for the sale of gramophones and the other for the sale of records, exclusively Gramophone Company products. A high standard of service was key to the store's success, of such importance that the premises included a school for its sales staff, where new assistants rehearsed the skills and techniques that they needed to become successful sales persons, including how to deal with customers and how to dress shop windows.

No doubt, Dame Nellie Melba would have volunteered to open the store, but she was back home in Australia, which left only one person to lead the grand event: Sir Edward Elgar. Elgar's opening address was suitably high-toned in its praise of the gramophone, promoting its use in schools and claiming that it had now taken its place in the world of the arts, bringing music to a wider public who could learn about it 'in a way that could not be learnt through books on harmony'.[29] The store was a success, a fixture on the West End shopping scene. Walk down Oxford Street in 2018, stop around number 363 and what will you see? The HMV record store, almost 100 years old and still in business.

High Culture Fights Back

When nineteen-year-old violinist Jascha Heifetz made his London concert debut in 1920, a reviewer noted that 'his fame had preceded him in a series of gramophone records'.[30] A few months after Heifetz's debut, an anonymous gramophone industry insider claimed that the music of composers such as Wagner and Stravinsky was outselling jazz, ragtime, comic song, and other popular records. No evidence was offered to back up this assertion, but the anonymous source suggested that the change was at least in part the result of industrial depression; a lack of work coupled with poor wages meant that fewer people could afford to buy records and so the purchase of discs was now confined to the 'cultured' classes. Implicit in this explanation was the suggestion that popular music was still popular, but its fans could no longer afford to buy it. Nonetheless, *The Times* felt able to subtitle its article '"Popular" Records Now Unpopular'.[31] On the following day, the paper published a counter article, refuting the anonymous interviewee's assertion that classical music was leading the market. The correspondent was full of praise for the gramophone and the quality of records now available but could find no evidence that popular music was no longer popular: 'The open windows on summer evenings do not suggest that the public taste in gramophone music is quite as "high-browed" as all that'.[32]

Whatever the situation, there was a market for classical music. Vocalion wanted its share but lacked the stars and the albums of complete works to be found on other labels. It decided that education held the key. If people were reluctant to buy opera and classical music discs because they could not understand them, why not help them to understand? On the reverse side of such recordings, the listener would find 'short spoken commentaries by eminent musical authorities'.[33] Such an advantage for listeners, exclusive to Vocalion discs, came at no extra cost; of course, a short, spoken commentary was likely to cost Vocalion much less than a second musical recording, however eminent the authorities might be, and eminent or not, the company did not consider them worthy of naming in the catalogue. For those who so loved their records that they wore them out or broke them, Vocalion also offered help: return a broken or worn record to your dealer and Vocalion would give you an allowance of 8*d* for each 10-inch disc or 1 shilling for a 12-inch disc, if they were exchanged for new records.[34]

Vocalion's educational commentaries were first and foremost a commercial activity, but others saw 'music appreciation' as an obvious field of education for the gramophone. Schools could buy a gramophone and start to build a collection of discs, enabling pupils to hear the works of the great composers and the talents of great musicians and singers. Enthusiastic and knowledgeable teachers could use these recordings to educate their pupils—much better than having to rely on the teachers' own talents as pianists or singers, which would surely fall short in any attempt to emulate the famous.

The Incorporated Society of Musicians saw the 1920s as a decade of great opportunity, with a revival of interest in music that gave it a central place in British life. A revolution in music teaching was at hand, with high-sounding phrases such as 'eurythmics', 'aural training', and 'musical appreciation' as its outward signs; however, *The Times* cautioned that there was a problem with music education: the nation's youth was listening to the wrong things. 'The moments of greatest joy to the youthful mind continue to be associated with sounds that are not [classical] music'. Young people were going to pantomimes (the article appeared on 1 January) and listening to the gramophone; without making prejudices explicit, the writer hinted that these young people were enjoying comic songs and dance music, 'and it is time that something was done about it.' Thankfully, help was at hand in the form of Mrs Douglas Hoare and her Ladies Orchestra, which promised two holiday concerts filled with 'Music melodious, tender, gay, from former days and modern score (Conductor, Mrs Douglas Hoare)'. It is doubtful if dance bands and comedians felt threatened.[35]

Music appreciation in schools was never intended to encompass every genre of music. It was a strategy in the war against the degenerate noises of dance tunes, popular ditties, and jazz—another weapon in the armoury of cultural snobbery. Genuine folk singers like Joseph Taylor did not sing authentic folk songs for children to appreciate; instead, classical singers backed by classical ensembles repackaged these songs for a middle-class audience, as researcher Lucy Wright puts it.[36] Folk songs of drunkenness, illicit sex, murder, or witchcraft were ignored or heavily censored. 'Degenerate' blues and jazz records were not appropriate for analysis or appreciation. The gramophone, still at times seen as the enemy of musical taste, was now being championed as its saviour. Exposure to music through gramophone records would give children a far greater appreciation of music than they could ever gain from acquiring basic skill at the keyboard or violin. A gramophone in a school could give children the experience of hearing 'all kinds' of music. A bold and worthy aim, although *The Times* correspondent's idea of 'all kinds' was really limited to all kinds of classical music, from Bach to Beethoven, Handel, and Purcell. Almost as an afterthought, the article suggested adding a few examples of the 'ultra modern excesses that nobody can understand', not with the intention of pleasing the young listeners, but to see if the children thought there was anything in it worth hearing.[37]

The gramophone's role in maintaining social order involved the highest in the land. For Empire Day 1923, the King and Queen recorded a message on disc for the children of the Empire. Each disc cost 5s 6d, often raised by collections from among the pupils; the Gramophone Company passed its profits to children's hospitals and wards across the country.[38] The record, on the HMV label, bore the legend 'To the boys and girls of the British Empire from HIS MAJESTY KING GEORGE THE FIFTH AND HER MAJESTY QUEEN MARY'.

The Word is Out: Reviews, Magazines, and More Disdain

As educationalists and critics established 'serious' roles for the gramophone and the instrument became a fixture in the majority of homes, the nation's press started to take it seriously. It was too popular to ignore or dismiss with a few sarcastic words, part of too many areas of British society and culture; by the end of the 1920s, 61.6 per cent of households owned a gramophone.[39] Newspapers that were previously unconcerned with record reviewing changed their perspectives. In 1921, the *Daily Telegraph* and *The Times* began publishing occasional record reviews. In 1922, both papers started regular review columns, as did the *Scotsman*.[40] *The Times* informed its readers that the gramophone influenced 'practically everything that appeals to human beings through the auditory sense'.[41]

Talking Machine News, first published in 1903, served Britain's gramophone trade and the more technically minded enthusiast, but most of the listening public was largely ignored until 1923, when *The Gramophone* appeared to meet the needs of the discerning listener rather than the manufacturer or retailer. Editor Compton Mackenzie declared in the first issue that it would be 'an organ of candid opinion'. The magazine covered a wide range of discs from opera to dance tunes, but most of its pages were devoted to recordings of 'serious' music. The first issue included an article on chamber music, reports from gramophone societies (and an article on how to start one), a Wagner Supplement, and a record review section. A quick glance at the pages gives the impression that 1920s gramophone records were exclusively devoted to the classical and operatic repertoires, but there were also brief reviews of dance and popular music, with reviewer James Caskett giving the thumbs up to discs by Paul Whiteman, America's so-called 'King of Jazz'.[42]

The forty-year-old Mackenzie was a writer and journalist who had served at Gallipoli and in the secret service. He would go on to write *Whisky Galore*, to be a co-founder of the precursor of the Scottish National Party, and to be knighted.[43] He was an enthusiastic and witty editor, happy to employ opinionated journalists and reviewers whose work seemed tailor-made to antagonise musicians, record labels, and gramophone fans alike. His magazine appealed to knowledgeable readers, mostly keen collectors who cared about the quality of their instruments as well as the quality of the recordings. Its influence extended across the Atlantic; its design and editorial style exerted a strong influence on the style and appearance of *The Phonograph Monthly Review*, an American magazine first published in October 1926. Reviews in *The Gramophone* could be detailed and lengthy, often extending to half a page or more, but brevity was also valued, especially if space was limited. The magazine devised a simple rating system for dance tunes: * indicated a 'good' tune and ** indicated an 'especially good' one. Each side was rated separately and no narrative review was added.

Reviews of live concert performances were well-established, but reviewers did not embrace recorded music with any enthusiasm in the early years of the talking machine. Reviews of gramophone records represented a challenge, or even a threat, to the authority of the music critic. By the time a concert review is published, the concert has passed. Only a small proportion of the readership can have experienced it and their memories have already started to fade. A contrasting opinion to that of the reviewer might be expressed in a letter to the newspaper, but there would be no evidence with which to back it up. The professional critic held the upper hand. A record review was a different matter. Once a critic gives his opinion on the contents of a gramophone record, any reader who offers a contrary opinion has, in the form of the record, ample evidence to back up their view. The critic's expertise is far more readily open to question, their reputation under greater threat.

Such concerns may have made critics wary of reviewing records, but once the process was under way, they leapt to their task with relish. They understood the gramophone was far from perfect, but advances in quality meant that it could now offer listeners a reasonably accurate representation of the live musical experience. Tone was the main problem; violins sounded 'fluty', lower strings (presumably the cello and bass) were 'reedy', and it was not always possible to differentiate instruments. On the bright side, these defects could be turned to advantage because they encouraged closer listening.[44] Concentrate the mind, learn to ignore the constant noise of the revolving disc, and you would develop a greater appreciation of the music; listen through the noise, as American broadcaster Michael Cumella puts it.[45]

The first of the occasional articles in *The Times* ignored dance bands, jazz, comedy, and opera, turning its attention instead to a series of records of Indian languages. This was a prime example of the gramophone as an educator— over 130 records featuring a variety of languages from the sub-continent including 'scores of unwritten tongues spoken by wild tribes [and] songs sung by peasants.'[46] *The Times*'s next attempt at enlivening the listening public's experience focused on Elizabethan madrigals, as recorded by the English Singers for HMV.[47]

Madrigals and Indian languages soon gave way to a more mainstream concern: how to programme a gramophone concert for the home. This article began from the premise that most people had little musical taste; when listening at home, they would even 'mix ragtime and Wagner and Clara Butt, and Heaven knows what not'. Advice was obviously called for, and offered. A gramophone concert, with an audience of one, gave the imagination the chance to 'do wayward and fantastic things'. For listeners unused to wayward or fantastic things, the critic gave an example: the playing of Mozart's Overture to 'The Magic Flute' and Debussy's 'L'Aprés-midi d'une Faune' in succession. With such a wayward and fantastic pairing at its heart, the writer proposed a gramophone concert programme taken 'at random' from the HMV catalogue; although the sampling technique managed to avoid the light opera, music hall singalongs and dance records that were by now taking up the bulk of the company's list.[48]

In 1924, *The Times* introduced 'Gramophone Notes', the first of which covered a selection of dance music records from three leading labels: HMV, Vocalion, and Columbia.[49] In contrast with the patronising attitude of many writers on music, the column was complimentary about dance tunes and the talents of dance bands such as the Savoy Orpheans but made one complaint: these dance records were all 10-inch discs; those who loved to dance at home would prefer the longer playing time of a 12-inch record. The column continued for the next few years, offering considered opinions on a range of records to help buyers make their choices. Most of these discs were musical, but occasional spoken word records merited consideration. One column recommended a Columbia release by Jack Hobbs, the famous cricketer, called with a notable lack of imagination 'My Cricket Record'.[50]

The time was ripe for a book and music critic Percy A. Scholes duly obliged. *The First Book of the Gramophone Record* was a guide to the fifty 'best' gramophone records to cover the period from Byrd to Beethoven, a guide *The Spectator* agreed was sorely needed. The enthusiast who followed Scholes's guidance would build 'a library of music that will not stale with time, and will also spare himself those dusty chimney-stacks of unused records possessed by most indiscriminate buyers.'[51] Books such as Scholes's, plus magazine and newspaper reviews, aimed to educate the general public in the subtleties of music appreciation. The authors were experts (by their own admission at least) and the readers needed enlightenment. Reviews went beyond discussion of the music or the performers and into the issues of sound quality and the thorny problem of 'cuts,' the editing of longer pieces of music so that a recording would fit neatly onto one side of a disc. Beethoven, Byrd, and Bach were inconsiderate enough to write compositions that did not fit neatly onto one side of a shellac disc, so when the playing time of a disc was no more than four minutes, such edits were necessary, but not always in sympathy with the music. A disc that ensured that a composition was cut at an appropriate moment would be a better investment than one on which the cuts were chosen at random.

Fans of popular music, a rapidly expanding group across Britain, would also find authors able and willing to help them build collections of interest. Edgar Jackson was one such authority, an expert in jazz and dance band records who produced a series of booklets listing the Parlophone label's *Rhythm Style* records from the late-1920s to 1940. Jackson's booklets provided exhaustive details of the records, songs, composers, and band members that fitted into his *Rhythm Style* genre. Luckily, Parlophone had an extensive catalogue of these discs, featuring the biggest names on the scene, including Louis Armstrong, Bessie Smith, Duke Ellington, and Count Basie, as well as a small, select bunch of lesser-known British artists, such as Jack Miranda and his Meanderers.[52] Scholes and Jackson were early examples of the discographer, individuals whose research into the recording activities of artists, bands, or orchestras would provide invaluable information to fans and later to historians.

In the world of fiction, the gramophone continued its roles as plot device and character indicator. James Joyce's vision of the noisy and rather pathetic gramophone was not unique. In E. F. Benson's *Mapp and Lucia* series, the snobbish Lucia Lucas is an affirmed gramophone-hater. Her first encounter in *Queen Lucia* makes her opinion abundantly clear:

> Lucia gave a little cry of agony and put her hands over her ears, just as if she had been seized with a double-earache of peculiar intensity. 'Gramophone,' she said faintly.... Only one, so far as was known, had ever come to Riseholme, and that was introduced by the misguided Robert Quantock. Once he had turned it on in her presence, but the look of agony which crossed her face was such that he had to stop it immediately.[53]

In *Dodo Wonders*, Dodo shares Lucia's disdain: 'A gramophone is much the most odious thing in the world for its size, worse than fleas or parsnips. I think I bought it because I hated it so.'[54]

Gramophones had their uses, whatever Lucia and Dodo might think. Sherlock Holmes solved *The Adventure of the Mazarin Stone* thanks to one of them. Cleverly placing a gramophone in one room of his flat, loudly playing violin music, Holmes takes shelter in another room. The villains are fooled by the trick and soon captured.[55]

In the real world, one devious criminal incorporated a gramophone into a carefully planned murder. William Gourlay, a young Englishman, disappeared from Boulogne in late 1920 after visiting a garage to buy a new car. Tricked into meeting garage owner Monsieur Daguebert alone in his house, Gourlay sat down, took out the £300 in cash, and prepared to sign a receipt. Under cover of loud music from the gramophone, Daguebert shot Gourlay twice through the back of the head.[56]

A Multimedia Future?
The Gramophone Comes Under Threat

Amid the excitement of new music, fashion, and social mores, business continued. By the mid-1920s, Columbia and HMV were 'practically unchallenged' in the British market, with HMV claiming around 25 per cent of British gramophone sales and Columbia 18 per cent. Their control of disc sales was even more emphatic, with HMV selling 46 per cent and Columbia selling 34 per cent of the total number.[57] Competition between the two companies ended in 1931, when they merged and became Electrical and Musical Industries Ltd (EMI). The new company would remain at the top of the British record market; Nipper continued to provide EMI's most arresting visual trademark.[58]

Talking pictures, a development with game-changing potential for entertainment and social life, eluded the jazz-age gramophone engineers. The idea of moving pictures that talked was as old as the motion picture industry itself, and early attempts to achieve this goal often centred on synchronizing the pictures on screen with a soundtrack on a gramophone record. Thomas Edison's Kinetophone controlled film and gramophone record together, ensuring that if one slowed or stopped, so too did the other, and controlled the level of sound emanating from the gramophone to suit the size of the hall. A London demonstration at the West End cinema in January 1914 impressed *The Times*'s critic, who particularly enjoyed a movie of a 'minstrel entertainment' with a xylophone quartet and a clog dance and claimed that the synchronisation of sound and picture was uncannily realistic.[59] The cinema gave daily exhibitions of the Kinetophone as part of its regular programme, billing it as 'The Greatest Invention of All Times', but talking pictures remained a novelty.[60]

In 1921, another demonstration took place in London, this time of George Webb's unnamed machine, which used a transmitter connected to projector and gramophone by telephone wire. A soundtrack of Caruso singing 'On with the Motley' and a film of an actor miming the song created an unusually effective illusion, but many problems were still to be overcome, especially in relation to damaged film or to the synchronisation of multi-reel features. The invention had its place; in one critic's opinion, a short talking picture would be an interesting novelty, but the gramophone and the movies would grow apart.

Despite its failure in the development of talking pictures, the gramophone was a post-war success, a technological advance that was part of the new and exciting 1920s society. Within a few years, it was almost dead. The wireless was on its way.

On the Record: 'The Love Nest', Jack Hylton's Jazz Band (Zonophone, 1921)

The Original Dixieland Jazz Band may claim the kudos for making the first jazz record, but others were quick to follow suit in Britain as in the USA. Pianist and bandleader Jack Hylton was one of Britain's most popular musicians, providing a politer and less swinging version of jazz for the flappers and their friends.

'The Love Nest', recorded at HMV's Hayes factory on 8 July 1921, is one of the first discs from Jack Hylton's Jazz Band, a septet featuring Hylton on piano and the splendidly named Wag Abbey on drums. The band recorded four tunes on that date and went on to record twenty-four sides in total between then and 14 November 1922.[61] The tunes were released on Zonophone, the 'budget' label of the Gramophone Company, rather than on the more expensive HMV label—an indication, perhaps, that they were not viewed as having sufficient appeal to wealthier record buyers. The 'Jazz Band' that recorded 'The Love Nest' was not a dedicated jazz combo, merely a renamed Queen's Dance Orchestra. A later session produced two versions of 'Coal Black Mammy' deemed suitable for release. Take four was credited to Jack Hylton's Jazz Band and released on Zonophone, and take five was credited to the Queen's Dance Orchestra and released on HMV; there is little to choose between the two in terms of tempo, instrumentation, or anything else.

'The Love Nest' is a jolly, medium-paced tune, with a few 'humorous' effects from the trombone and a melody played on alto saxophone. The musicians are skilled, but the tempo is strict, the playing restrained. Hylton was a lover and defender of jazz—'that savage rhythm of jazz' as he described it—but decided to sweeten the savagery, combining 'the colour of jazz music with that element of harmony that is so beloved of our race'.[62] None of the musicians sound like they are improvising, there is no sense of competition between players, energy levels are low, and no one is likely to become breathless. Contrast this record with the Original Dixieland Jazz Band's releases and the difference in energy, inventiveness, and instrumental power is obvious. 'The Love Nest' harks back to a different musical era; it would not have sounded too far out of place in a 1913 musical evening. The jazz is all in the band's name.

The record epitomises the way in which British record labels jumped on the jazz bandwagon, promoting 'jazz' records that did not come close to living up to the real thing. By name, Queen's Dance Orchestra sounded like the sort of staid, dull ensemble your parents would listen to, whereas Hylton's Jazz Band sounded like an exciting new musical adventure. If Hylton led a 'Jazz' band, then the band must be playing jazz, so 'The Love Nest' must be a jazz tune. For music fans across Britain who never heard the ODJB, or Jim Europe's Hell Fighters, this was the real thing. When the recordings of King Oliver, Fletcher Henderson, and Louis Armstrong made it across the Atlantic, they must have provided a real shock to the system.

BBC Sundays and the Gramophone Pirates

It was all going so well. Cylinders and phonographs were as outmoded as the horseless carriage, cinema was in the ascendant but posing a threat to live theatre and variety rather than to entertainment at home, the war was over, and Britain was rebuilding. The Jazz Age was in full flow and dance music was quite the thing, despite the establishment's attempts to send it packing back to the United States. The future was bright.

The Jazz Age was a boom time for the British gramophone industry. HMV and Columbia dominated disc and gramophone sales, but competition was keen as new companies entered the market and older firms fought to hold on to their profits. Vocalion, Edison Bell, and the Crystalate Gramophone Record Manufacturing Company (with the Imperial label) were the leading budget record companies, with small companies such as Decca, Fullotone, and Dulcetto each having a small share of the gramophone market.[1] The shellac producers of India saw their incomes rise along with disc production; by the end of 1921, raw shellac was fetching £350 per ton.[2] Britain was proving to be a goldmine for record and instrument sellers and W. Lionel Sturdy reported that price cuts were generating increased sales of instruments.[3] At the top of the market, Sonora gramophones ('The Highest Class Gramophone in the World') ranged in price from £25 to an eye-watering £178.[4]

The industry regularly trumpeted new 'improved' equipment or claimed better sound. The Gramophone Company produced an improved tool for testing the accuracy of turntable speed, a new tool kit for repairing instruments, and a filing cabinet for up to 100 discs, with a lever system that enabled any disc to be popped out of the cabinet without fuss.[5] Sewing needle makers W. R. Steel of Redditch broke into the gramophone business with its 'Perfect Points' needles, and Stead and Co. of Sheffield produced the 'Vulcan' mainspring.[6] From its premises on London's Old Street, Rifanco Gramophoneries sold twenty-five different instruments and parts in abundance—eighteen tonearms, fifteen soundboxes, twenty-six motors, numerous different gramophone cabinets, and 'thousands' of horns—servicing a small but lucrative section of the market.[7] The company sold many of its products to repair shops, but do-it-yourself gramophone builders were also keen customers. An estimated 4 per cent of gramophone owners built their own machines in the 1920s.[8] In some cases, this would be for economic reasons, but many of these amateurs would build their own instruments for fun and personal satisfaction, just as others would service their own cars or repair their own bicycles.

What the public really needed was an added element of danger, or so Scientific and Projections Ltd seemed to believe when it produced one of the most intriguing new instruments. The 'Flame-Phone' combined sound and light by the simple expedient of attaching the soundbox not only to the amplifying horn but also to a gas supply. Two small gas burners directed flames horizontally across the horn through 100 jets, to be reflected in the protective aluminium shield as they flickered and flashed in response to the music; in a darkened room, the jets of flame were 'very pleasantly reflected'.[9] This now-forgotten machine showed once again how the early gramophone industry was ahead of the pack with a psychedelic light show in the comfort of your own home over forty years before the emergence of Pink Floyd, although the thought of sending naked flames shooting across one's music room might have given prospective purchasers pause for thought.

In October 1925, the Gramophone Company introduced the HMV 'New Gramophones', all made in the Hayes factory.[10] The company claimed that these new instruments solved the two remaining problems of sound reproduction—an over-prominent treble and weak bass notes—by the use of a redesigned tone arm and sound box. Tone would now be richer and rounder than ever, with surface noise 'practically eliminated'. There were ten models in the range, from the newest portable, the HMV 101, to the impressive Cabinet Grand Model 211, a 4-foot high, 2-foot wide, electrically powered instrument with an automatic speed regulator and an automatic brake, finished in mahogany with gold-plated and enamel fittings, at a cost of £110. The Gramophone Company called on some of its most famous artists to endorse the 'New Gramophones'. Sir Edward Elgar called them, 'The most important invention in the history of the Gramophone'. Sir Landon Ronald spoke of their 'amazing tone'. The advertisements emphasised the instruments' technical advances, with no recourse to images of idyllic riverside picnics, stylish society parties, or glamorous dances. It was the pinnacle of the gramophone's success in the era of acoustic recording.

How could the gramophone buyer get past the advertising hype and slick marketing? For many buyers, price and size were the most important factors when considering a purchase—namely, a small and cheap instrument, to fit neatly into a small sitting room and a small weekly income. For the more discerning, *The Gramophone*'s annual tests gave useful information. The

1923 test compared five instruments, from a Decca portable to an HMV Cabinet Grand, with the £10 Cliftophone Model 6 proving triumphant.[11] Within two years, the test expanded to include ten gramophones and was now a public affair, with audience members voting for their favourites after a demonstration. This time, the Orchorsol Gramophone Company took the honours.[12]

Upmarket stores continued to advertise their gramophone and record departments, emphasising the quality of the products on sale. Waring and Gillow of Oxford Street did not have departments, it had 'Galleries' filled with top-end instruments. Yet, the discerning consumer wanted more. Waring and Gillow offered audition rooms and supplied gramophones in custom-made cases; decorated and period cases were the store's specialties.[13] Selfridges offered the latest audition rooms, ensuring that customers could sit comfortably at a table while listening to records rather than in a 'necessarily stuffy' soundproof room.[14] Keith Prowse Gramophone Salons countered by promising 'ideal conditions' in which to hear a range of instruments from their extensive stock.[15] The ever-resourceful Selfridges responded to the Prowse Salons by introducing its 'Telephone Audition Service'. Customers were invited to telephone the service on Gerrard 1, request to speak with 'Telephone Auditions', and ask to listen to any disc that took their fancy. Once you made your choice, the discs would be dispatched 'by the first available delivery van'.[16] Then it all started to go wrong.

The Wonders of the Wireless

Wireless technology capable of broadcasting entertainment programmes had been around since Guglielmo Marconi gained his first UK patent for radio communications in 1898, having sent a wireless transmission between two buildings owned by the General Post Office.[17] In the USA, Reginald A. Fessenden sent a radio broadcast from Brant Rock, Massachusetts, to a few ships belonging to the US Navy and the United Fruit Company on Christmas Eve 1906.[18] Such limited early successes posed no threat to the gramophone. Amateur radio enthusiasts (the 'hams' of Ham radio) started to broadcast from their sheds or bedrooms, but they were not building up large audiences or broadcasting concerts from the top dance bands of the day. Then the BBC arrived.

The British Broadcasting Company formed in October 1922, prompting the City of London Phonograph Society to add 'Radio' to its title.[19] The company made its first radio broadcast, from station 2LO in the Strand, on 14 November. The audience was small. To receive broadcasts, you needed a wireless receiver set and a licence; by the time of the first broadcast, just 30,000 licences, at 10 shillings each, had been issued. Also, the range of the transmitter was limited, but the broadcast worked and radio was here.[20] Within twelve months, the BBC set up seven more main stations and eleven relay stations, giving coverage to most of the population on the British mainland, with a Belfast main station bringing the wireless to Northern Ireland.[21] The *Radio Times* appeared in September 1923, described as 'The Official Organ of the B.B.C.'[22] Arthur R. Burrows, director of programmes, gave readers a jovial welcome on the front page, describing the magazine as the 'Bradshaw of Broadcasting' and making a bad joke about the 'wave-train'.[23] Since 2LO's first day less than a year before, Burrows wrote proudly, the BBC had transmitted for 8,000 hours, producing 1,700 programmes. For those more concerned with the future rather than the past, the *Radio Times* gave programme listings for the next week.

Each main station broadcast its own programmes, occasionally joining others for a network-wide broadcast. London operated from 11.30 a.m. on weekdays and from 3 p.m. on Sunday, most other stations began later in the day and broadcasts ending at 10 or 10.30 p.m., usually after a news bulletin. Programmes ranged from live concerts (opera, organ recitals, piano solos, and vocal duets) to stories for children, news for farmers, and talks 'for women' (*Women's Hour* lasted for thirty minutes) and 'for men' (a 'Men's Talk' on motoring from Captain Richard Twelvetrees). On 2 October, a special treat was on offer: speeches from the Duke of Connaught, W. MacKenzie King (the prime minister of Canada), and General Smuts (the prime minister of South Africa), live from the Royal Colonial Institute dinner at the Hotel Victoria in London. Light entertainment was limited, although dance music programmes were a common feature of late broadcasts, with a forty-five-minute programme of dance music by the Savoy Band direct from the Savoy Hotel a regular highlight. Across the week, it was possible to find something for almost everyone, but famous entertainers were notably absent from the schedules; for the flappers and bright young people of Britain, there was little to recommend the wireless.

The wireless may have been a revolution in home entertainment, but the revolution was not an immediate success. By the middle of 1923, wireless sales were in a slump. W. Lionel Sturdy reported that the fall in sales experienced early in the year showed no sign of ending and suggested that the wireless might prove to be a seasonal trade, like the trade in portable gramophones. More realistically, he noted that in late summer 1923, large parts of Britain were still out of reach of the transmitter stations, and he was hopeful that the trade would grow again as more new stations went on air. A month later, Sturdy claimed that amateur wireless builders were partly to blame as self-build was a much cheaper way to obtain a set and easy enough, he claimed, for the average man or boy to do.[24]

Three years after 2LO began broadcasting, problems with signal quality and programming remained. The *Radio Times* dealt with both of these areas of concern. K. P. Hunt offered helpful tips on the impact of the weather. Music, said Hunt, sounded clearest on wet and windy nights—a piece of good news for the inhabitants of the British Isles—but rain meant that signal strength dropped. Fog caused signals to fade, dry and warm weather created static in the headphones of crystal set users, snow could short out the aerial, and moisture could cause leakage of energy. As for poor programme quality, A. Corbett-Smith complained that listeners must take some of the blame as they were 'largely neutral' towards the BBC and so failed to demand improvements even when they knew which areas of the service needed to be better.[25]

Slumps, foggy fades, and criticisms no doubt boosted the gramophone trade's optimism that it could meet the threat from this new competitor, or even benefit from its presence; after all, from the start of the BBC's broadcasts, gramophone records were a part of its programming. At first, local gramophone dealers hired or loaned gramophones to the broadcaster.[26] Record companies supplied discs free of charge, and in return, the announcer would give details of each disc's artists, title, label, and serial number when it was played. Such announcements were valuable advertisements for the record companies, but even so, some of them insisted that the BBC should return the records after they had been broadcast.[27] In the summer of 1927, the BBC decided to build its own gramophone library, ensuring that a large number of recordings were always to hand.[28]

For some listeners, the BBC's use of records was lazy, an easy and cheap way of filling up time without concern for the nature and quality of the performances on the discs. The BBC's 'celebration' of three years of broadcasting incurred the wrath of Captain Granville Soames, who claimed that too many of its programmes, even in a week where it promised shows of particular interest, were filled with 'uninteresting padding', including an 'irksome succession of gramophone records'. In the good captain's opinion, such padding was unsuitable for broadcasting and reached its nadir when an announcer was 'constrained to cut off an uncompleted record on account of its mediocrity'.[29]

From April 1924, one regular weekly programme—on Thursday afternoons from 1–2 p.m.—gave exposure to new gramophone records, but the debate about the quality of the BBC's output continued, and many listeners felt that Sunday programmes were particularly lacking in interest. The gramophone and record companies took advantage of such programmes by advertising on foreign stations on Sundays 'when, since many people consider the British Broadcasting Corporation's programmes for that day a trifle tedious, there is a good chance of getting people to listen'.[30] In parliament, Lieutenant Colonel John Moore-Brabazon put it a little less harshly: 'our own British broadcasting programme on Sunday is not particularly good.'[31]

The First DJ?

Something had to be done to improve the BBC's gramophone broadcasts. Compton Mackenzie announced that he would take charge of the gramophone hour on 12 June 1924, with the stated aim of speaking about the records being played during the programme and the implicit aim of making the programme more interesting and informative by doing so.[32] Whether Mackenzie achieved his aims or not is not clear, but it seems he did not take up the presenting role on a permanent basis and the gramophone hour continued on its steady but unexciting way. Three years later, Mackenzie made a brief plea in his regular *Gramophone* editorial: 'I hope that all of you will give us your support in trying to make the B.B.C.'s gramophone hour on Thursdays more entertaining than it used to be'.[33]

Christopher Stone (the army officer who transported his Decca portable across France and Belgium during the last eighteen months of the Great War) was the man to achieve Mackenzie's aim. Mackenzie was married to Stone's sister, Faith, and Stone was an early contributor to *The Gramophone*, becoming its London editor and then its co-editor with Mackenzie. When Stone was the guest on the BBC's *Desert Island Discs* in 1957, he intimated that it was all his own idea: 'I suddenly came to the conclusion that the BBC were not having, really, the best new records that were coming into my office.' He wrote to the BBC to make his conclusion clear and was invited to take over the Thursday show. On 7 July 1927, the first gramophone hour under his charge was broadcast. Stone did not appear on air but prepared some notes on each record for the duty announcer to read out; his first broadcast as the presenter was in October.[34]

By 28 November, Stone's growing popularity was reflected in the *Radio Times*, when it began to describe his programme as 'A Recital of Gramophone Records arranged by Mr Christopher Stone' (although that particular programme was on a Monday evening and lasted just twenty minutes). Stone's relaxed approach (for the time) is clear on recordings he made in the early 1930s. On 'Christopher Stone's Medley', released as HMV C2371 in 1932, he chats amiably about his love of music—'I grew up, you might say, with a song in my heart'—and introduces a few of his favourites, even singing one or two himself. A year or so later, he recorded 'The Decca ABC', a record promoting the company's catalogue on which he takes listeners through the alphabet of Decca releases.[35]

By the late 1920s, Stone was also presenting a weekly programme of film criticism.[36] His popularity with the public suggests that his broadcasting career was an unqualified success, but the BBC was not always in favour of his ideas. When he proposed a series of talks on the gramophone (care and use of the machine, choosing records, how to ensure that you received good service in gramophone shops, and a programme of jokes with gramophones), the broadcaster rejected all of them.[37] Stone's approach to programming his shows came under BBC scrutiny. The BBC's standard practice was to use records supplied by the record companies, most of which by this time were kept in the corporation's gramophone record library. Stone, however, used his own records, which he obtained from companies in his role at *The Gramophone*. A series of memos from 1932 outlined BBC concerns that some companies were paying Stone to give exposure to particular recordings; such record-plugging was not BBC policy. One BBC staff member suggested that it should exert more direct control over record broadcasts, possibly taking over responsibility for programming Stone's shows from the man himself.[38]

Whether or not such drastic steps were taken, Stone continued to broadcast for many years and his BBC fame led to his starring role at the London Palladium, when he took to the stage of the famous theatre for a week, topping a variety bill that included comedian Vic Oliver. According to *The Times*, Stone's bid for theatrical stardom was a failure.[39] Stone appeared on stage with a gramophone, played a recording of '*La Donna è Mobile*' by Caruso, and demonstrated a process for playing records backwards, 'though why anybody should ever want to play a record in that way he does not explain.' For the rest of the time, Stone drifted on and off the stage, 'a nebulous spirit of wireless who seems to have turned in the wrong direction at Oxford Circus'.

Stone weathered that critical storm. In 1934, he became one of the radio personalities immortalised in a series of W. D. and H. O. Wills cigarette cards, alongside Paul Robeson, Elsie and Doris Waters, announcer A. Stuart Hibberd ('He is one of the tallest men at Broadcasting House' his card helpfully explained), the Two Leslies, Gracie Fields, and bandleaders Jack Hylton, Ambrose, and Roy Fox. On *Desert Island Discs*, the presenter, Roy Plomley, introduced him as 'the first gentleman of the gramophone ... The man who started it all ... The very first to present gramophone records on the air in an individual way', which was rare praise indeed. Today, he is often referred to as the first disc jockey, a phrase that was not in common usage until the 1940s, and it is difficult to see this gently spoken, articulate, and gentlemanly broadcaster being comfortable with the title. His place in the history of DJs is assured, however—the start of a line that joins Stone to DJs such as Jimmy Young, Tony Blackburn, John Peel, Annie Nightingale, Jo Wiley, and Pete Tong.

Pirates and Bootleggers

Pirates threatened the nascent BBC, but not in the way that 1960s lovers of under-the-covers radio listening might have understood the term. The first radio pirates were listeners, not broadcasters, and the gramophone played no part in their nefarious activities. The piratical act was a simple one: listening to BBC programmes without buying a wireless broadcast licence. The Post Office struggled to supply licences to every listener who wanted one. There were 260 wireless manufacturing firms producing 1,450 approved types of receiving apparatus and amateur wireless engineers built many more sets at home, with little incentive to buy a licence. For the postmaster general, managing the transmission side of broadcasting, rather than the receiving side, was the priority.[40] By 31 May 1924, around 800,000 licences had been issued. The scale of unlicensed sets was not clear, but Sir Harry Brittain suggested that in Edinburgh alone, there were 5,000 sets without a licence.[41] No doubt, there were many listening pirates, but they still failed to attract the wrath of the Post Office; in the two years to March 1925, the Post Office acted against just two pirate listeners.[42]

The relationship between the BBC's wireless broadcasts and the gramophone brought a new concern for performers: the threat of being bootlegged. The Earl of Shaftesbury explained the process to his compatriots in the Lords:

> Broadcasting can be used by any person who is in possession of a receiving set and a loud speaker, for purposes which were certainly never intended by the Broadcasting Company—namely, the illicit mechanical reproduction of a performance transmitted by the Broadcasting Company. If you and I were the happy possessors of a recording instrument and also of a wireless set with a loud speaker, by placing the recording instrument in close proximity to the loud speaker we could get a record of any performance, and we could make that record into quite a number of gramophone records.[43]

Bootleg discs, recorded illicitly, could be made at little cost to the bootlegger with no chance of payment for the artist. The fear of being bootlegged was real and may explain the absence from the airwaves of the major stars of music. As Sir Martin Conway MP explained on introducing the Dramatic and Musical Performers' Protection Bill:

> [An] illicit gramophone negative can be used to produce records which can be sold. That sale has the effect of breaking contracts between artists and the various gramophone companies, and in order to save their contracts it is impossible for most of them to have their performances broadcast.[44]

Shaftesbury and Conway's use of the word 'illicit' is notable as the activity was not illegal until the Dramatic and Musical Performers' Protection Act gained Royal Assent on 31 July 1925, giving performers some protection against the massed ranks of British record bootleggers.[45]

Pirate listeners were joined by pirate broadcasters. If bootleggers threatened artists' financial and contractual status, the pirate broadcasters threatened the BBC's monopoly of the airwaves, and the gramophone was a central weapon in their armoury. Amateur wireless enthusiasts operated legally before and after the start of BBC broadcasts, licensed by the postmaster-general, but they were limited to a frequency range below the BBC's frequencies and they usually broadcast on a one-to-one basis as they contacted other enthusiasts across the world.[46] The pirate broadcaster was a different beast. This enthusiast, Captain Ian Fraser declared, 'grinds out bad gramophone records after broadcasting hours, and generally makes the night hideous.'[47] It is hard to understand how these amateur broadcasters, working after the BBC closing time of 10.30 p.m., could impinge on the night-time peace of British citizens unless those citizens slept with their wireless sets switched on and retuned to a pirate's frequency. The postmaster-general, Sir William Mitchell-Thomson, was less concerned than Captain Fraser about this scourge of the late-night airwaves, at least for the time being, but eventually the authorities would act.

The pirate broadcasters were an innocuous bunch, driven by an enthusiasm for wireless technology and the chance to show off their know-how and skills. This was not an organised movement dedicated to the downfall of the state-sanctioned BBC, or a group of fake-news-spreading anarchists. Occasionally, however, one or two of them were caught and prosecuted. Punishments were mild, usually just a small fine or the removal of their wireless equipment. Defences were often rather naive. George Skinner, a young Brighton labourer, built his own broadcasting set based on a second-hand blueprint and used it to broadcast mouth-organ music, though whether from records or his own performances was not made clear. He claimed that he did not believe the signal carried beyond his own house, but he was fined £1.[48] When 2HD, a licensed amateur broadcasting station in Manchester, broadcast a concert (presumably on records, rather than a live performance) on its authorised wavelength, it incurred the wrath of the Post Office for a different reason, receiving a letter from the postmaster general that accused the station of breaching its licence by broadcasting entertainment. The Manchester Radio Scientific Society stood by its member station, stressing that the broadcast was an 'experiment' and so was within the terms of the licence. As its chairman, J. E. Kemp, put it, 'if the public choose to regard it as an entertainment to follow [the station's] tests … that is not the affair of the society'.[49]

George Skinner and the Didsbury station were minor thorns in the side of the BBC and the General Post Office compared to the Barker Brothers of Norwich. Wilfred and Gerald Barker's regular Sunday morning gramophone show became so popular that the Post Office sent its detection van to the city in order to track down and close the brothers' pirate station, creating a couple of local heroes in the process. The van tracked Wilfred, the nineteen-year-old younger brother, to his home in Petersfield Road.[50] The officials confiscated his equipment, bringing an end to the brothers' broadcasts, but they gained sufficient notoriety to attract the attention of *Amateur Wireless* magazine, which printed an exclusive and laudatory interview with Wilfred, giving him the chance to explain his activities in detail.[51] As Wilfred explained, the brothers built two transmitters, both using frequencies around 260–270 metres. Wilfred operated Norwich 2, while his brother took charge of Norwich 1 from his own home 3 miles away. Wilfred claimed that they started simply as a way of speaking to each other by radio-telephone on Sunday mornings until he realised that local people were listening in to these conversations and he had the idea of putting together programmes of gramophone records; the BBC still did not start its Sunday programmes until 12.30 p.m., so the brothers saw themselves as 'filling a gap'. Norwich 1 and 2 soon found a regular listening public around their home city until the fateful morning of Sunday 4 March 1934. Wilfred broadcast for a few hours, then at 11.45 a.m., he decided to shut down for the day and put on a record of 'God Save The King'; even pirate broadcasters were loyal to their monarch. As the anthem was playing, the Post Office officials walked in and ended Wilfred's show for good. *Amateur Wireless* made its position on the matter clear—the Barker brothers' activities were 'Very laudable, but quite unconstitutional, of course!'

The Post Office won only a partial victory. Due to a technical failure, Norwich 1 did not broadcast on that Sunday morning, and the detector van failed to find the equipment. Wilfred and Gerald dismantled Norwich 1 and hid it away, but the lure of illicit broadcasts proved too strong for Gerald, who restarted his activities and was tracked down a few months later. Norwich magistrates confiscated Norwich 1 and fined Gerald £4 10s with £5 5s costs for operating a wireless transmitter without a licence and, in so doing, defrauding the Revenue. Gerald had been broadcasting for four years before being discovered.[52]

The BBC weathered the threat of piracy, just as the gramophone industry survived the best efforts of bootleggers. By 1930, the wireless and the gramophone lived a harmonious existence. 'Broadcasting has proved, indeed, an enormous advertisement for reproduced music', the *Merchandising Survey of Great Britain* concluded. Britain's love of cinema musicals was another source of optimism for the gramophone industry as songs made popular in the movies were eagerly bought on disc. The survey was upbeat:

> Eight years ago, the establishment of broadcasting facilities was considered in Great Britain ... to have sounded the death-knell of the gramophone. Today the popularity of the gramophone is greater than it has ever been, and a steadily increasing demand for records testifies to the beneficial effect ... of broadcasting and talking films.[53]

Bell's Elementary French Picture Cards.   *IV.—LE SALON.*

Above: A convivial evening at home with the piano. The gramophone would soon put a stop to such sophisticated family entertainment.

Right: Oxford Records make the grandiose claim that their cylinder recordings are 'Good'. (*Courtesy of the Accademia Nazionale del Jazz, Siena*)

Charing Cross, early 1900s—home to the Edison-Bell Consolidated Phonograph Company Limited.

The Cecil and Savoy Hotels on the Strand, early 1900s. William Barry Owen based himself at the Cecil when he arrived in London—the Strand would become the epicentre of the Gramophone Company's emerging empire.

Above left: Gertie Millar, *c.* 1907. Miss Millar was a musical comedy star who took advantage of the gramophone to record her best-known songs.

Above right: Isabel Jay, *c.* 1906. Miss Jay was a star of light opera and the London stage, who, like Miss Millar, seized the chance to record some of her most popular songs.

Below: The Recording Angel fills up the 'blank' side of a Gramophone Company 7-inch record. (*Courtesy of the Accademia Nazionale del Jazz, Siena*)

"His Master's Voice" Record Albums

More Records are scratched or broken through lack of proper storage than ever become worn out by actual playing. The simple solution is to store your records in "HIS MASTER'S VOICE" Albums, which are strong and neat in appearance.

Left: HMV warns of the dangers of improper storage and recommends its record albums as the perfect solution.

Below: The Songster Company's Gramophone Hint No. 5 offers some advice on keeping your records in tip-top condition.

200 LOUD TONE

THE CORRECT

Songster NEEDLES

USE ONCE ONLY

FOR ELECTRICAL

PLAY ALL RECORDS BETTER

GRAMOPHONE HINT No. 5.

Don't leave your records uncovered. When not in use they should be kept in record envelopes or albums to keep them clean. An occasional dusting (circularwise) with a velvet pad is essential to keep the dust out of the grooves.

Above: Nipper adorns the lid of a tin filled with loud tone needles. (*Courtesy of Dave Guttridge*)

Below left: Luigi Mancinelli, composer of the undistinguished 'St Agnes', which even gramophone effects failed to enliven. (*Courtesy of the Norfolk and Norwich Festival*)

Below right: A Salkind's advertisement from the 1908 Norfolk and Norwich Festival programme: pianos still reigned supreme although 'Genuine Gramophones' were now available. (*Courtesy of the Norfolk and Norwich Festival*)

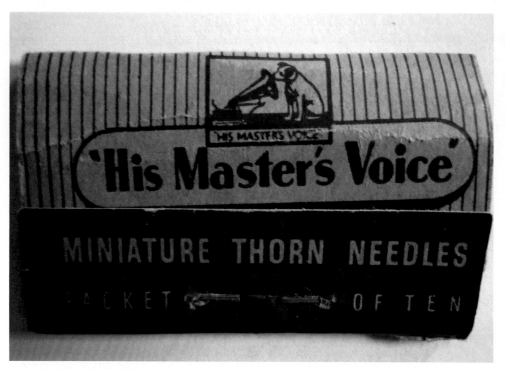

Thorn needles—an alternative to the more usual metal needles. (*Courtesy of Dave Guttridge*)

Songster Loud Tone needles—200 in one small tin. (*Courtesy of Dave Guttridge*)

Above: A 'Trench Decca' portable gramophone. (*Courtesy of Paul Buck*)

Below left: A Beatall Records version of 'Alexander's Ragtime Band' by the Beatall Military Band, an anonymous orchestra on a budget label. The Yorke family of Erddig in north Wales owned a copy of this disc, indicating that budget labels appealed to the gentry as well as the poorer music fans.

Below right: Bessie Smith sings 'St Louis Blues' accompanied by Louis Armstrong. Recorded in New York in 1925, this is the real thing and a far cry from attempts at 'jazzing' by the Coldstream Guards.

Left: Edgar Jackson's 'Rhythm Style Series No. 2'—a discography of Parlophone releases, vital for serious fans of jazz, swing and boogie-woogie.

Below: Oxford Street *c.* 1910, featuring Waring and Gillow, the department store that sold gramophones in its 'Galleries'.

WILL'S CIGARETTES

CHRISTOPHER STONE

WILL'S CIGARETTES

LESLIE HOLMES AND LESLIE SARONY

Above left: Christopher Stone, the first disc jockey.

Above right: The Two Leslies— a favourite of Christopher Stone.

Right: Wilmott's of Norwich. This 1930 advertisement notes that HMV has recently reduced the prices of all of its gramophones and radiograms. (*Courtesy of the Norfolk and Norwich Festival*)

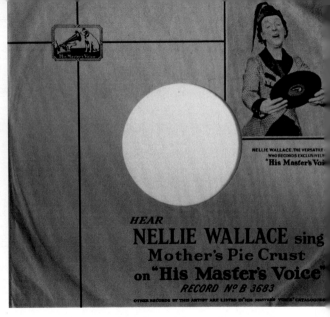

Above left: A Tuck Gramophone Record Postcard, *c.* 1929. The company stuck small discs onto pre-existing postcards, ensuring, in this case, that the 'maiden fair to see' could not be seen.

Above right: Nellie Wallace sings 'Mother's Pie Crust', as advertised on an HMV record sleeve. Wallace was a popular comedy performer on stage and screen; she recorded this song in 1930.

Below: V-Disc 274A, featuring the legendary Benny Goodman Trio. (*Courtesy of the Accademia Nazionale del Jazz, Siena*)

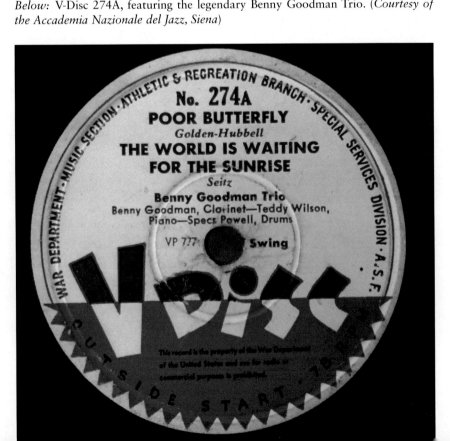

A Columbia Records advertisement from the 1947 Norfolk and Norwich Festival
programme. The label's stars include Sir Malcolm Sargent and Dennis Noble.
(*Courtesy of the Norfolk and Norwich Festival*)

The following artists appearing at the NORFOLK & NORWICH MUSICAL FESTIVAL have recorded for

"HIS MASTER'S VOICE"

SIR MALCOLM SARGENT · LONDON SYMPHONY ORCHESTRA · HEDDLE NASH

DENNIS NOBLE · PETER PEARS · GLADYS RIPLEY · SOLOMON · NORMAN WALKER

Your "H.M.V." dealer will give you full details of their records

Records of Music from the programmes

Cockaigne — Concert Overture - - *Elgar*
B.B.C. Symphony Orchestra
Conductor : Sir Edward Elgar - - DB 1935-6

Violin Concerto No. 4 (K.218) - - *Mozart*
Yehudi Menuhin with the Liverpool Philharmonic Orchestra
Conductor : Sir Malcolm Sargent - DB6146-8

Piano Concerto No. 3 - - *Rachmaninoff*
Rachmaninoff with the Philadelphia Orchestra
Conductor : Eugene Ormandy
DB 5709-12, DBS 5713

Piano Concerto No. 4 in G Major - *Beethoven*
Artur Schnabel with the Philharmonia Orchestra
Conductor : Issay Dobrowen - DB 6303-6

Symphony No. 3 in F Major - - *Brahms*
Boston Symphony Orchestra
Conductor : Koussevitzky - - DB 6276-9

Symphony No. 2 in D Minor - - *Dvořák*
Czech Philharmonic Orchestra
Conductor : Vaclav Talich - - DB 3685-9

Symphony No. 9 — "Choral" - - *Beethoven*
The Philadelphia Orchestra and Choir
Conductor : Leopold Stokowski - DB 2327-35

Sinfonia Concertante - - - *Walton*
Phyllis Sellick with the City of Birmingham Orch.
Conductor : William Walton - C 3478-80

Jesu, Joy of Man's Desiring - - - *Bach*
Myra Hess - - - - - B 9035

The Magic Flute — Overture - - *Mozart*
B.B.C. Symphony Orchestra
Conductor : Toscanini - - - - DB 3550

For details of the following Choral Recordings see
"H.M.V." Catalogue — 1946-7

Requiem Mass — *Verdi* - - - DB 6210-9

***Dream of Gerontius** — *Elgar* - C 3435-46

Recorded under the Auspices of the British Council

GREATEST ARTISTS FINEST RECORDING

THE GRAMOPHONE COMPANY | "HIS MASTER'S VOICE" | LIMITED, HAYES, MIDDLESEX

PRINTED BY THE GOOSE PRESS, NORWICH

HMV advertisement from the 1947 Norfolk and Norwich Festival. This label also lays claim to Sir Malcolm Sargent and Dennis Noble. It was just a spot of friendly competition, as both labels were part of EMI. (*Courtesy of the Norfolk and Norwich Festival*)

Above left: An unknown library makes an apparently unsuccessful plea for the return of Ray Ellington's 'very valuable' 1948 recording. Ellington (no relation to Duke) is probably best remembered for his regular musical contributions to radio's *Goon Show*.

Above right: A 'limited edition' Jazz Collector release of the Original Dixieland Jazz Band's 'Barnyard Blues', which may or may not be a bootleg disc. (*Courtesy of the Accademia Nazionale del Jazz, Siena*)

Below: The Cromer Secondary Modern School Choir's three minutes of fame, thanks to Jack Bryant's Cromer Recording label.

This record has been made on a lacquer disc. The following notes will assist in securing the best results and longest playing life.

1. If your reproducer is fitted with a lightweight pick-up (weight not exceeding 1½ ozs at needle point) use a sapphire or fine steel needle.

2. If the record is to be played on any other type of reproducer use only the special TRAILER needles obtainable from us.

3. Never use on this record a needle which has played a commercial (shellac) record. Thorn or fibre needles are harmful to lacquer records.

4. Ensure there is no stiffness in the movement of the pick-up or tone arm of the reproducer.

IMPORTANT - STORAGE Dust, scratches and finger marks will impair the quality of reproduction and lead to the early deterioration of a lacquer record. Therefore, always handle the record by the edge and keep it in the envelope when not actually playing it.

Jack Bryant's detailed instructions for the care of Cromer Recording discs. The discs would quickly wear out if these instructions were not followed.

The iconic Dansette record player. (*Courtesy of Mike and Liz Delf*)

Right: Dave Guttridge, in contemplative DJ78 mood, with a Songster Gramophone Hint at hand. (*Photograph by Tascha Dearing*)

Below: Karla Richards, as her DJ alter-ego Karla Chameleon. (*Photograph by Alice Peperell*)

Karla Richards's Pramophone. (*Photograph by Karla Richards*)

As with any relationship, the partners occasionally argued. When Vocalion introduced its Broadcast record label, the disgruntled BBC was quick to act. The label was misleading as Vocalion had no connection with wireless broadcasting, and to add insult to injury, the company released discs by Harry Bidgood and his Broadcasters, a band that had never been broadcast. It had also had the temerity to record parts of the BBC's religious services from St Martin-in-the-Fields without permission. Three strikes and you are out—the BBC banned the Broadcast label from its airwaves for three years.[54]

The Pedagogical Gramophone

The gramophone industry enthusiastically supported education for all, as long as such support was profitable. Music appreciation was not the only sphere of education that relied on the gramophone. With suitable discs, it could provide music for school assemblies, physical fitness exercises, or the illustration of lessons in history (the great classical composers placed in the context of important historical events) or geography (the 'folk musics' of other lands helping children to understand life in far-away places). The gramophone companies promoted these educational benefits to teachers and parents alike; this was potentially big business, and the Gramophone Company established its own Education Department soon after the end of the Great War.[55]

The department produced educational records that it advertised in catalogues headed 'The Gramophone in School'.[56] These records had the full support of Sir Edward Elgar, the company's ever-faithful celebrity: 'I should like to see a Gramophone and a suitable selection of Records in every school and great teaching institution', he proclaimed from the pages of each catalogue. Music appreciation was to the fore in the extensive list of records, starting with the teaching of basic rhythms and moving on to music from the great classical composers. For children still in nursery classes, the catalogue offered simpler musical fare. Its Playways series included simple dances, rhythmic exercises, and ear-training discs; also, there were plenty of nursery rhymes, including 'Us Two', a poem about Winnie the Pooh written by A. A. Milne. Children were also given the chance to hear music from contemporary composers. Just sixteen discs were listed, under the heading of Tuneful Modern Orchestral Works. 'Modern music is by no means all discord', the catalogue declared before listing compositions by Gustav Holst, Fred Delius, Claude Debussy, and a few others. In the spirit of a comprehensive education, the Gramophone Company offered a few lighter pieces of music (the baritone John Goss singing 'What Shall We Do With The Drunken Sailor', Paul Robeson singing spirituals such as 'Sinner, please doan' let dis harves' pas', two tunes from Northumbrian piper Tom Clough, and a selection of nursery rhymes for the youngest pupils), but genuinely popular contemporary music—be it jazz, dance bands, or music hall ditties—was almost completely absent. The single exception was a set of discs recorded at the *Daily Express* 1928 Remembrance Festival, which included a medley of community singing, featuring wartime favourites 'It's a Long Way to Tipperary' and 'Take Me Back to Dear Old Blighty'.

Other discs included music 'For marching in and out of school and to give pianoforte and pianist a rest', records for quiet listening at the end of a busy school day, and English folk dances collected and arranged (to ensure no possibility of any risqué dance moves) by Cecil Sharp. Children's patriotism could be reinvigorated by listening to recordings of the King, the Prince of Wales, and the Duke of York, whose disc coupled his lecture on 'My Camp, Its Purpose', with a singalong recorded at one such camp in New Romney. How many young children grew up associating the Duke (later King George VI) with a rousing chorus of 'Dashing Away with the Smoothing Iron' is yet to be established. For schools on a budget, the company offered discs on its low-cost Plum label, mostly popular classics performed by little-known orchestras or singers, although an organ recording of Bach's 'Prelude and Fugue in E Minor' was credited to theologian, philosopher (and organist) Dr Albert Schweitzer. There was also a course on colloquial French, contained on fifteen double-sided records and recommended for pupils of all ages who did not have a French-speaking teacher. This was, claimed the catalogue, 'the greatest contribution to self-education, apart from music, that the gramophone has made in any country'.

Adopting the gramophone into the school day was not simply a matter of finding a suitable spot in the classroom and building up a disc collection; teachers needed to be taught the intricacies of this new educational technology. The Gramophone Company provided everything the teacher needed to master this new skill in a series of free booklets: *How to Use the Gramophone in School*. As for choosing an instrument for the classroom, the company took the guesswork out of that particular task by recommending its own instruments, such as the £20 Model No. 157 upright grand, finished in oak and available on special purchase terms. Teachers were invited to send comments to the Gramophone Company's education department, reminded to make sure that their local dealers sent them the lists of new issues of records and advised that the company could provide the complete recorded works of any composer listed in the specialist education catalogue.

The Gramophone Company was especially astute in promoting its products to schools. Its 1929 'Win a Gramophone for your School' essay competition promised prizes of gramophones to the winning essays on the subject of 'Why I like (or would like) a gramophone in my school'.[57] Not to be outdone, Columbia released its own educational records on behalf of the International

Educational Society. This extensive collection, produced mostly as two-disc sets for lectures of around fifteen minutes, included 'The Englishman Through the Ages' by Professor F. G. Parsons, Julian Huxley's lecture on 'Ants and their Habits', Mr H. J. Massingham's rather poetic talk on 'Woodland Birds' ('the pebbly-bright percussions of black-capped coal or marsh tits rummaging in the leafy upper world'), and the Rev. F. E. Hutchinson's 'Famous Books of the Seventeenth Century'.[58] The gramophone was thriving and it was about to make its biggest advance since the great days of Berliner.

On the Record: 'Ain't It Grand to Be Blooming Well Dead', Leslie Sarony (Imperial Records, 1932)

A curiosity and a reminder that the British record industry could always produce surprises, Leslie Sarony's 'Ain't It Grand to Be Blooming Well Dead' may have been intended as a comedy song but seems today to be more macabre—an eccentric disc that combines music and black comedy as Britain attempts to recover from the Great Depression.

The song takes up both sides of the disc, over six minutes in all, as Sarony sings of the benefits of being dead. His character is not really dead—he is singing about a dream he has had—but the lyrics and delivery suggest that he is looking forward to the day he breathes his last. He is poor and miserable; death will be a blessed relief. The musical accompaniment is jaunty, full of comedy whistles and a cheery marching beat, occasionally referencing tunes such as 'John Brown's Body' or 'Little Brown Jug'. Sarony sounds like a misanthropic eighty-year-old despite being just thirty-five when he made the record. He repeatedly sings the title, using the phrase to link a series of insulting and accusatory comments about friends, neighbours, family, and professionals (florists, lawyers, sextons, and pallbearers) involved in his funeral. The comments are often insightful, usually hilarious, and sometimes scurrilous. His family is not grieving too strongly; his wife is laughing, his sister has bought a new hat, and his brother is celebrating with a fat cigar.

'Ain't It Grand to Be Blooming Well Dead' has within it the seeds of The Goons, Monty Python's Flying Circus, and Spike Milligan's scatological flights of fancy. Another Sarony song, 'Jollity Farm', was popularised by the Bonzo Dog Doo Dah Band in the late 1960s.

In the 1930s, Sarony was one of The Two Leslies, a popular duo on the wireless and on stage. Christopher Stone chose their recording of 'Why Must We Keep on Working?' as one of his Desert Island Discs. In his later years, Sarony became a character actor, appearing in TV shows such as *Crossroads, Victoria Wood as Seen on TV*, and *Z-Cars*, and in movies including *Monty Python's Meaning of Life*.[59]

The Most Famous Zebra Crossing in The World

Electrical sound recording arrived in 1925, thanks to research from Western Electric and Bell Telephone Laboratories (both part of American Telephone and Telegraph). The development rendered the old acoustic recording systems redundant overnight—the electrical microphone was more powerful and more sensitive than the old recording horn, revolutionising the recording process, and as the new technology and equipment were made available to the record industry on payment of a royalty for their use.[1] The recording engineers needed to learn new skills or become redundant themselves, the performers found a new freedom, and Britain's record buyers fell in love with a boy soprano.

When the Revolution Comes

The new technology was not the first electrical system to be used to produce a gramophone record. In 1920, Columbia used Lionel Guest and Horace O. Merriman's system to record the burial of the Unknown Soldier at Westminster Abbey and released part of the recording, including 'Abide with Me'. Sound quality was poor, worse than the acoustic recordings of the time.[2] The Guest and Merriman system disappeared and the Western Electric system became the industry standard.

J. P. Maxfield and H. C. Harrison, two of the Bell Laboratories staff, authored a detailed paper in early 1926, describing the merits of electrical as opposed to acoustic recording.[3] They wrote of maximum amplitude, sine wave curvature, vacuum tube amplifiers, and the coordination of resonances, but two photographs taken at the studios of the Victor Talking Machine Company and included in their paper sum up exactly what the science meant for performers. The first photograph shows an orchestra at an acoustic recording session. A huge recording horn dominates the room. The conductor stands on a high platform to one side of the horn, the clarinettists stand immediately to his left, and the trombonist stands as far from the horn as possible without leaving the room. The cellist, also on a raised platform, sits behind the violinists and the bassoon player. The entire orchestra is cramped, almost shoulder to shoulder. Most of the violinists use the Stroh model of the instrument. Strung like a standard violin, the Stroh had a small amplifying horn attached to the bridge; the violinists pointed their instruments' horns directly at the recording horn to ensure that the sound was amplified sufficiently to be recorded. It is a scene far removed from the orchestra on the concert hall stage.

In the second photograph, the orchestra has much more space. The musicians sit comfortably, with space between each of them at the same level. The violinists use their standard instruments, the percussionist sits next to the cellist, and the harp player sits alongside the clarinets. It is a recognisable set up, just as if the orchestra was playing in a theatre or concert hall. Front and centre, just behind the conductor and on a stand about 4 feet high, is the microphone. It is remarkably unobtrusive, easily missed on a casual glance at the photograph. As Maxfield and Harrison put it, at the acoustic session, 'it is very difficult to arouse the spontaneous enthusiasm which is necessary for the production of really artistic music', but the electric session allows the musicians to relax and find that spontaneity. The use of a microphone, placed a distance away from the musicians, had another benefit for recording and for the listener. The microphone picked up the sound of the musicians after it had blended with the walls and furnishings of the room itself, receiving the sounds just as a listener at a concert would experience them.[4]

The spread of domestic electric power forever changed the act of playing a record. The disc still needed to be put on the turntable and the needle still had to be lowered onto the disc, but the machine was now more sensitive to sound, the wind-up clockwork motor was redundant, and volume could be controlled electrically rather than by changing the position of the amplifying horn or adjusting the extent to which the gramophone doors were opened. Another development proved to be a boon to the more relaxed gramophone fan, who felt that rising from the comfort of their sofa or armchair every four minutes to change the record was merely tiresome. The autochanger, capable of automatically changing to a new disc as the previous one finished, began appearing in the late 1920s—stack a few discs onto the autochanger, start the machine, and relax as the gramophone provides a continuous stream of musical entertainment.[5]

For the lazy fan of the classical repertoire, the autochanger was not, at first, an obvious advantage. A symphony might have to be divided across six, eight, or more sides, gathered together in a record album and presented in sequence. The symphony started on disc one side one, then carried on through side two, disc two side one, and side two, as so on. Playing these discs on an autochanger would mean that the symphony would be heard out of sequence:

disc one side one would be followed by disc two side one, disc three side one, and so on. Record companies began to pair the discs in a new sequence—1:8, 2:7, 3:6, and 4:5. The music lover could now play the entire symphony from start to finish, rising from the armchair only once, to turn over the pile of discs at the midway point.[6]

Electric gramophones arrived soon after electric sound recording, although acoustic gramophones could play the new electrically recorded discs. The Brunswick Cliftophone of 1927 boasted a new 'tubular amplifier' whether you chose a portable model or a top-of-the-range cabinet model.[7] The company's more upmarket Panatrope Junior came equipped with a five-valve electrical amplifier in its mahogany cabinet, at the hefty price of 65 guineas.[8] The continued popularity of hire-purchase meant that around 50 per cent of purchasers bought their gramophones on 'easy terms'.[9]

Once the wireless joined the gramophone as an indispensable home entertainment technology, it did not take long before the two were combined, creating the radiogram. Once again, the stylish home was required to find space for a large, ungainly, and immovable piece of furniture, although the occasional model was portable to a degree; the Burndept Ethogram was apparently 'Movable from room to room'.[10] Music lovers unfortunate enough to live in rural areas without reliable electricity supplies were not forgotten as the Lisenola Radio Gramophone was available in both battery-powered and mains-powered forms. At the top end of the market, radiograms were designed to fit in with the décor of the grandest homes. Society hostess Margaret Greville bought an HMV radiogram in a walnut case for Polesden Lacey, her country home in Surrey. When it was sold at Christie's in 1943, after Mrs Greville's death, it fetched £115; by contrast, her Pye television sold for just £35.[11]

The speed regulator's time was also coming to an end as electric recording and electric motors in the gramophones meant that a consistent and correct playing speed was available to everyone—well, almost consistent and correct. Electric power was available in many homes by 1925, but the supply provided varied from place to place across Britain and this could affect the speed at which the turntable revolved, although not to the extent of the mechanical speed regulator. It was not until the National Grid began to supply power across the country in the mid-1930s that a uniform supply was available, and record and radio fans could expect consistent, high-quality signals and accurate turntable speeds.[12]

Playwright and political activist George Bernard Shaw was so concerned about the problem of speed regulation that he made a gramophone record about it; the Linguaphone label released 'Spoken English & Broken English' in 1927. Shaw opens the disc by explaining with precise diction and intonation that he has been asked to provide an example of spoken English, 'But first, let me give you a warning.' The warning is about using the gramophone properly, a vital skill because unless this is done, you will not be hearing the voice of George Bernard Shaw, but something 'grotesquely unlike any sound that has ever come from my lips.' For the next four minutes, Shaw tells a story of how he used the speed regulator on a gramophone to 'find' the voice of Ramsay MacDonald, the leader of the Labour Party, on a record. At first, in the hands of an inexperienced 'gramophone operator', Shaw hears 'a high-pitched, sharp, cackling voice, most unmusical, suggesting a small, egotistical, very ill-mannered man complaining of something.' Taking charge of the speed regulator, he slows the record down gradually until the high-pitched cackles changed to the 'fine, deep, Scottish voice and … remarkably musical and dignified delivery' of the politician.

At the wrong speed, Shaw warns, even the greatest of singers 'sound quite horrible and silly'. He acknowledges the difficulty of finding the correct speed for each record but offers a helpful hint to listeners who have never heard him face-to-face or on the wireless:

> If what you hear is very disappointing and you feel instinctively 'that must be a horrid man,' you may be quite sure the speed is wrong. Slow it down until you feel that you are listening to an amiable old gentleman of seventy-one with a rather pleasant Irish voice. Then that is me. All the other people that you hear at the other speeds are imposters, Sham Shaws, phantoms who never existed.[13]

It is probably the finest lesson on gramophone speed setting ever committed to disc, even though, by 1927, it was becoming unnecessary.

For lovers of outdoor music for picnics, punting, or cross-channel swimming, the clockwork gramophone was still valuable. The lightest portable machines could be carried easily in a rucksack; John Buchan, novelist and MP, reported that many hikers taking advantage of bracing country walks did so with portable gramophones and concertinas in their packs.[14] A portable gramophone could also make longer journeys more enjoyable. Robert Ketton-Cremer took his Odeon Orion portable (covered in smart, red leather) around the world on the SS *President Monroe*, as attested by the shipping agent's address label and the stickers from Sydney and the Galle Face Hotel in Colombo, which still adorn the gramophone today.[15] Placed in his stateroom, the machine helped to while away the long hours between ports. Portables were pressed into political service as a means of attracting the attention of potential voters when candidates set out on the campaign trail. Arthur Henderson, Labour candidate for Clay Cross, was an early adopter of this approach, playing music on a portable gramophone in his car as he drove around the constituency in search of support.[16]

In the home, old machines could still find a useful role. The Melly family in Liverpool preferred the wireless to the gramophone (although they would go on to buy a radiogram), so they relegated their old wind-up gramophone to the nursery where, along with a few old shellac records, it gave their son, George, his first experience of recorded music. This was an early and formative experience for George, who would become a popular jazz singer and writer.[17] The portable gramophone proved invaluable to Melly and his fellow pupils at Stowe school in the late 1930s. Melly and many of his compatriots brought their machines to the school and his first exposure to jazz came from a fellow pupil's gramophone—a recording of cornetist Muggsy Spanier playing 'Eccentric'. His own machine came in handy when he took part in a Surrealist art exhibition at Stowe, when he used two or three gramophones not to play music, but to revolve a series of objects placed on their turntables.[18] Melly might have been inspired by the Dadaist Stefan Wolpe, who used eight gramophones to simultaneously play eight records at different speeds at a 1920 event.[19]

Mechanical technology would never totally fall out of favour, and at its best, it still challenged the new electrical models. Author and war correspondent John Langdon-Davies happily recommended the EMG Mark X as the finest gramophone available, with the exception of the most expensive electrical instruments.[20] EMG was a British company, named after its founder, Ellis Michael Ginn and noted for high-end instruments. The Mark X was a table-top wind-up instrument with an enormous external horn 'like a ship's ventilator, which will upset the symmetry of any drawing-room', wrote Langdon-Davies. *The Gramophone* and the broadsheets continued to educate their readers about the best records and equipment. EMG and record retailers Imhof's and Rimington, Van Wyck joined in, producing their own monthly magazines for their customers.[21] These three companies were at the top end of the gramophone market, with a wealthy and educated customer base. The magazines were educational, but their primary aim was to help retain free-spending clients.

I Know a Maiden Fair to See

As recording and reproduction advanced and electricity took over from clockwork, Raphael Tuck and Sons solved the problem that had worried T. C. H. way back in 1890, by producing a gramophone record that could be readily sent by post. Tuck's Gramophone Record Postcards were flimsy, thin, and tatty, but the addition of a postage stamp was all that was needed to send them to a friend or loved one. Tuck's was a well-established firm, producing stationery including Christmas cards, postcards, *Zag-Zaw* picture puzzles, and calendars, holding a Royal Warrant as art publishers to the King and Queen. It was not the first company to produce miniature gramophone records, but it was the most successful in the British market. In about 1929, the firm began selling series of postcards with 3-inch wide, dark brown, single-sided records stuck to them. Each series consisted of four cards, costing 1s the packet; customers could choose from popular songs, orchestral tunes, instrumental solos, birthday wishes (two series, one male vocal and one female vocals), and others, all performed by anonymous artists and with a playing time of around a minute.

Tuck's development process was primitive. Instead of producing a new line of cards specially designed to incorporate a miniature record, the company simply glued each disc onto the picture side of a postcard from its existing stock and drilled a centre hole through the disc and the postcard, so that the entire object would have to be placed on the turntable in order to play the record. This was a cheap way of making these novelty items, but it meant that most of the images were almost totally obscured by the disc. One noteworthy example is 'Birthday Wishes' (male voices), stuck firmly on a card titled 'I know a maiden fair to see'. The disc obscures all but the young woman's hat, hair, and right eye; if she is fair, she cannot be seen.[22] Three decades earlier, Tuck's gramophone cards would have been a revelation. By 1929, they were nothing more than a novel way of sending greetings through a selection of sentimental songs and tunes that failed to reflect the British love of dance bands, let alone the adventurous energy of the Jazz Age.

Playing Favourites

As the electrical age dawned, *The Gramophone*'s editor, Compton MacKenzie, decided to explore the favourite music of the wider arts community, publishing the results in December 1926 as *Our Symposium*.[23] The title was rather grandiose; MacKenzie had simply written to a selection of musicians, actors, poets, and others, asking them to name their favourite song, singer, composer, and tune. These apparently easy questions confused some, angered others, and led still others to ignore one or more of them when responding. MacKenzie published the replies of thirty-four contributors, noting that people from literature and the stage predominated. The scarcity of musicians and clergy, he noted, was due to their unwillingness to commit themselves. The absence of members of the legal profession was his responsibility: 'you can't very well ask a judge to admit that he has favourites, and you can't very well ask a KC [King's Counsel], because he is liable at any moment to become a judge.'

Essayist and caricaturist Max Beerbohm did not own a gramophone: 'Had she made any gramophone records of her voice, I should certainly buy

a gramophone, and Jenny Lind would become my favourite singer.' Hilaire
Belloc's favourite singer was 'a man who sang tenor in the puppet show in
Rome in '21.' D. H. Lawrence's was 'a Red Indian singing to the drum, which
sounds pretty stupid.' Novelist Sheila Kaye-Smith chose the Italian soprano
Amelita Galli-Curci: 'on the gramophone. I am afraid I have not heard
her in the flesh.'

Most of the contributors to the symposium made high-culture choices—
Mozart, Richard Strauss, Wagner, Dame Nellie Melba, Chaliapin—but a
diverse range of favourites was displayed. Beerbohm declared a love of tunes
from burlesques and musical comedies. Noël Coward gave his favourite
composer as George Gershwin, his favourite tune as Rodgers and Hart's
'Mountain Greenery' ('I am doing this during a rehearsal' he wrote, 'so it may
sound rather peculiar.'). G. K. Chesterton and Irish writer and politician T.
M. Healy chose traditional Scots and Irish songs. Father C. C. Martindale
selected 'It's A Long Way to Tipperary'. Composer, novelist and painter Lord
Berners revealed that his favourite singer was the music hall star Little Tich.
Walter De La Mare did not want to answer, but 'at pain of being jazzed to
death,' he made the effort. Sir John Lavery had no favourites: 'How dreadful.
I don't like music.'

The questions attracted abuse, mostly humorous and good-natured (after
all, MacKenzie and his symposium members moved in the same social circles).
Hugh Walpole made this plain: 'If it had not been you as the artist who had
asked, well, I would not have answered.' W. Somerset Maugham answered
each question but complained 'What a devilish fellow you are to ask a harmless
and respectable gentleman like myself to answer such questions … Curses on
your head.' George Bernard Shaw was succinct: 'only people in a deplorably
elementary stage of musical culture have favourite tunes'; he considered the
question 'a monstrous insult'. If MacKenzie just wanted to fill a few pages
of the Christmas edition of *The Gramophone* with some light banter from
leading artists and thinkers, then he succeeded. If he hoped for their unfettered
endorsements of the gramophone, he would have been disappointed. None of
his contributors voiced the opinion that it was the instrument of the Devil, or
that it should be banned from the households of Britain, but neither did they
declare it to be the finest invention of the past 100 years.

A Million-Selling Angel

Images of the 1920s—the Jazz Age, the Roaring Twenties, dance bands,
jazz, cocaine, flappers, and bright young things—emphasise the energy and
vibrancy of the decade. The economic boom of the late '20s coupled with
electrical recording brought new record companies to market (Goodson

Gramophone Records, Guiniphone, Dominion Unbreakable Records, and many more), but when the economy slumped, many of them disappeared. Most of Britain was not living the high life, it was working for low wages in factories, mines, shops, or domestic service. For every London socialite who got a kick from cocaine, thousands of working men and women made do with a trip to the pub and a Sunday service in the parish church. The taste in music displayed by Compton MacKenzie's symposium members did not reflect the nation's favourites either. The 1920s equivalent of the Metropolitan Liberal Elite was as far removed from the rest of the country as its twenty-first-century descendants.

Ernest Lough, a fifteen-year-old chorister at Temple Church in London, recorded Mendelssohn's 'Hear My Prayer' and 'O, For the Wings of a Dove' in April 1927, accompanied by the church's choir and organ. In six months, the disc sold 316,000 copies and by the end of the year the stampers, from which copies were made, had worn out. HMV brought Ernest back with his accompanists in April 1928 and recorded the songs again. Within three years of the original recording, Ernest had sold over 700,000 discs, and by the early 1960s, it had become a million-selling record.[24] With my rock, funk, and jazz-addled ears, it is hard to figure out the appeal, even with the improved sound of the electrical recording process. Lough's voice sounds forced; in the 1927 version, he seems so focused on enunciation that he fails to convey any sense of genuine emotional connection with the song and the accompaniment is hackneyed and uninspired. Yet this is one of the biggest-selling 78 rpm records to be made in Britain, a disc that drove Compton MacKenzie to write 'I am quite sure that no boy's voice has ever been recorded nearly as well as this, and I am equally sure that I never heard such a beautiful one.'[25] It is a salutary reminder that the pastimes and parties of the privileged young do not necessarily reflect the predilections of the country as a whole. No doubt, the comforting sound of a teenage chorister singing Mendelssohn songs to the accompaniment of choir and organ brought more comfort and joy to people around the country than did the raucous jazz and seductive dance music that has become synonymous with the age.

As for the voices of the dead, ultimately, every disc and cylinder will hold such voices, as no one (so far) lives forever. Berliner's prediction of twenty-minute recordings of an entire life may never have achieved popularity, but as the men and women who first committed their voices to disc reached the end of their lives, the record companies began to sniff another potential income stream. No marketing department decided that 'voices of the dead' was a suitable name for this new genre; the Gramophone Company's team went instead with the cheerier 'The Art of a Past Generation'.[26] In the early years of electrical recording and reproduction, the Gramophone Company rereleased many of its earliest mechanical recordings, listing them in its catalogue of

'His Master's Voice Records of Unique and Historical Interest'. In the first part of this catalogue, the company took great pains to justify making these recordings available. 'Where tradition could only speak with an uncertain voice, the Gramophone will recreate the past with absolute fidelity', it wrote. These records gave insight into 'the art and personality of many famous figures—now, alas, removed by the hand of death.' Such a worthy and vital act excused the fact that these recordings were now technically imperfect when compared with those made with cutting-edge electrical processes.

The recordings went back to the earliest days of the British gramophone industry: recitations by Sarah Bernhardt, some of Enrico Caruso's first recordings, a series of music hall comic Dan Leno's discs from 1900, and Sir Henry Beerbohm Tree enacting scenes from Shakespeare. The selection included some less likely recordings. Count Leo Tolstoy's reading from 'For Every Day' was coupled with a speech on education from the Cardinal Archbishop of Westminster, another record featured the Victorian divine and orator Reverend Canon Fleming reading Edgar Allan Poe's 'The Bells', and a third disc coupled Fleming's recitation of Tennyson's 'The Charge of the Light Brigade' with actors Julia Neilson and Fred Terry portraying a scene from Baroness Orczy's 'The Scarlet Pimpernel'. They may not have set the nation rushing to its nearest disc dealer, but they served as a reminder of how much history the gramophone could already claim to have saved from oblivion.

A Studio at The Crossroads

Efficient and effective reuse of old recordings was a handy way of squeezing every penny from the back catalogue, but the Gramophone Company looked to the future as well. The company started to record electrically in 1926 and decided that it would have the finest recording facility in the country. It acquired property in Abbey Road, in London's St John's Wood, for the purpose; in November 1931, the studios opened for use.[27] Sir Edward Elgar, the Gramophone Company's faithful supporter, conducted the London Symphony Orchestra in a performance of 'Falstaff' for the studio's first recording session, on 12 November.

There were, in fact, three separate studios in the building, with Studio 1, the largest, able to hold 250 musicians. This was a major investment for the company, costing around £100,000 at a time of economic depression. The money bought the largest and best-equipped studio in the world.[28] The pioneering Fred Gaisberg was present at the opening; so, too, were a Mr Bernard Shaw and a Mr Cedric Hardwicke. The report in *The Times* did not expand on the identities of these two guests, but if they were Shaw the writer and Hardwicke the actor, then the studio opening brought together three major artists from three major arts.[29]

Abbey Road studios were at a physical crossroads—a junction now notable not only for the studios but also for the zebra crossing that featured on the cover of *Abbey Road* by the Beatles (which remains a place of pilgrimage for fans of the Fab Four)—and also at a cultural one.[30] By the time they opened, only the most reactionary or eccentric cultural commentator or music lover was dismissing the gramophone as a worthless toy. *The Gramophone*, broadsheet newspaper reviews, the huge catalogue of discs, and the sonic improvements gained by electrical recording brought the instrument the credit it deserved. John Langdon-Davies welcomed these sonic improvements: he would now rather hear his favourite artists on disc than in the Albert Hall, and in his 'Gramophone' column for *The Spectator* he treated the gramophone as 'a vehicle of culture'.[31]

Studios were not reserved solely for professional musicians. It was possible to hire a studio to make a private recording of professional quality if you had the money, and occasionally, such an act could have unforeseen benefits. Collector Paul Buck tells of a woman who owned a private recording of her husband duetting with the famous bass-baritone Peter Dawson. Her husband, a competent amateur singer, hired a studio (which Buck thinks may have been one of the Abbey Road studios) at the same time as Dawson was recording elsewhere in the building. The two men met and Dawson offered to sing with the amateur on a recording, which his widow treasured.

Talking Books

In the early days of the phonograph, Thomas Edison predicted that audiobooks would be used in the asylums of the blind but did little if anything to bring this prediction to fruition. During the Great War, many soldiers were blinded in action, returned to their homes rather than to asylums and started the long and often lonely process of dealing with their inability to see. Captain Ian Fraser, blinded at the Somme in 1916, came up with the idea of the talking book as he listened to gramophone records while recuperating at St Dunstan's, a charity for blinded ex-servicemen. His first experiments involved the use of cylinder-based dictaphones, but Fraser's idea of books to listen to was thwarted by the constraints of talking machine technology as neither cylinders or discs lasted long enough. By the mid-1930s, EMI—working with St Dunstan's and the National Institute for the Blind (NIB)—developed 12-inch discs that could be played at 24 rpm, enabling each side of a record to last for twenty-five minutes, and the gramophones needed to play at this much-reduced speed. Electrical recording was key to this development, enabling acceptable sound quality for recording and reproduction to be achieved at this slow speed. St Dunstan's and the NIB announced their Talking Book Service in the spring of 1934, making the first talking books available on 7 November 1935.[32]

From the outset, the Talking Books Library, operating much like a book lending library but sending discs by post, offered a wide range of audiobooks. Typically, each book was recorded onto as many as ten double-sided discs. The first talking books were Agatha Christie's *The Murder of Roger Ackroyd*, Joseph Conrad's *Typhoon*, and the 'Gospel According to St John'.[33] The catalogue expanded over the years, and though the relatively high cost of producing the recordings and the need for each title to be approved by the Talking Book Selection Committee slowed the process somewhat, by the end of the first year, fifty-five titles were available.[34] Fraser (now Sir Ian) chose his narrators with care. One of the first was BBC announcer Stuart Hibberd, who narrated the Gospel of St John.[35] Radio broadcasts were widely available by 1935, and the British Wireless for the Blind Fund had started to supply free radios in 1929.[36] Talking books remained popular, however, because they offered a different listening experience. The BBC was not in the business of broadcasting lengthy readings of novels, and its programmes were not to everyone's tastes. The talking book library offered the choice of what to hear and when to hear it.

A Criminal Use of the Gramophone

Over thirty years after it arrived in Britain, the gramophone was a commonplace object. An expensive model or a new-fangled electric instrument might act as a conversation piece, but few people were likely to be surprised by the appearance of a gramophone in a friend's home, on a picnic, or in a novel or short story. Dorothy L. Sayers was no longer impressed by its use as a plot device. In her introduction to 1932's *The Second Omnibus of Crime*, she wrote about the clichés of the crime writer:

> The substituted corpse, the gramophone alibi, the murder by means of an animal, ... the reader knows them all and knows how to detect them as well as the detective himself. In the novel they can still be used—or some of them. (Personally, I think the gramophone should be given a rest.)[37]

Sayers's advice fell on some famous but deaf ears. Agatha Christie had already mentioned the gramophone in *The Murder at The Vicarage* in 1930. She went on to make the gramophone a potential alibi in 1938's *Hercule Poirot's Christmas*, and a year later, a gramophone record became crucial to the plot of *And Then There Were None*. Graham Greene was similarly unmoved by

Sayers's opinion; Pinkie, the anti-hero of *Brighton Rock*, also published in 1938, records a disc for his wife, Rose. T. H. White used a gramophone alibi in *Darkness at Pemberley*, even going into detail about the technology, a handy 'how a gramophone works' primer for the uninitiated. The book was published in 1932, so we can at least excuse White from the crime of ignoring Sayers. James Joyce made his own appearance on disc in 1930, reading from *Anna Livia Plurabelle*. Despite a 'particular distaste' for Joyce's works, John Langdon-Davies found the Irish writer's recording to be delightful and praised his 'beautiful diction'.[38]

Theodor Adorno, the German philosopher and cultural critic, was one of the first European academics to take the gramophone seriously as an object to be critiqued. Adorno wrote *The Curves of the Needle* in 1927, when electrical recording had established itself. He was not a fan, either of the object, its recordings, or the people he believed to be its consumers. He was even unkind to the faithful Nipper (who he did not even have the decency to name). 'The relevance of the talking machines is debatable', he wrote:

> The spatially limited effect of every such apparatus makes it into a utensil of the private life that regulates the consumption of art in the nineteenth century. It is the bourgeois family that gathers around the gramophone in order to enjoy the music that it itself ... is unable to perform ... Most of the time records are virtual photographs of their owners—flattering photographs—ideologies ... The dog on records listening to his master's voice off of records through the gramophone horn is the right emblem for the primordial affect which the gramophone stimulated and which perhaps even gave rise to the gramophone in the first place.[39]

Adorno recognised some of the practical problems associated with the gramophone—the aesthetic and psychological problem of the external horn, and the difficulty of achieving the correct pitch—but he did not seem to be familiar with the improvements brought about by electrical recording. He gave no indication of an awareness of 'low culture' discs, although his derogatory use of the term 'bourgeois' suggests he considered any use of the gramophone to be beneath him. Like many critics that followed, Adorno seemed immune to the idea of being entertained by this 'piece of bourgeois furniture'.

Blue Discs and Blue Pencils

When John Langdon-Davies declared that he would treat the gramophone as a 'vehicle of culture', he was being complimentary, declaring the instrument's social value, but there were other aspects of the gramophone that the guardians of Britain's morals were less keen on. In his attempt to justify his ideas, Langdon-Davies recommended that 'Every highbrow' should buy a copy of Julian Lester's vocal version of 'She's Funny That Way'.[40] This was because 'It has deep psychoanalytic meaning, I am told; and rumour alleges that Augustus John broke it in two as being a disgrace to decency.' On the surface, it is an innocuous ditty (albeit one that places the woman in a secondary role). Lester sings about a woman, a 'fallen star,' who is crazy for him and slaves for him in his kitchen. He does not understand why she loves him, concluding that it is simply because 'she's funny that way.' So, what drove John—an artist 'whose rampant sexuality and over-arching egotism were altogether at odds with conventional notions of marriage'—to commit so violent an act as the wanton destruction of a shellac disc?[41]

The song, by Richard Whiting and Neil Moret (a.k.a. Charles Daniels), has been recorded many times. Post-Lester versions include those of Frank Sinatra, Nat King Cole, Kurt Elling, and Billie Holiday, but few of these include the opening lines about the woman (or in Holiday's case, the man) being a 'fallen star'. Perhaps Lester is singing about his mother, whose illegitimate pregnancy caused her to fall and who he remains with for Freudian reasons, or perhaps Langdon-Davies is joking.

'She's Funny That Way' may be open to interpretation, but other gramophone records were more obviously morally suspect. Music hall artists like Marie Lloyd had a long history of risqué songs, jokes and recitations filled with double entendres, and some of these found their way onto disc, perhaps after a bit of self-censorship to tone down their worst excesses. The Durium Dance Band's 'She Was Only A Postmaster's Daughter', for example, is a comic song about the daughters of various tradespersons ('She was only a postmaster's daughter, but she knew how to handle her mail') that the BBC banned from its airwaves.[42] Major stars such as George Formby ('With My Little Stick of Blackpool Rock' and 'With My Little Ukulele in My Hand') enjoyed the double entendre, as did their audiences. At the more sophisticated end of the British entertainment spectrum, a cut-glass accent, a tailcoat, and a bow tie could hide a multitude of sins. Harry Roy's recording of 'Pussy!' (a.k.a 'My Girl's Pussy') may start with a few meows, but as soon as the singing starts, it is obvious that the pussy in question does not need cat food.[43] These British recordings were the aural equivalent of Donald McGill's saucy postcards, but some of the discs making their way across the Atlantic were made of stronger stuff.

'Ol' Man Mose' was one such recording. It is an innocuous song, as the jaunty 1960s version by Britain's own Swinging Blue Jeans ably demonstrates, but Eddy Duchin and his Orchestra's Brunswick label recording has become notorious for its (possible) inclusion of the F-word. Mose has died, so the chorus repeatedly informs us that he has kicked the bucket. Patricia Norman,

Duchin's vocalist, appears to deviate from the narrative when she replaces the 'b' of bucket with an 'f', altering completely the meaning of the intended 'buck-buck-bucket' lyric. Does she, or does she not? It seems clear that she does, to the delight of the musicians.

Some blues artists left nothing to the imagination, eschewing even the single entendre. Lucille Bogan went straight to the heart of the matter on her second version of 'Shave Em Dry', opening the song by announcing 'I got nipples on my titties big as the end of my thumb, I got something 'tween my legs 'll make a dead man come.'[44] However, blues records were rare in Britain at this time, and it is unlikely that anyone at the BBC ever considered playing one of Bogan's songs. Sexual content (explicit or merely suggested) was an obvious reason for the BBC to ban a record from the airwaves. Drug references would also result in a ban; Fats Waller's 'If He's A Viper', about reefer smoking, fell foul of that particular rule. Concern about obscene gramophone records reached the House of Commons in 1930, when two MPs (Daniel Somerville and Harry Day) asked the Home Secretary if he or the police had taken any action about what Day called 'offensive gramophone song records'.[45] Unfortunately, neither man named any of these songs, or gave examples of their offensive lyrics. The Home Secretary, John Clynes, replied that neither he nor the police had seen any information about offensive gramophone records. He was clearly disinclined to look for any.

On the Record: 'Falstaff', Sir Edward Elgar and the London Symphony Orchestra (HMV, 1932)

Electrical recording techniques revitalised the British gramophone market and were eagerly adopted by leading composers and conductors such as Elgar. This disc was the first to be recorded at Abbey Road Studios, on 12 November 1931. If Leslie Sarony's irony and dark humour represented the more eccentric side of British working-class life, 'Falstaff' was rooted firmly in aspirational high-culture.

Elgar composed 'Falstaff, A Symphonic Study In C Minor' in 1913, the study being of Sir John Falstaff, William Shakespeare's comic character from *Henry IV Parts 1 and 2* and *The Merry Wives Of Windsor* (although Elgar based his work only on the character's appearances in the *Henry* plays, rejecting his appearance in *The Merry Wives Of Windsor* as a 'caricature').[46] A grand symphonic work, based on a character from Britain's greatest playwright and already twenty years old at the time of recording, the choice of 'Falstaff' as the first recording at Abbey Road made the record company's credentials as a supporter of the country's cultural history and its ruling class abundantly clear. What could be more British than a work by Sir Edward Elgar, based on a character by William Shakespeare?

Elgar, who was seventy-four years old at the time of recording, received a knighthood in 1904.[47] In 1924, he was appointed as Master of the King's Musick. He had a long-established association with EMI, going back to the days of the Gramophone Company. Elgar was one of the company's trophy signings, like Melba or Caruso; Fred Gaisberg described his association with the company as 'chiefly decorative, his name carrying the prestige of England's greatest composer'.[48] Such a statement might be code for 'he gave us prestige but not much profit', but decorative or not, the association lasted until the composer's death in 1934.

The 1931 recording, on four discs, retailed at 6 shillings per disc or as an album set for 24 shillings. The company went to town on the advertising campaign, adding a cartoon of the portly and jolly Falstaff alongside its usual trademark of Nipper the dog.[49] In a nod to the emergence of new gramophone technologies for the listener, the records were available coupled for use with an autochanger, where side one was paired with side eight, side two with side seven, and so on.[50]

The recording was well-received. Writing in *The Gramophone* soon after the recording's release in early 1932, W. R. Anderson called it 'a gold standard of recording. It is grand, ripe work, worth our closest, most loving study; and the performance (it seems) ripens with the humanity of the music', a review that EMI was happy to quote on its advertisement. The critic in *The Times* was equally effusive about the composition, performance, and recording, which the critic described as 'extraordinarily good … we cannot remember to have heard the auxiliary percussion instruments (tambourine, triangle, side-drum, &c.) so faithfully reproduced before.'[51] Even after numerous later recordings, broadcaster and commentator David Nice was able to say, in 2016: 'There's no more volatile "Falstaff" on disc than the conductor's … sounding plump and luxuriant on bass clarinet, bassoons and cellos right at the start.'[52]

It was an auspicious start for Abbey Road. Ninety years later, it is still one of the world's most prestigious recording studios.

Al Bowlly's Dead and Gone

The sensitivity of the electrical microphone made it possible to record artists whose talent lay in their vocal subtleties rather than power and volume and enabled a new breed of musical singing star to emerge. In the United States, Bing Crosby would become a huge star thanks to the electric microphone. In Britain, Al Bowlly would become famous for a similar reason. Both men lacked Enrico Caruso's vocal power, but their intimate and personal styles were perfectly suited to the electrical recording era and a public that craved a new kind of celebrity artist. Crosby stayed at the top of the entertainment tree for fifty years, but Al Bowlly's career came to a sudden end in 1941. A second worldwide conflict brought fresh opportunities and problems for the gramophone industry, and by the end of the war, new communications technologies posed yet another threat to the 78-rpm record's supremacy.

Crooners and Cosy Nights In

Al Bowlly and his singing partner Jimmy Mesene (a guitar and vocal duo by the name of The Radio Stars with Two Guitars) played the Rex Theatre in High Wycombe on the night of 16 April 1941. After the show, Bowlly returned to his flat in Piccadilly and stayed there even after the air raid siren sounded; in the early hours of 17 April, a Luftwaffe bomb exploded nearby, killing the singer.[1] With commendable foresight, Bowlly's last recording was 'When That Man is Dead and Gone'.[2]

Bowlly's recording career began in Berlin, in July 1927, when he recorded half a dozen songs with Arthur Briggs's Savoy Syncopators. After that, he recorded every year, especially in the period from 1930–35. Bowlly was a crooner, a type of singer characterised by an understated, soft style usually employed in performing romantic ballads. He owed his career to the microphone and electrical recording. Before they appeared, on stage, his intimate vocals would have been overwhelmed by a band's instruments (if not by the chatter and heel clicks of the dancers), and in the studio, his voice would have struggled to move the diaphragm of the horn with the force required to cut a disc. Afterwards, he thrived in both environments.

Crooners could thrive on stage or in the studio because of new recording technologies, but this does not explain their popularity. If the public demanded Caruso, Dame Nellie Melba, George Formby, and instrumental jazz and remained unmoved by the sweet and intimate vocal stylings of Al Bowlly or Bing Crosby, new technologies would not have been enough to bring them fame and fortune. Their popularity in Britain as elsewhere was the result of a combination of factors—a bringing together of social change, artistic developments, and technological advances.

More and more homes owned gramophones. By the mid-1920s, writers such as Cole Porter and Irving Berlin were creating the body of work that became known as the Great American Songbook, which includes some of the most popular love songs of the last 100 years—songs that were a perfect match for the crooner's voice. At the same time, social change gave young men and women more freedom to form relationships and to meet in private. Records of romantic love songs, sung by attractive singers, were the perfect background to intimate dates. Crooners were a product of a new age, responding to the desires of a new generation of record buyers just as much as they were driving the fashion for this new musical style.

'Crooner' was a term applied to male singers, but electrical recording brought a new group of female singers to prominence just as easily even though no one seems to have coined a neat, catch-all, term for them. In the USA, Ella Fitzgerald, Sarah Vaughan, and Billie Holiday epitomised the new style of singing. In Britain, Vera Lynn became a huge star thanks to her renditions of songs such as 'We'll Meet Again', becoming 'the Forces' Sweetheart' and establishing a career that lasted into the twenty-first century. Like Bowlly, Lynn cultivated an intimate style—a sympathetic voice that could effortlessly echo the combination of optimism and melancholy felt by millions of young Britons as they were separated from their partners and lovers. The BBC did much to bring these new singers into people's homes, but the family gramophone ensured that people could hear their favourite songs whenever they were wanted and, if that gramophone was portable, wherever they wanted as well.

Keeping Up Morale

As Europe moved closer to another major conflict, French writer Maxime Baze suggested recording the sound of artillery and other weapons onto discs that could then be replayed repeatedly through loudspeakers on the battlefield to destroy the morale of opposing troops. This was psychological warfare that posed little physical risk to either army, with the force with the largest and loudest collection of explosions on disc gaining the upper hand without a real shot being fired. *The Times'* Paris correspondent was unimpressed by the idea, seemingly disappointed that future battles might simply be loudspeaker contests.[3] Sadly, battles by disc did not catch on.

By spring 1939, the government was preparing for conflict with civil defence, the protection of the British population at home, as a key area of planning. Air raid shelters were necessary and while physical protection from the Luftwaffe was the main aim of these shelters, planners recognised that people's psychological well-being was also important. During the debate on the Civil Defence Bill, Sir Francis Freemantle was aware that people would take their portable gramophones into shelters, but less convinced of their efficacy as morale-boosters: 'When they get down [into the shelters] what are they going to do?... somebody may have a gramophone, but they would soon get tired of that'.

David Logan was more scathing: 'To imagine that a crowd of people will only need, perhaps, a few gramophones playing underground when bombs are rattling overhead, is to live in a fool's paradise, in the atmosphere of a pantomime and not of an air raid.'[4] Nevertheless, official advice issued immediately prior to the 3 September 1939 declaration of war suggested that gramophones in shelters would be welcome distractions during raids.[5] In Oxford Street, the basement of the HMV store was designated as an official shelter: one place, at least, where access to a portable gramophone would not be a problem.[6]

The government needed to recruit thousands of new soldiers, sailors, and air force personnel, young men and women who would be unused to a military life, away from home for the first time and desperate for a few home comforts. Labour MP Arthur Creech-Jones was particularly worried about the effect on the more studious, sensitive, and active-minded of these conscripts. Educational and social facilities would be vital for those young people, especially during their initial training as they became accustomed to life in the armed forces. Leslie Hore-Belisha, the Secretary of State for War, agreed with Creech-Jones. Referring to the conscripts as 'militiamen', he said that they would be able to share in all of the army's various 'institutes', where they could play billiards or darts, buy glasses of milk and bars of chocolate, and spend their money in any number of agreeable ways, 'perhaps to the accompaniment of the gramophone and wireless'.[7]

As war service sent people long distances from their homes, maintaining contact with family and friends was vital for morale. Gramophone records could be sent to relatives on active service, but the discs were notoriously fragile, so in November 1939, an advertisement for HMV, Regal Zonophone, and Parlophone discs advised readers to 'Send Him Some Records' by means of record tokens: 'A New Gift Idea'.[8] This was a great idea for troops on the home front and with easy access to a record shop, but not helpful to those on the front line in mainland Europe or beyond, whose access to record shops was restricted, to say the least.

The BBC's early response to the outbreak of war gained mixed reviews. By early October, it was allotting less time to gramophone records than it had given them before the war—a positive move, according to the Lord Privy Seal, Samuel Hoare. Cecil Poole's experience was different:

> I may be unfortunate in regard to the time at which I switch on my radio, but I either get a programme of gramophone records or Sandy Macpherson at the B.B.C. organ. I have nothing against Sandy Macpherson. He has played a noble part, but by now he must be feeling exhausted.

During the early months of the 'phony war', the BBC appeared to run out of news on a regular basis and filled in the time with music on disc. This was not a popular move and Cecil Poole extended his complaint to encompass repetitive news bulletins and a preponderance of tedious gramophone records:

> After I had had the devastating experience of hearing the news three times over recently, the first record that came on was, 'What noisy noise annoys an oyster most.' I would ask the Minister whether that is the kind of elevating stuff that will fill the British public with courage and confidence to win the war.[9]

The BBC claimed that it had been planning for war for nearly a year and promised that its broadcasts would not consist solely of gramophone records and news but would feature plenty of live shows, entertainment, and talks: 'ordinary broadcast programmes—only probably of a rather higher standard than those we know in times of peace!'[10] Despite this planning, it took the BBC a little while to get into its stride. On Monday 4 September, in a total of seventeen hours of broadcasts, gramophone records occupied nine hours. For 'Platterbug', this was not enough. The gramophone fan wrote to the *Radio Times* to ask for more:

> What a debt the BBC [owes] to Edison, Berliner, and other pioneers up to the present-day workers on gramophonics! My wish is for more specially arranged and presented 'absentee broadcasting' (to use Carroll Gibbons's term).[11]

The BBC's gramophone programmes catered to most tastes (they included variety acts as well as music), but such variation also brought a vitriolic and racist attack from one Member of Parliament. Andrew MacLaren MP was a supporter of the wireless as a propaganda tool and morale booster but concerned that the 'wrong' sort of gramophone records, performed by the wrong sort of people, were being broadcast. According to MacLaren, crooners and jazz bands were 'a foreign importation and are not native to this land. They come here from the backwoods of America and have the rhythm of the nigger running through them, with all that it implies. They do not belong to our people.' John Parker took a more inclusive perspective, emphasising that propaganda should unite the people of the Commonwealth, not divide them and criticising MacLaren for using a term 'that gives great offence to many coloured subjects inside the Commonwealth'.[12]

The BBC eventually made good on its promise to feature fewer gramophone records on its home service. On Monday 4 March 1940, it offered just half an hour of records in *Tunes of Yesterday*. The following Saturday, with no schools programmes, it broadcast only two programmes of records, totalling eighty minutes. The Forces Service featured a few more records but still fell well short of two hours per day.[13] The BBC began this special wireless service for the armed forces on 18 February 1940, its schedule including popular music, classical music, drama, comedy, religious services, and sport. On its opening day, after a short morning worship and a summary of the day's programmes, the service's first programme was devoted to recordings of American jazz star Paul Whiteman playing songs by the Russian-born composer Irving Berlin.[14] Mr MacLaren's response to such multi-cultural programming is unknown.

The BBC Forces Service and, from 1943, the American Forces Network (AFN) brought entertainment to serving men and women worldwide, so the need for front-line gramophones was less than it had been in the First World War, but the instruments still found their way into the billets of combat troops. RAF aircrew passed the time between missions by reading, listening to the wireless and playing gramophone records in their home bases. At RAF Oulton in Norfolk, the RAF personnel were billeted at Blickling Hall, a seventeenth-century mansion near Aylsham. They established a 'Music Circle' that met in the hall's solarium and enjoyed performances from some of the station's more talented members, before the base's accounts officer, Flight Lieutenant David Collins, was prevailed upon to buy some records, enabling the Music Circle to present two gramophone record recitals each week.[15] Armed forces personnel who found themselves in German POW camps made more ingenious use of records; one group of intending escapees hid maps in record sleeves, while MI9 sent German currency to Colditz hidden in a record that could be split in half to reveal the banknotes.[16]

Outside the confines of the BBC and the armed forces, gramophone records remained crucial to people's day-to-day entertainment; Waterloo station staff connected a gramophone to the loudspeaker system to entertain train passengers.[17] Sir Cyril Entwistle, Chairman of Decca Records, stressed the importance of the industry. Records brought entertainment to the troops, relaxation to those at home, brightened the working lives of those engaged in factories and other arduous work, disseminated education and culture, and were vital for the broadcasting of propaganda at home and abroad: 'the gramophone record performs a vital service in the life of the community'.[18]

The public wanted and needed entertainment, but the British war effort needed men and women and conscription soon impacted on the recording industry. Jack Hylton's experience was typical. Between 14 September 1939 (his first recording session after war was declared) and 6 March 1940 Jack Hylton and his Orchestra recorded seventy-four sides for HMV. The numbers included four with comedian Arthur Askey, standards such as 'Have You Met Miss Jones' and 'My Heart Belongs to Daddy', patriotic numbers including 'Oh, Ain't it Grand to be in the Navy', a version of Irving Berlin's 'It's a Lovely Day Tomorrow' and the risqué 'The Organ Grinder Grinds All Day' ('He is grinding Annie Laurie for quite a little while' sings Sam Browne over Hylton's cheerful orchestral backing).[19] By April 1940, seven key members of the orchestra had been called up, so Hylton disbanded the orchestra and never recorded again.[20]

As it had during the First World War, the gramophone industry gave over part of its production capacity to war work, producing electric fuses, instruments, and shells. At first, the industry produced gramophones and discs for export and brought in much-needed foreign income as well as promoting British entertainment. A picture special for *The Times* showed discs and instruments being packed for destinations including Mombasa, Palestine, Rangoon, and Malta. Unwanted discs were recycled—an estimated 6,000,000 were available each year—and used for war materials. Dustmen and rag 'n' bone men agreed to collect the discs from homes and warehouses.[21] By 1942, a shellac shortage threatened to bring record production to a halt. Fearful of a negative impact on morale, the Ministry of Supply stepped in, agreeing to the continued production of records using shellac in stock, but at a rate 30 per cent lower than in 1941. The Ministry allowed record companies to 'debase' their shellac; this made it go further and allowed additional recycling of salvaged discs.[22] The British Legion appealed for 10,000,000 used discs, and although King George VI and his daughters (Princess Elizabeth and Princess Margaret) contributed a few records from their personal collections, their largesse still left the appeal short of its target. The British Legion was surprisingly fussy in its demands—no cylinders and no cracked or broken discs (although minor chips to the edges were acceptable). It even stipulated acceptable record labels: HMV, Columbia, Parlophone, Regal Zonophone, Zonophone, Brunswick, Decca, Rex, and Panachord. The records were needed for one specific purpose: to maintain 'the production of oversea [*sic.*] propaganda'.[23]

War work, reduced production, shellac shortages, and conscription all impacted on the gramophone industry, but it was still functioning and it still wanted to sell its products. Imhof's, the London retailer, carried on selling gramophones and records but also offered instrument cases, amplifiers, press work, and metal handles produced by its parent company, emphasising that such products could only be made if they were 'priority work'. It ensured that customers were aware of its role in the war effort without giving too much away: 'We cannot at present tell you of the immense scope of our activities during the war except to say that we are contractors to the Admiralty, Air Ministry, Ministry of Supply, G. P. O., etc.'[24]

Gramophone companies may not have indulged in the sort of gung-ho jingoism they had practiced in the First World War, but they were still quick off the mark in promoting themselves as patriotic, morale-boosting providers of fun. Nipper was, of course, part of the war effort from the start. 'Here's a picture of happiness,' HMV declared beneath its much-loved logo of gramophone and dog, 'a key to the cheerfulness we must have on the home front'.[25] 'Don't stop buying our products,' the advertisement pleaded, 'just because there's a war on': 'money outlayed on a first-class radiogramophone, even in these days, is MONEY WELL SPENT'. Brunswick Records stood out from the rest by advertising its American artists—Duke Ellington, Art Tatum, Deanna Durbin, and Bing Crosby were some of its biggest stars— and by ignoring the war altogether, with the possible exception of a version of 'There'll Always be an England' by 'The Famous International Tenor' Alfred Piccaver.[26]

Gramophone production plummeted. In the first nine months of 1945, only ninety instruments were exported compared to 31,000 in the first nine months of 1938.[27] By June 1945, HMV was ready to give thanks for victory and to help the British public to do so as well. The company released a series of celebratory records: King George VI's victory broadcast of 8 May, a disc featuring two of Winston Churchill's victory speeches, excerpts from the thanksgiving service at St Paul's Cathedral, and a complete recording of Sir Edward Elgar's 'Dream of Gerontius'.[28] Profits from the King's speech and Churchill's disc would go to their nominated charities; Elgar and the St Paul's service would help to swell HMV's own coffers.

Many people might have decided to make the best of the night-time blackout by snuggling together with a selection of Bing Crosby or Al Bowlly records but Linguaphone had other ideas. Learn a new language, it suggested, for this was 'An Ideal Occupation for long Black-out Evenings.'[29] Linguaphone offered twenty languages, noting that any of them would help to ensure an understanding of the wartime situation. Birth rates suggest that Crosby and Bowlly's recordings were more popular than Linguaphone's; although births fell at the beginning of the war, by 1941, the rate was rising sharply.[30]

Occasionally, people questioned the gramophone industry's patriotism. Sir Geoffrey Mander MP accused it of acting as a fifth column for the German forces when he discovered that a manufacturer was producing records of 'German soldier songs in German' including '*Deutschland Über Alles*'. The unnamed manufacturer was producing these discs on demand but had made no more than twenty-two copies in the previous few months. This was still too many for Sir Geoffrey, who expressed his concern that British labour was producing such anti-British material.[31] Linguaphone, the company that saw the blackout as a business opportunity, was accused of having commercial dealings with the enemy. In 1940, the company had sent gramophone matrices via New York to Norway (after the German invasion in the early part of the year) and Sweden; in 1942, it arranged for records to be supplied to Norway and Denmark from its Berlin representative, without paying the appropriate royalties. Did these actions pose a real threat to Britain? Mr Justice Stable thought that they did not, but the company had still knowingly acted illegally and so he fined the company £1,000 and its managing director, Jacques Roston, £500.[32]

Back on the Front

On the front line, the gramophone brought comfort to troops as part of entertainment packages that also included books, games, and even a mobile cinema.[33] The Royal Air Force Comforts Fund benefitted from the profits from two contrasting charity records. HMV produced a recording of a nightingale's song—'a simple and authentic document that stirs the imagination by its beauty and strangeness'—taken from a live BBC broadcast of the bird's song, which was cut short for security reasons due to the sudden appearance of the sound of bombers taking off for a raid on Mannheim. On the disc, the nightingale's song is loud and clear and so, too, are the aircraft. Decca released Charles Gardner's commentary on an air battle over the English Channel, which had been broadcast live on the BBC on 14 July 1940.[34]

Gramophones were in short supply by the summer of 1942, and the Entertainments National Service Association (ENSA) launched an appeal for instruments.[35] Decca arranged for its dealers to collect donated instruments and send them to the Decca factory for refurbishment. The company stressed that it was no longer making gramophones because of war work, but that it would reimburse its dealers for the costs of post and packaging. Flanagan and Allen, the popular variety act, supported the ENSA appeal.[36] The more resourceful members of the armed forces built their own instruments while on active service, which *The Times* referred to as 'camp-made' gramophones.[37] Others ensured that their portable gramophones formed part of their belongings as they moved from posting to posting; they included a young George Melly, who took his own wind-up gramophone and cases of 78s to sea when serving in the Navy at the end of the war.[38]

A short-form disc recording was proposed in 1943 as a more personal form of communication than the letter or postcard. Small discs, similar in size to a letter and postable in the same way, could be recorded by men and women on service and sent to loved ones back home. Each disc could hold a maximum of around 170 words (depending, presumably, on the garrulousness of the speaker and the number of syllables in each word) and messages would have to be written out and checked by censors before being committed to disc.[39] It is impossible to gauge the popularity of this form of personal communication. The discs were small, but the recording equipment was presumably larger and not a priority for front-line transport, while checking a 170-word audio recording would have taken the censors much longer than checking a brief postcard.

The Special Operations Executive (a body devoted to espionage and irregular warfare) decided that the gramophone could play a more offensive role in the war and proposed its use in countering what it viewed as the pro-German sympathies of many Moroccans. The idea was simple, if bizarre; the distribution of obscene gramophone records casting aspersions on Hitler's sexual prowess. The plan was not put into practice.[40] Another SOE plan took place at the beginning of the D-Day landings, when two five-man teams of SAS soldiers parachuted into the Cherbourg peninsula. Each team carried Very pistols, a portable gramophone and a few records, key equipment in a deception plan. The Very pistols fired flares to light up dropping zones, the discs contained recordings of small arms fire and soldiers' oaths to be played as a means of confusing German forces; Maxime Baze's notion of the gramophone as an offensive weapon was clearly not as far-fetched as all that.[41]

V for Victory—On Vinyl

The United States entered the war after the Japanese attack on Pearl Harbor on 7 December 1941, and American forces began arriving in Britain in 1942, bringing their own records, instruments, and ideas about entertainment with them. The Clubmobile was one of these ideas—a converted bus stocked with American newspapers, magazines, cigarettes, coffee, and records. Each Clubmobile was staffed by three young American women who drove to isolated bases and played the latest American discs through roof-mounted loudspeakers.[42] The Clubmobiles would have been busy; around 3 million US troops passed through Britain during the war.[43] Mostly young, these troops demanded the latest music from their homeland. Jazz musicians, crooners, swing bands, and dance orchestras were all popular, but they were rarely part of the BBC's programming. The records had to be brought from the USA.

America shipped gramophone records to its troops, but in 1942, the American Federation of Musicians initiated a recording ban in a dispute over royalties.[44] The supply of new records dried up and so the American government (specifically, the War Department's Special Services Athletic and Recreation Branch Music Section) established its own V-Disc label. V-Discs were special recordings of major American stars, made outside the ban and outside existing recording contracts, for distribution free of charge to US forces in Europe. Between October 1943 and May 1949, over 900 V-Discs were produced. Each one was a double-sided 12-inch disc, with a playing time of up to six minutes per side, so one record could contain four tracks. The series started with a now relatively unknown act; Bea Wain appeared on V-Disc 001 with her big band arrangement of 'Comin' In on a Wing and a Prayer'.[45] After her, the cream of the American entertainment industry contributed recordings. Frank Sinatra, Paul Robeson, Duke Ellington, Dinah Shore, Arturo Toscanini, Fats Waller, Glenn Miller, and many more artists made V-Discs into one of the most diverse and star-studded record labels of all time.

The discs may have been distributed free by a department of the US government, but they stand out even today for their quality. Each label gives full credit to the composers and songwriters as well as to the ensembles who made the recording. Soloists and vocalists are credited, and on recordings made by smaller combos, each member of the group is listed. While Glen Gray and the Casa Loma Orchestra is too big a group to list every member, the label of the orchestra's V-Disc 375A does note that Sonny Dunham plays trumpet on 'Memories of You' and Pee Wee Hunt sings on 'Lazy Bones'. V-Disc 274, by the Benny Goodman Trio, has space to list all three musicians—Goodman on clarinet, Teddy Wilson on piano, and Specs Powell on drums. This information would prove to be of great interest to British music fans during and after the war, especially lovers of modern jazz who were keen to explore the new music emerging from the USA. A fan of the piano playing on the Goodman record could seek out Wilson's own recordings, for example, and such knowledge would help to spread the word among the fervent jazz aficionados of the post-war years.

Two more pieces of information adorned the V-Discs' labels. The music was categorised according to its style or mood—the Casa Loma record was 'Sweet', the Goodman was 'Swing'—which helped soldiers looking to programme music for a party or dance. The labels also noted that each disc was to be played at 78 rpm and required an 'Outside Start', an instruction most useful to the presumably very small number of people whose listening experience was confined to Pathé's quirky discs which played from the inside out.

V-Discs were not for sale, and the labels made it clear that they were not for general broadcast either; 'This record is the property of the United States Government and use for radio or commercial purposes is prohibited' ran the warning on each record's label. If British citizens were going to hear these records, it would be with the help of US troops, at dances on bases, in local pubs when some of the troops brought a few discs with them, or perhaps at a summer picnic with a portable gramophone. V-Discs were important for Axis jazz fans and musicians, too. In Germany and Italy, they listened to V-Discs on American radio broadcasts at a time when their home countries banned such music from the airwaves and the discs remained important until record production re-started after the war—so important that they gained almost legendary status among fans and musicians alike.[46]

Although V-Discs were not supposed to be sold, given, or traded to civilians, many of them found their way into private hands and remained in Europe to be sought after and cherished by collectors. It is easy to understand their appeal. The catalogue contains some of the greatest musicians of the mid-twentieth century, a V-Disc's playing time approaches that of a 45-rpm extended play record, and the red, white, and blue labels (carefully chosen, one assumes, to link the flags of the US, Britain, and France) are visually striking.

The V-Disc label brought something else to Britain that would soon have a widespread and devastating impact on the primacy of shellac. The wartime shellac shortage forced the V-Disc's producers to look for an alternative material. Vinylite was the first substitute, a resin that was already in use for radio transcription discs and created a flexible but almost unbreakable disc. However, it was also used for military equipment such as electrical insulation and life rafts and so it, too, was in short supply. It was replaced by Formvar, a polyvinyl acetal resin developed by a subsidiary of Monsanto.[47] Few listeners were likely to care about the material used to make V-Discs, but within a decade, it would render shellac obsolete.

On the Record: 'It's a Lovely Day Tomorrow', Al Bowlly (HMV, 1940)

Bowlly's recording, one of his last, epitomises the smooth, sophisticated romance of the crooner. A generation swooned.

Al Bowlly recorded 'It's a Lovely Day Tomorrow' with the Ronnie Munro Orchestra on 15 February 1940, in London.[48] Irving Berlin wrote the song in 1938 as his response to the Munich Agreement between Hitler and Neville Chamberlain, which had upset him and many of his friends. He later referred to it as his first war song of the Second World War and included it in his 1940 show *Louisiana Purchase*.[49]

The song is not typical of Great American Songbook composers such as Berlin; they rarely made overtly political statements (Yip Harburg and Jay Gorney's 'Brother, Can You Spare a Dime' is perhaps the best-known example of an overtly political Songbook classic) and, indeed, the lyrics to this song are not obviously making a political statement. The title encapsulates much of the mood of the song. It is a hopeful lyric but acknowledges that things are not going well just now; today is sad, but tomorrow will be beautiful. The sentiments were particularly appropriate when Bowlly recorded his version; soon after its release, the British and French forces were retreating to Dunkirk.

Bowlly sings 'It's a Lovely Day Tomorrow' quietly and with restraint. The song is driven by the rhythm guitar; the arrangement emphasises the orchestra's string section (which today sounds rather syrupy and clichéd) and muted brass. Bowlly barely rises above a whisper, a conversational vocal that a listener could easily imagine was being directed at them and them alone, a comforting and warm voice that helps to soothe away the terror of the conflict and the fear of losing a loved one on the battlefield. With Al Bowlly on the gramophone, things might feel just a little more optimistic. It is a style that suits the song, but it would have been impossible without electrical recording.

Lyrically, 'It's a Lovely Day Tomorrow' shares some common ground with First World War songs such as 'It's a Long, Long Way to Tipperary' or 'Take Me Back to Dear Old Blighty' (all three long for a change, for things to return to normal), but Bowlly's performance is a million miles away from singers like John McCormack or Florrie Forde. Acoustic recording makes McCormack work hard, pushing out the air to get the diaphragm moving. An emphasis on jaunty sing-along arrangements to keep the spirits up, with a few novelty sound effects, means that Forde has no chance of creating a one-to-one intimacy (although her version sounds positively romantic compared to Ella Retford's dire rendition). Thirty years later, Bowlly, Vera Lynn (despite an amusingly kitsch organ solo), Frank Sinatra, and others made the most of their chance to do justice to Berlin's song. It is Bowlly who wins the prize, though, and it is still a lovely disc today.

9

Multimedia Mayhem

Britain welcomed victory and peace, voted out wartime Prime Minister Winston Churchill in favour of Labour's Clement Attlee, and looked forward to a lovely day tomorrow. The gramophone looked forward to an uncertain future. By the late 1940s, 78s had been around for half a century; the basic technology of the gramophone itself would still be recognisable to an enthusiast from 1900, and even electrical recording was over twenty years old. The time was ripe for change.

In the next decade, exciting new ways of recording and reproducing sound would emerge; recording onto tape, commercially available vinyl discs, 33⅓-rpm records with over twenty minutes of sound on each side, and 7-inch diameter discs rotating at 45 rpm would all be part of the sonic mainstream. The BBC would continue to monopolise the British airwaves but its services would expand and its television service, cut off in its prime by the outbreak of war, would return. In this brave new world, would there be a place for the clunky old gramophone and its fragile shellac discs?

There's Life in the Old Dog Yet

In the immediate aftermath of the war, the gramophone industry might have looked forward to a return to growth. After all, Britain was emerging from almost six years of conflict and an entertainment-focused industry could expect a boom. Hugh Dalton, the Chancellor of the Exchequer, promised to reduce purchase tax on instruments and discs.[1] Men and women were being discharged from the armed forces in their millions, adding to the industry's potential market.[2] Television, when it eventually restarted, would remain an option for the wealthy few and so offered no immediate threat. As for the dear old BBC, it was failing to live up to the standards of its relatives overseas. Lord Sandhurst openly criticised the BBC for its poor-quality broadcasts, complaining that the corporation's approach to the broadcasting of gramophone records was 'frankly paralytic' compared with the radio stations of France, Holland, the USA, and even Germany.[3]

Such complaints could signal a boost for the gramophone industry—poor BBC programmes might encourage more people to buy records to play at home, rather than listen to the wireless—but the BBC was a source of free advertising for the record labels, and if its presentation of records was poor, this could make it less likely that listeners would go out and buy them. The industry carried on with record and instrument production, hoping that improved sound would help to keep markets buoyant. In 1945, Decca introduced *ffrr* (full frequency range recording), which improved sound quality through advances in recording technology. Although Decca used the term for some time, it did not catch on as a generic name for the new and improved sound; customers preferred another new term, with much the same meaning: 'High Fidelity'.[4]

Social and cultural life underwent major changes in the aftermath of war, and some of those changes brought benefits for the gramophone industry in the form of new markets. Communities from mainland European countries such as Poland and Italy and from many Commonwealth countries began to establish or enlarge themselves. As these communities grew, entrepreneurs established small shops and record labels to provide them with the music of their homelands; as collector Paul Buck puts it, 'Discs for the diaspora'. The Polonia label was British but mainly repackaged recordings from Melodiya, a record label operating in the Soviet Union whose output included music from Poland.[5] Stern's record shop in central London specialised in discs from West Africa. Collet's in Charing Cross Road sold records from Eastern Europe, including discs on Melodiya and Bulgaria's Balkanton label.[6] Other shops specialised in records imported from the USA, especially jazz and blues. Bandleader and record collector Chris Barber bought his first blues discs from Millers in Cambridge and soon frequented Dobell's in London, which he called 'the first record shop that was really special'.[7]

Some shops sold second-hand records, ex-jukebox records, and bankrupt stock, or licensed releases from small American labels. Others took a slightly less legal approach to satisfying their customers' needs. Kensington's Jazz Collector carried an extensive stock, including copies of rare jazz and blues records made by the shop's owner Colin Pomeroy. Garth Cartwright writes of these discs as 'bootlegs' while others refer less critically to them as 'reissues'; maybe they were a mix of both. The Jazz Collector rerelease of the Original Dixieland Jazz Band's 'Barnyard Blues' looks legitimate enough. It sports a professionally produced label, with the Jazz Collector logo in greenish-yellow against a white background, credits the composer and the musicians, and gives the date of the original recording (although there is no mention of the original US or British labels on which the tune first appeared). In Morpeth, local hairdresser Mr Barnston set up his own gramophone record lending library. It proved popular and won the praise of the local press, which did not bother to inform its readers of how Mr Barnston acquired his discs or how much he charged borrowers.[8]

The demand for workers, especially in the public services, brought men and women from the West Indies to Britain—the so-called Windrush Generation, named after the *Empire Windrush* that brought one of the first groups from the Caribbean to Britain in 1948. Among the passengers on the *Windrush* were the calypso artists Lord Kitchener and Lord Beginner. Their presence was perhaps an indication that the Caribbean migrants would soon form a population large enough to provide work for Caribbean musicians, but they were not the first artists to arrive from the West Indies. In 1927, Parlophone released a series of seven discs by West Indian artists including Sam Manning and Slim Henderson, recorded in New York. Although sales were disappointing, Manning and Lionel Belasco arrived in Britain in 1934 to record for Decca, and in 1938, Brunswick released six calypso recordings from Decca's US catalogue. Once again, sales were poor and no further issues followed. These pre-war releases appear to have been aimed at a white British audience, rather than migrants with a knowledge and love of the music: the Brunswick label felt the need to explain calypso to its readers, comparing the singers to 'old Elizabethan Troubadours'.[9]

The post-war arrival of workers from the West Indies provided a different kind of audience for Caribbean music—an audience that knew and loved the music, for whom it offered a connection to the homes they had left behind. Musician and composer Courtney Pine CBE, whose parents came to Britain at the end of the 1950s, remembers the important place the gramophone held in the homes of the early arrivals from the Caribbean. Many people brought records with them, while record stores in Paddington sold more discs which would be shared around the members of the West Indian community. For Pine, the gramophone was crucial:

> ... it inspired West Indian families, 'cos you know we had single-room apartments ... a zinc bath, Lifebuoy soap. The gramophone was the iconic piece in this one-room apartment.... the gramophone, that was the science of the day, trust me. I can actually remember learning how to stand on my feet by holding onto the side of the gram. The sound that came out of the speaker, that's what inspired me to walk. That's how important the gram was. The family would take off their pork pie hats, sit down at the table, have some vodka and rum and food, chit-chat and the gram would be there providing the entertainment.[10]

The music that came out of these gramophones was a link to the homes that had been left behind, as well as a link with friends and relations. In Pine's telling phrase, 'The gramophone was a ray of light'.

The land-owning upper classes of Britain, happily inhabiting the same country estate for generations, built up their own collections of gramophone records. Two large estates, now in the care of the National Trust, offer some insight into the listening habits of the gentry. Robert Ketton-Cremer lived at Felbrigg Hall in Norfolk. In Wales, Philip Yorke III owned Erddig, near Wrexham. Their collections of 78s are remarkably similar and display eclectic and occasionally surprising taste.

At Felbrigg, Ketton-Cremer bequeathed to the Trust around eighty shellac discs alongside his reliable Odeon portable gramophone. A few 'high-culture' artists appear (Caruso, Pablo Casals, and Theodor Chaliapin, although there is nothing from Dame Nellie Melba), but the vast majority of his collection is from the more popular end of the entertainment spectrum. Ketton-Cremer was clearly no label snob as his collection includes records from Brunswick, Zonophone and Imperial as well as HMV and Columbia; his copy of HMV's recording of Wagner's 'Wotan's Farewell' is labelled 'Factory Sample'. Famous artists are featured but so, too, are anonymous performers such as the Zonophone Light Opera Company and Edison-Bell's Radio Melody Boys. A night's entertainment at Felbrigg could feature dance music from Lew Stone and his band or Jack Hylton and his orchestra, Ukulele Ike's version of 'Singin' in the Rain', Elsa Lanchester pleading 'Please Sell no More Drink to my Father', slow hulas from Sol Hoopii and his Hawaiian Quartette (an Australian pressing, possibly bought in Sydney), or a selection of songs from the animated movie *Snow White* (an HMV disc with a special bright yellow label featuring a scene from the film). If guests were open to the risqué, they could be regaled by Betty Bolton's 'She Jumped on her Pushbike and Pedalled Away' or Gracie Fields's seminal 'What Can You Give a Nudist on his Birthday?'.

Meanwhile, almost 250 miles to the west, the Yorkes were building their own collection of 78s. Some 200 of these discs survive, as do two Columbia Viva Tonal Grafonola portables. The Erddig collection covers more than fifty years, from a single-sided Gramophone Company disc (Olly Oakley's 'Danse Arlequin') with the Recording Angel logo pressed on the reverse, to 1950s pop records such as Johnnie Ray's 'Texas Tambourine'. The Yorkes bought their records from a range of retailers, including Manchester's The Talkeries, John Dunn of Princes Street in Edinburgh, and Walter Roberts, Sports Outfitters of Wrexham. HMV and Columbia predominate among the labels, but there are plenty of examples from rarer labels such as Currys, John Bull, Regal, Winner, Sterno, and Beatall ('Alexander's Ragtime Band' played by the Beatall Military Band, pressed in Prussia). A record from the Durium label, with the playing material pressed onto cardboard, and a bright red, flexible disc from Filmophone are also part of the Erddig collection. The land-rich but cash-poor Yorkes also appear to have acquired a few discs second-hand, as a couple of records still sport handwritten labels from a G. Walker and a Miss West and another pair of discs are kept in sleeves made by cutting up an envelope that previously held a 'Fine Art Calendar'.

Melba is again absent, but Caruso is in the collection, as are the Italian tenor Giovanni Zenatello (whose facsimile autograph is pressed into the centre of his Columbia recording of 'Cavalleria Rusticana') and Master Ernest Lough with his version of 'I Know That My Redeemer Liveth'. The Yorkes shared Ketton-Cremer's preference for popular entertainment and it is this love of the lighter side that characterises most of their record collection. Songs from musical theatre sit alongside swing, dance and jazz records from Artie Shaw, Charlie Kunz, Victor Sylvester and Bing Crosby. Sentimental ballads ('When Irish Eyes are Smiling' or 'God Send You Back to Me') join music hall favourites like Harry Lauder's 'Roamin' in the Gloamin' (sung by Jock MacLean) and, more surprisingly, a disc by the great Fado singer Amália Rodrigues. There is comedy: Mel Blanc's 'I Taut I Taw a Puddy Tat', Charles Penrose's 'laughing songs' ('A Nice Old Maid' and 'Away with Melancholy'), Spike Jones and his City Slickers, Angela Baddeley and L. du Garde Peach's comic dialogue 'Motoring Without Tears', and Joe Hayman's 'Cohen Gets the Wrong Phone Number' (the Jewish equivalent of the Casey sketches and equally unfunny).

Neither of these collections bear out the assertions of labels like HMV that 'high-culture' was the staple listening of the upper classes. Even though the Yorkes and Ketton-Cremer were not at the absolute top of the British social scale, they were still far, far wealthier than the average family. The Erddig and Felbrigg collections are not only strikingly similar to each other, they also bear a strong resemblance to my own father's collection of 78s by Mario Lanza, Crosby, Glenn Miller, Arthur Askey, and Gilbert and Sullivan—the collection of a Post Office electrician. Wealth and social status were clearly not indicators of the breadth of entertainment to be found in a record collection.

Cut, Chop, Splice, and Stick

Few gramophone fans were interested in the nitty-gritty of the recording process, but the post-war shift to tape recording from the direct-to-disc process opened up a whole new world of possibilities. Tape recording was almost as old as the gramophone, the first system having appeared in 1899, but high-quality, commercial systems took some time to appear.[11] The BBC used the Blattner-Stille system of recording magnetically onto steel tape in the 1930s, enabling the rebroadcasting of programmes and allowing programme producers to 'demonstrate any mistakes which artists may make during a rehearsal'.[12] Tape recording advanced during the Second World War, particularly in Germany where some early stereo recordings were found after the war.[13] When Jack Mullin returned to the USA from Germany with two Magnetophon tape recorders and began to develop the technology, Bing Crosby took an interest, eager to record his radio shows but unimpressed by the existing disc technology. On 1 October 1947, the Bing Crosby show became the first radio show to be broadcast from a tape recording.[14] In Britain, EMI started to manufacture magnetic tape and tape recorders soon afterwards. Most of this production was for sale, but EMI soon used tape recording in its own production of records.[15]

Tape recording offered the gramophone industry two advantages. It enabled much longer recordings to be made, and it enabled those recordings to be manipulated by editing—a physical process of cutting the tape, removing sections, moving sections, mixing tapes from two or more different takes, and sticking the tape back together again. Performers were free from the tyranny of the single take, mistakes made mid-song could disappear, fluffed phrases could be replaced, an inspired solo from take six could be spliced into an earlier attempt at the tune. Such freedom meant that even minor errors had no place on gramophone records: perfection was the new normal. Gramophone recordings were no longer 'live' performances in the way that concert-goers experienced them. A record might consist of two, three, or more performances, chopped up, shuffled around, and stuck back together again.

Tape could also be a threat to the gramophone industry's profitability. *The Times*' music critic predicted a time when music lovers would buy their own tape-recording equipment and record wireless programmes in the comfort of their own homes. There would be no need to buy a disc, the critic feared: the practice would 'destroy the market of record dealers ... deprive musicians of fees and impinge upon the rights of broadcasting organisations.'[16] The critic's fear of such wholesale bootlegging was groundless, at least until the late 1960s, when inexpensive, portable, cassette recorders enabled an entire generation of music lovers to record friends' albums, the BBC's weekly *Top Of The Pops* TV show, radio shows, and live gigs and concerts onto cheap, poor quality, and unreliable ninety-minute tape cassettes, causing the record industry's catchphrase, 'Home taping is illegal—and it's killing music', to be printed onto millions of LP sleeves. The accusation had been levelled at the gramophone many years earlier and it would be levelled at recordable CDs, downloads and streaming services. None of them have killed music, yet.

Size Matters—But So Does Speed

Tape recording opened up the possibility of longer records, but only if the limitations of the 78-rpm disc could be overcome, which they soon were. Experiments with disc speeds, microgrooves, new materials for disc production, and tape editing produced two new products that would come to dominate the market. The long-playing record (the LP, or 'album') was 12 inches in diameter and rotated at 33⅓ rpm, making twenty minutes per side easily attainable and allowing for the possibility of even longer times. The single was 7 inches in diameter and rotated at 45 rpm. It did not extend playing time beyond the four minutes per side achieved by the old technology, but it did squeeze this time into a much smaller, lighter, and less fragile package.[17] Both of these discs were manufactured from vinyl and used narrower grooves than those found on shellac 78s, enabling them to be played with a narrower diameter stylus, hence they were referred to as 'microgroove' discs.[18]

The LP was the first of the new discs to hit the British market. The basic technology was already in place as early movie soundtracks were recorded on 17-inch discs rotating at 33⅓ rpm and RCA Victor had attempted to market LPs in the USA in 1931, although poor sound and the need to buy specialist gramophones to play them meant that they sold poorly.[19] They reappeared in the USA in 1948 thanks to Columbia Records. Made of vinyl, they were noticeably lighter than their shellac counterparts and less likely to break (although more likely to warp). The 45-rpm single arrived just a year after the LP. Once again, America got there first, with RCA Victor marketing singles from 1949.[20] British record labels were not far behind as Decca introduced the first LP in 1950 and HMV released LPs on its own labels including HMV, Columbia, Parlophone, and MGM in late 1952: 'Non-breakable, superb recording, silent surface.'[21] Gramophone manufacturers soon developed machines capable of playing discs at the new speeds.

Murphy Radio and Television was one of the first British manufacturers to produce a three-speed record player, to meet the demands of buyers with a collection of 78-rpm, 45-rpm and 33⅓-rpm discs, as part of the £78.10s A182R radiogram.[22] This was as solid a piece of furniture as one would expect for the price, but it was an indication of an acceptance of the new discs and their speeds. British access to LPs was initially limited when compared to the American market, but companies such as Decca and Nixa imported recordings from smaller American labels and HMV and Columbia quickly built up their own catalogues. If there was a problem with the range of LPs available by 1953, it was one of over-supply, the wide range of recordings forcing all but the wealthiest collectors of classical music to be selective about which discs to buy. The 45-rpm disc was still in its infancy, but HMV started to reissue some of its older discs as 45s: 'midgets of seven inches diameter with a huge hole in the middle' as *The Times*' columnist described them. As for the 78, the columnist was optimistic that it had a future: 'it hisses more than its little-grooved offspring does, but it can offer us treasures from the past'.[23] Decca Records made rapid progress with these new formats after introducing the LP to Europe in 1950.[24] In 1952, it released 500 LPs on the Decca label, plus others on associated labels such as Brunswick, Capitol and London, and by the start of 1954, it offered 1,350 LPs on its various labels, plus around 100 of its 7-inch MP discs (Medium Play, known more commonly as EP or Extended Play, which rotated at 33⅓ rpm); by the end of the year, it added over 100 45-rpm discs, featuring popular light music.

Carry on Campaigning

Politicians were experienced in using recorded speeches during election campaigns as the practice dated back to around 1900, but cannier candidates now made use of other recordings, including music on records played through loudspeakers fitted to car roofs, to attract crowds to speeches and meetings. A spot of light music could enliven the electoral process, but was it prohibited under law? A Parliamentary debate on the 1948 Representation of the People Bill brought the issue to a head and put the gramophone centre stage in the House of Commons. It proved to be an entertaining few minutes, a debate that seemed to belong to a bygone age or to the script of a *Carry On* film and changed absolutely nothing.[25]

The debate centred on an amendment to an amendment of Clause 42 of the Bill, 'Miscellaneous amendments as to election expenses and propaganda'. Some expenditure during election campaigns was acceptable, some was not; the details were contained in the Corrupt and Illegal Practices Prevention Act of 1883. This act banned the payment of expenses for such items as banners, torches, flags and, more controversially, 'bands of music'. It was this phrase that exercised the minds of MPs. Did 'bands of music' refer solely to bands performing live at election events or did it also exclude bands who performed on gramophone records when these records were played at election events? The Corrupt Practices Act became law well before recorded music appeared, but if its prohibitions were to be contained within the proposed Representation of the People Act, how was 'bands of music' to be defined?

Kenneth Younger, an Under-Secretary of State in the Labour government, proposed an amendment to Clause 42, by inserting the phrase 'except in so far as it relates to bands of music, torches, flags and banners', thereby ensuring that payments for these items would continue to be prohibited. Osbert Peake, Conservative MP for Leeds North, proposed an amendment to Younger's amendment: the insertion of the phrase 'other than music reproduced by gramophone records' after 'bands of music'. The debate began. Peake's proposal seems clear—a gramophone record is easily identifiable and readily distinguishable from a 'band of music' in the form of living, breathing musicians. He had no wish to prohibit 'the quite common practice of playing a gramophone record in a motorcar to attract by a suitable tune a crowd before embarking upon an open-air speech', though Peake's fellow MPs had other ideas.

Viscount Hinchingbrooke foresaw a problem with another modern technology: the radio. What would happen, he asked, if a car fitted with a radio were to park close to a candidate during a speech in a public space and the driver were to turn on the radio and play music from a BBC station? Would that breach the Corrupt Practices Act? Charles Williams raised concerns about a much older form of entertainment, the Welsh choir: 'I have some excellent Welsh supporters in my division, and I do not wish to see them stopped from singing if they think it necessary, because they were mostly Socialists but now they are sensible people.' James Ede, the Home Secretary, attempted to clarify the situation. The key issue, he said, was whether or not payment was made. Volunteer bands, or volunteer gramophone owners, who supported a candidate, or drowned out an opponent's voice, would be permissible but payment would not be allowed.

Sadly, his clarification was insufficiently clear. Commander Thomas Galbraith pointed out that payments for the hire of a loudspeaker van, through which a candidate could speak or play recordings of their speeches, were acceptable. Would additional payments for the hire or purchase of gramophones and records be allowable on that basis? Mr Ede made another valiant attempt, answering the Commander's question regarding the purchase of records:

> ... if the expenditure to which he referred was on music for the election, I
> think it will be caught by the words; but if the hon. and gallant Member has
> his own records at home, brings them along and plays them, and no expense
> is incurred at the time, I would have thought it would not be caught.

It was now 9 p.m., but despite the late hour, Thomas Reid introduced another point for debate: when is a band not a band? He argued that 'if I choose to produce either a singer or a solo instrument, either alive or in the 'canned' form of a gramophone record, it seems to me that I am not breaking the law'. Mr Reid believed that 'a singer or a choir or a solo instrument, whether alive or through the medium of a gramophone, is plainly exempt'.

> [On the other hand] ... it is equally clear that a live band—and a band need
> not consist of more than two persons I should think, but I will not go into

these niceties – is prohibited if one pays for it, but what about using a record, or, as my noble friend says, the B.B.C. programme? That is a difficult point. Is that a band of music or is it not?

Sanity returned in the shape of the Lord Advocate, John Wheatley, who suggested that Mr Peake withdraw his amendment to the original amendment.

> I do not think that the law as it stands refers to gramophone records playing music. When reference is made to 'bands of music' it refers to live bands ... Therefore, if my construction is correct, that bands of music refer to live bands, and do not refer to gramophone records, and we leave the law as it stands, I think the interests of all parties will be served.

Mr Peake agreed and withdrew the amendment to the amendment, so an entertaining but ultimately futile debate drew to a close.

The debate's comic potential can be enhanced by reading the speeches aloud in the voices of Kenneth Williams, Sid James, or Charles Hawtrey, but it does highlight a more serious issue. Parliament was playing catch-up with new recording and reproduction technologies. Improved amplification and loudspeaker systems made the playing of records in public a more contentious issue than it had been when a small portable gramophone was the only available instrument. The gramophone's role in electioneering was just one issue that would impact on government in succeeding decades.

'Now I've Got the Telly'

LPs and singles would see off the 78, but they were simply replacing one sound reproducing format with a couple of new, improved ones. Television threatened to destroy the record industry completely, along with radio and the cinema. The most pessimistic proponent of the gramophone predicted that the cultural life of the nation would cease, to be replaced by a lowbrow entertainment medium sending its worthless programmes into the heart of the nation's homes. Yet again, a charge that was levelled against the gramophone when it was the emerging technology was being levelled at the latest upstart.

Britain, or at least a small part of it, first got the television on 2 November 1936 when the BBC began broadcasting.[26] Television manufacturers busily produced new models for what they must have assumed was a market ready for expansion. The 1939 National Radio Exhibition opened on 23 August, displaying the latest in broadcasting technology and though most of the exhibition was devoted to radio receivers, including portable models 'particularly useful when outdoor holidaymaking', Baird, Phillips, Scophony, and HMV all exhibited their latest televisions. HMV's most expensive TV, the Model 900, was a combined television (picture size 10 inches by 8 inches) and radio, with provision for the connection of a gramophone.[27] Ten days later, the BBC television service ended, drawing to a sudden halt midway through a cartoon on the afternoon of 1 September 1939, in the prelude to the Second World War.

The BBC restarted transmission at 3 p.m. on Friday 7 June 1946, with an official re-opening by the Postmaster General (the Earl of Listowel) and a 5½-hour extravaganza featuring Margot Fonteyn, Mantovani and His Orchestra, and Leslie Mitchell as the Master of Ceremonies, as well as a full showing of *Mickey's Gala Premiere*, the cartoon that had been rudely interrupted in 1939.[28] For the first couple of years, the service struggled as viewer numbers were still limited and there was no regional transmitter to take the signals beyond the home counties. The winter of 1946–7 was severe and caused a fuel shortage that forced BBC TV off air for a month. The daily programme schedule was intermittent, the service shutting down for an hour or two between some programmes. Most importantly, the programmes lacked variation and Britain's favourite stars of radio, stage, and record were mostly absent.[29]

Television programmes made no use of gramophone records nor, at first, did they spend much time showcasing performers whose work was available on disc, so they seemed to have no upside for the record labels. Equipment manufacturers did spot an opportunity, however. Once regular television broadcasts returned, it was only a matter of time before the radiogram welcomed this new medium. Pye's Model LV21RG squeezed a 'large-screen' TV into the cabinet, alongside the radio and the gramophone.[30] For the early adopter with seriously deep pockets, Decca produced a combined television, radio receiver, and record player for £595 (inclusive of purchase tax). The company had the honesty to remark that this set was for 'the fortunate few'.[31] Teleradiograms, if that is what they might be called, never matched the popularity of the radiogram. The television would find its own place in the nation's living rooms.

That place was firmly established on 2 June 1953, with the televising of Queen Elizabeth II's coronation. By that time, regional transmitters were in place across Britain and an estimated 20 million or more people watched the live broadcast of the event (7.8 million in their own homes, 10.4 million in other people's homes, and the rest in pubs, cinemas and other venues), far more than the audience for the BBC's radio coverage.[32] Television was firmly in place as the third major source of home entertainment, alongside the gramophone and the radio. In 1955, commercial television came to Britain (initially, only to the London area), courtesy of ITV. It brought another alternative to evenings at home with the gramophone, but its focus on family entertainment also held promise for record sales.³³ By the end of the year, EMI was happy to report that television appearances were leading to increased record sales for popular entertainers such as Max Bygraves, Ruby Murray, and Alma Cogan.³⁴

In the midst of all this technological upheaval, on 2 September 1951, Fred Gaisberg died at his home in Hampstead, aged seventy-nine. A somewhat hagiographic obituary from P. G., a self-proclaimed friend for twenty-five years, painted Gaisberg in the most glowing terms, as a strikingly modest and courteous man: 'Singers and instrumentalists, being temperamental creatures, he did not find too easy to handle … but soothed by his gentle persuasion they would give of their best until perfection was attained.' He would, of course, be sadly missed.³⁵

On the Record: 'I Hate A Man Like You', Ottilie Patterson with Chris Barber's Jazz Band (78rpm and 45rpm single, Decca, 1955)

The mid-1950s was a turbulent time for Britain's youth. Jazz (albeit a revised version of the trad jazz of the 1920s and '30s) was hip, but skiffle and rock 'n' roll were on their way. Patterson and Barber's version of this venerable song had its roots in the early years of the gramophone as a 78-rpm record, but as a 45-rpm single, it represented a new way of producing and listening to discs, signalling the transition to the new music of the younger generation.

Ottilie Patterson was from Northern Ireland; her father was Irish and her mother was Latvian. A singer and pianist, she first heard Jelly Roll Morton (who wrote this song), blues singer Bessie Smith, and boogie-woogie pianist Meade Lux Lewis when she was studying art in Belfast. On holiday in England in 1954, she met trombonist and bandleader Chris Barber and performed with him on a few occasions. Barber offered her a job with the band a few months later and she returned to England. Patterson sang with the Barber band for ten years and was married to Barber from 1959 until they divorced in 1983. Her time with the band coincided with the British trad jazz boom and the band enjoyed great success, touring the USA and playing the Washington Jazz Festival. However, by the early '60s, trad was out and pop was in. Soon after, Patterson retired from the band.³⁶

The title of 'I Hate A Man Like You' is not ironic. The man in question is violent and thuggish, the singer's life is one of domestic abuse. He stays out on their wedding night, tries to have her thrown into prison, gambles and walks around armed with a switch (blade) and a rod (pistol) while his wife is forced to sneak pans of food from the 'white folks' yard.' He's unfaithful, too, 'like a rooster at a hen' whenever her back is turned. Patterson's voice is raw and bluesy, filled with anger and disgust at the man—no trace of her County Down childhood filters through to her accent. The band's backing comes nowhere near matching Patterson's impassioned delivery, with the exception of a lively clarinet solo.

Morton's own solo version, recorded in 1938 for the Library of Congress by Alan Lomax, describes an even more abusive man, one who uses physical violence against his wife. After the song ends, Morton speaks briefly to claim that the song was a true story.

'I Hate A Man Like You' exemplifies its time as a period of cultural change. It is an old song, looking back to a past that its British audience envisaged with an unwarranted degree of nostalgia and romance, played by a jazz band whose line-up was increasingly out of step with the small, electric guitar led, combos emerging from modern America. The song was recorded at the Royal Festival Hall in London, 'under the auspices of the National Jazz Federation' as the label of the 45-rpm version informs us. Rather coyly, the label describes the song as 'Southern Music'.

One of Patterson's bandmates was a young singer and guitarist called Anthony James Donegan. Influenced by the blues, Donegan adopted the first name of legendary blues guitarist Lonnie Johnson, became Lonnie Donegan and went on to be one of the creators of skiffle, a peculiarly British hybrid of folk, blues, and early rock 'n' roll that influenced thousands of teenagers across the country including young Paul McCartney and John Lennon in Liverpool, two men whose new approach to popular song would finish off trad jazz and skiffle for good.

Dansettes and Teens

Four months after the Clause 42 debate about bands on records, an advertisement appeared in *The Times*. It was a small, plain display advertisement, just one of a series promoting the latest books. This one advertised two works of fiction from publishers T. V. Boardman and Co., giving most of its space over to *Anny*, a novel by Marc Bernard, but mentioning R. J. McGregor's new book, *The Secret of Hangman's Wood*, as being 'The Ideal Book for the Teenager'.[1] This was the teenager's first appearance in the venerable newspaper. The word was unfamiliar to many of the newspaper's readers, as were the young people it described, but such unfamiliarity would not last. Within a few years, this strange new phenomenon would be everywhere, exerting its influence on British fashion, dance styles, hairdressing, magazines, and music. The gramophone, like many other aspects of British life, would never be the same again.

Splack, Splack

The 1950s teenagers enjoyed music and dancing just as much as their parents and grandparents had enjoyed them in the 1920s and '30s, but like every succeeding generation of young people, they wanted to do it in their own way. The dances would be new, the music would be (mostly) new, the records would be new, and so, too, would the machines to play them. In public settings such as youth clubs and coffee bars, the jukebox promised an easy and cheap way to listen to popular hits in the company of like-minded music lovers: make your choice, drop in a coin, and let the machine do the rest. At home, the unwieldy, immovable radiogram could stay in the living room or the parlour. The clockwork portable lacked any sense of modernity, in function, design, or materials. Teenagers wanted something different, something that was their own personal possession. Even the names their parents used ('gramophone' or 'radiogram') were old-fashioned; the younger generation wanted record players.

'Record player' was a modern term, one that the teenagers could claim as their own, or so they thought. There is nothing new under the sun, as mum or dad might say, as record players had been around for over twenty years. In 1929, Automatic Records Player Ltd of Salisbury House, London Wall, began selling its Automatic Record Player for 35 shillings. This was a piece of equipment to be fitted to any make of gramophone, enabling it to play ten discs automatically without the need for the listener to intervene—in other words, an autochanger. The company promoted this 'ingenious and efficient accessory' with some persuasive claims:

> It will be popular in the home to enable users to listen in uninterrupted comfort to a whole selection or programme of records. It will be popular for private dances, dinner parties and concerts. It will be used in dancing and educational schools ... in hotels, restaurants and cinemas.[2]

Unfortunately for the Automatic Records Player Ltd, this ingenious accessory was not that popular. Gramophone manufacturers added their own autochangers to their instruments, making accessories superfluous. HMV produced two electric 'record players' in 1931 (the Standard and the Automatic) and redefined the term. These HMV record players were instruments that could be added to a wireless set to create what was in effect a radiogram: the Standard played one record at a time, the Automatic played eight records without interruption, or one record eight times.[3] HMV's All Electric Record Player appeared in 1937 and would play any record on any radio receiver.[4]

In fairness to the younger generation, the record player beloved of the 1950s teenager was a different beast—a self-contained instrument, often portable (but usually mains powered, so it could provide entertainment at house parties but not on hillside picnics), capable of playing singles, albums and even 78s if necessary, covered in brightly coloured cloth, operated by twisting and turning plastic knobs and reproducing sound in glorious mono. If the dull, brown wood gramophone looked at home in an Edwardian parlour, the record player's futuristic styling ensured that it would not look out of place in a spaceship, much less a teenager's bedroom.

The Dansette was the iconic record player of the time; for many young music fans, Dansette and 'record player' were synonymous. J. and A. Margolin of Old Street, London, produced the Plus-a-gram, their version of a record player attachment for radios, in 1934.[5] In 1952, the company registered the Dansette trademark and began producing a range of portable record players.[6] The basic technology was not new, although the autochanger turntables were a new design from another British company, Birmingham Sound Reproducers.[7] The company's target market was new, however. Dansettes were made to appeal to the teenager; the machines were covered in 'leatherette' vinyl in a range of gaudy colours like pink, cream, green, or red, fitted with carrying handles and autochangers, ready to carry to friends' houses and parties with a selection of records. Everly Brothers fan Liz Delf was given her two-tone blue and cream Dansette Conquest Auto, with autochanger, four-speed turntable, carrying handle and bass and treble tone controls, as a fourteenth birthday present. Fifty-six years later (and after forty years spent in the loft of the family home), it still worked beautifully when I visited Liz and her husband, Mike, pumping out at surprisingly high volume the music of the Everlys and others on shellac 78s.

The Dansette's appearance was timely as 1952 could be considered a watershed year for popular culture in Britain. As this brightly coloured and futuristic instrument hit the high street, EMI started to release 45-rpm singles on its labels, *New Musical Express* started publication, and then, on 14 November, the NME published Britain's first record chart.[8] The chart, or 'Hit Parade', was intended to list the top twelve discs in the country, but due to equal sales for one or two records, the first chart listed fifteen different discs. It was an odd combination of variety artists (Vera Lynn, with three entries, and Max Bygraves), genuine international stars (Bing Crosby and opera singer Mario Lanza), and one or two proto-rockers (Frankie Laine and Johnny Ray). Only Lynn, Bygraves, and bandleader Ray Martin were British; the number one song was 'Here in My Heart' by the Italian-American singer Al Martino. Modernity had not yet consigned the shellac to history; every one of these songs was recorded on 78-rpm discs and only Lanza's 'Because You're Mine' was also available as a 45-rpm single.

Eager teenage record buyers continued to take record players to their hearts, customising their cabinets to make them even gaudier and making full use of their autochangers. One famous fan, actor Joanna Lumley, summed up the joys of the record player (although she still preferred to call it a gramophone):

> My gramophone was, I think, a *Dansette*; it was white vinyl covered with small black stars and had a terrifically tall spindle, which allowed the records to fall, splack, splack for over half an hour, and if they were LPs ... well, music could fill your home for nearly two hours.[9]

The Dansette's golden period was a brief one. Dansette Products, the Margolin company's new name, went into receivership in 1969, a victim of cheap, imported record players and transistor radios and the rise of stereophonic hi-fi separates for the homes of wealthier audiophiles.[10] The teenagers' golden period would be far longer than the Dansette's, as their needs and their economic power grew. In 1959, it was estimated that the average teenage boy had around £5 per week to spend as he liked, the average girl £3. These were significant sums for the time and the teenage market was an important one as the group accounted for 25 per cent of all consumer spending on cinema, bicycles, motor cycles, records, and record players.[11]

By 1960, even the rarefied world of luxury cruises was attempting to cater for teenage tastes. SS *Canberra*, a new P&O liner, provided a 'rumpus room' for teenagers that the company proudly claimed would meet the needs of boys and girls; alongside soft drinks, modern lighting, and plenty of plastic decoration, a selection of records in a jukebox would make it easy for youngsters to dance to 'rock 'n' roll' or 'rhythm rock'.[12]

The members of the Houses of Parliament were still fond of the idea of the gramophone as an insult, a suggestion that someone was simply repeating the words or opinions of others or was fond of repeating their own tired ideas time and time again. The more creative parliamentarians, their fingers on the pulse of the modern world, developed the insult to take account of the new recording technologies. In a debate on food prices Frederick Willey, MP for Sunderland North, showed his awareness of the LP:

> I am told that one of the difficulties about the new long-playing gramophone records is that the needle is apt to stick in the groove and that the gramophone goes on repeating itself. That is equally true of the Parliamentary Secretary.[13]

Anthony Crosland became the first MP to mention long playing records in the House, just a month before Mr Willey, but this was in an appropriate context—a discussion of company profits during periods of research and development—and he was not attempting to be funny.[14]

Smash the Shellac

Long-playing records, 45s, Dansettes, and other new-fangled technologies were all very well, but many British households still owned gramophones that would only play 78s. The machines worked, the families' shellac collections could still be enjoyed, and even if the younger generation was keen to adopt the latest records on 45 or LP, plenty of older listeners were happily sticking with what they knew. Cartwright, author of *Going for a Song*, a history of the record shop, notes that specialist shops such as Dobell's, a jazz and blues dealer, were happy to trade in 78s as these were still popular with fans of these genres while shops catering to the West Indian community, many of whom brought their gramophones with them to Britain, would also keep stocking 78s. As 1955, EMI reported a 5 per cent increase in the sale of 78s over the year, although this was driven mainly by exports.[15]

By the late 1950s, however, the record companies wanted to move wholesale into the new technologies. Cartwright notes that the new formats held advantages for the retailer; 45s were smaller and lighter than 78s so were easier to store, and LPs took up the same space as 78s but sold for much more money. It would take some time to persuade record buyers to follow the retailers' example. A soft-sell approach emphasised the LP's advantages: much longer playing time, better sound quality, and less likely to break. Decca made it clear that the company's existing 78-rpm gramophones could play these newer discs simply by adding a Decca LP Player from as little as 9 guineas.[16] Most new machines, from cheap portables to expensive models such as the Grundig Arundel, boasted three- or four-speed turntables. These machines played 78s, singles, and LPs (four-speed turntables also played spoken word 16-rpm discs), thus ensuring that the shellac discs were not obsolete.

Advances in stylus technology were impressive. In the late 1930s, Imhof's had introduced the IM Long-playing Needles, claiming that each needle could play 100 sides without needing replacement, although they needed resharpening after every ten sides using Imhof's Pointmaster sharpener.[17] By 1952, record collector Alan D. Dare claimed that a sapphire stylus could play 1,500 to 2,000 LP sides without needing to be replaced (or re-sharpened) and suggested that diamond-tipped styluses could last for 15,000 sides. He found that the new three-speed turntables were prone to slippage but cured the problem by applying lighter fluid then rubbing with a typewriter eraser.[18]

Some shellac aficionados criticised long-playing records, especially from pop or jazz artists, for containing too much poor-quality material, much as the first double-sided discs had been criticised for providing unwanted content. *Jazz Journal* kept faith with the 78; at the end of 1952, it was still reviewing eight 78s for every one of the new long-playing discs.[19] Many fans were in no hurry to move away from the old format. Even at the end of the 1950s, new pop and rock records were being released on 78s, and many families still had not bought a new-fangled record player.

Rock 'n' roll fan Mike Delf was thirteen years old when he saw Buddy Holly play in Ipswich in 1958. The experience started his lifelong love of the music, but his family did not own a record player of any description. Mike persuaded his parents to buy him a second-hand, portable wind-up gramophone of long-forgotten make, costing, as he remembers, around £2 10s. He started building up his record collection with 78s by Dion and the Belmonts, the Everly Brothers, and Buddy Holly. As he remembers, 'Forty-fives were coming but a lot of people didn't have the equipment to play them on, so they kept buying the 78s.' A couple of years later, Mike bought a new record player and began collecting 45s: 'but I still played the 78s 'cos you could play either of them on record players.'[20] Mike still owns those first three 78s, and they continue to thrilling, raw sound when played through the family Dansette.

The music critic of *The Times* welcomed jazz rereleases on 45s rather than LPs as they gave fans the chance to buy new but relatively inexpensive copies of recordings that were now worn out in their 78-rpm format, so if a purchase proved disappointing, 'at least you haven't had to pay through the nose for it.'[21] The BBC moved over to the new formats, but decades of record collecting left it with a huge library of 78s. In the early 1960s, the BBC's gramophone record library held 500,000 different recordings; the oldest was an 1888 cylinder recording of the poet Robert Browning, and the oldest discs were an experimental 5-inch recording by Emile Berliner and a 7-inch Berliner disc of George Gaskin, an American baritone, singing 'Sweet Marie'.[22] Within this extensive collection, 336,500 discs were 78s.[23]

The end came suddenly. UK record companies released 287 78-rpm discs in 1960; in the first quarter of 1961, they released just eight.[24] At least one wholesaler took drastic action to get rid of now-redundant stock, with the help of a young Australian worker called Barry Humphries. Humphries was some years from his triumph as Dame Edna Everage and working in the wholesaler's offices in Melbourne, supplying LPs to record retailers. Eventually, he was sent to the storage area and ordered to destroy thousands of 'obsolete' shellac discs.

> ... the terrible task ... entailed spending days, and sometimes weeks ... literally smashing records with a hammer. Hundreds and thousands of records, popular and classical: Bing Crosby, Beethoven, Sibelius and Whispering Jack Smith were all shattered and flung in boxes which were carted off to some remote furnace.[25]

That was one way of ensuring scarcity of supply.

Many record retailers operated healthy mail-order businesses during the 1950s and this decade also saw growth in the number of small, independent record shops like Dobell's, which specialised in particular genres of music in contrast to the large department stores whose record departments catered for fans of the most popular discs. These shops, often owned or staffed by enthusiastic music fans, served as more than simply retail outlets; many of them also acted as social clubs or communities where like-minded fans could meet, listen to the latest discs (often imported from the USA, sometimes second-hand, occasionally bootlegs), offer each other advice on what to buy or not to buy, and catch up on gossip.[26] Cartwright refers to these shops as 'community hubs', vital neighbourhood centres and networking spaces.

The shop that did the job for Mike Delf and his schoolmates was on Ipswich's Buttermarket: 'we'd go down there on a Saturday and look through the racks. One of my schoolmates told me to buy the Dion record. I'd never heard of him but I did and I've been a Dion fan ever since.' Unusually, Mike's boarding school did a similar job when he entered the sixth form, providing him with another environment in which to learn about this exciting new music—a room where senior pupils could go to relax, chat, and drink coffee. 'There was an electric gramophone' says Mike, 'We'd all bring along different records, you'd listen to your friends' records, they'd listen to yours, we'd mix and match.'

However quirky, esoteric, or well-connected these record shops were, they had to make money to survive. As the record producers moved away from shellac 78s, so, too, did the record sellers.

Meanwhile, on the Norfolk Coast

July 1954 was a momentous month for the record industry, a month that can with just a little exaggeration be referred to as earth-shattering. It did not seem too momentous in Britain, where vocalist David Whitfield was starting a ten-week run at the top of the charts with 'Cara Mia', a melodramatic, string-laden, sub-operatic and woefully over-produced ballad. However, on the fifth of the month, in Sun Studios in Memphis, Elvis Presley, Scotty Moore, and Bill Black recorded 'That's All Right'. The record was the first in Presley's series of rock 'n' roll greats and heralded a new era in entertainment.

In the Norfolk seaside resort of Cromer, a couple of weeks after Presley's legendary session, the Cromer Secondary School Choir took its own small place in British recording history, with its recording of 'The Happy Wanderer' and Johann Sebastian Bach's 'Jesu, Joy of Man's Desiring', a notable production. Cromer record dealer Jack Bryant made the recording, a 78-rpm disc, on lacquer (or acetate) rather than shellac, released it on his A Cromer Recording label and pressed copies on demand to meet the needs of the children, teachers, parents, grandparents, and interested friends. Record collector Paul Buck has established that Bryant owned a portable 78-rpm recorder, which recorded direct to disc. Each succeeding record would have been cut from this first, master disc. Buck suspects that Bryant would have made a recording, advertised it locally, then cut copies to order rather than having a number of each disc in stock.

Catherine Clarke was a member of the Cromer school's choir. Eleven years old in 1954, she remembers that Bryant brought his equipment to the school hall to record the choir, which was drawn from pupils of all ages. Mrs Clarke was already familiar with 'The Happy Wanderer' but did not know the Bach piece. A few days after the recording, Bryant returned to the school to play the disc to the choir and its music teacher, Mrs Taylor. It was an exciting moment for the young singers, but as Mrs Clarke's family home did not have a gramophone, they did not buy a copy and she did not hear it again until 2018, when I played an extract on a Radio Norfolk show in the hope of contacting choir members.[27]

Bryant may have been running nothing more than a small independent label, but he took a professional approach to the business. His label's logo was a monochrome picture of Cromer pier, an iconic feature of the town to this day, with 'A Cromer Recording' overlaid in gothic script. Each side was given a serial number and a date—the Bach was VC 26 and 'The Happy Wanderer' was VC 27; both sides were dated 19 July 1954. The serial numbers suggest that Bryant built up a catalogue of a few dozen discs at least, but only a handful are now known to exist.[28] Bryant helpfully included an instruction sheet with each copy of his discs, noting that they were lacquer, not shellac, and so needed careful handling. For the best sound and longest life, the gramophone (which Bryant called a 'reproducer') needed a lightweight pick-up, not exceeding one and a half ounces and fitted with a sapphire or fine steel needle. Any other equipment needed special Trailer needles, which Bryant's sold. It was especially important (for unspecified reasons) that the record should not be played with a thorn or fibre needle, or any needle that had been used to play a shellac disc.

'Jesu, Joy of Man's Desiring' and 'The Happy Wanderer' make for an intriguing combination. On the surface, the mix of a well-known classical piece and a cheery sing-along song from the 1950s is just the thing to showcase the talents of a school choir and to demonstrate the musical awareness and open-mindedness of the school's teaching staff, but there is possibly more to it. Both Bach and the composer of 'The Happy Wanderer', Friedrich-Wilhelm Möller, were German, as was the writer of the Happy Wanderer's original lyric. Möller wrote a tune to fit lyrics written around 1800, and in 1954, a German-language recording by the Obernkirchen Children's Choir, released by Parlophone, reached number two on the British pop charts. The Cromer Secondary School Choir's version may not have been a bestseller, but it showed that the school had its finger on the pulse of the nation's big pop hits (at least, on the inoffensive, old-fashioned, end of the pop charts) and maybe the pairing was also intended as a display of unity with the children of the new, post-war Germany. The recording is energetic and enthusiastic. To piano accompaniment, the choir sings 'The Happy Wanderer' with great gusto and a degree of technical ability that suggests the school took pride in its musical education.

Jack Bryant was one of a band of small-scale local sound recordists, who spotted a niche in the market and invested in portable recording technology. Hornick Recordings of Birmingham was one of the more ambitious of these entrepreneurs, offering its services for recording weddings, choirs, orchestras, speeches, and 'crooning contests'. Wedding recordings cost 7 guineas; Hornick guaranteed that they would be ready for the happy couple to enjoy in just seven days.[29]

Indecent and Undesirable

The children of Cromer and Obernkirchen showed that the humble gramophone record could be a force for good, but the seedier side of the record industry still raised its head from time to time and gramophone records 'of an indecent character' briefly troubled the Commons in 1956. In June, Marcus Lipton, MP for Lambeth Brixton, reported on two such discs and demanded to know what action Gwilym Lloyd George, the Home Secretary, was going to take. Lloyd George's reply was to the point: 'None, sir.' Lipton continued, asking if it was in the public interest that these 'wretched things' should be on sale. Lloyd George thanked him for providing details but denied having heard the records and suggested referring the matter to the police. A few weeks later, another MP, Kenneth Thompson, raised the same issue, referring to the discs as records of 'undesirable character'.[30] He wanted to know how many prosecutions had taken place regarding the sale and distribution of such undesirable discs. William Deedes, Under Secretary of State for the Home Department, replied as succinctly as Lloyd George had done: 'None.'

'Blue discs', 'party records', 'stag records', 'adult records', or just plain old obscene recordings have a history that's almost as old as the gramophone's. Britain's guardians of morality expressed outrage over the disgusting nature of these records from the first years of the record industry, probably beginning their campaign just a few short months after a section of the gramophone-owning public began collecting these discs and playing them to their friends. Their existence is not in doubt, but just how obscene did they get and what impact did they have?

DJ and collector Dave Guttridge suggests that most blue discs were imported from the USA and that some of these records 'were like hard core pornography in audio form'. New York DJ and broadcaster Michael Cumella has a different perspective, believing that such discs are 'all innuendo, I think'. Most gramophone records that can be heard on the internet do not bear out Guttridge's assertion. They are mostly songs, rarely more than mildly risqué, with suggestive lyrics filled with double entendres or jokes that rely on the listener's capacity to fill in the blanks with a rude word or two. Others are comic monologues or sketches featuring a duo of actors (usually one male and one female) in a conversation where one character misunderstands the other, or where the exchanges are sufficiently ambivalent to confuse or excite the listener before resolving to a more benign closure. The rowdier of London's nineteenth-century music halls no doubt offered an obscener class of entertainment.

Some cylinder recordings from the 1890s went much further.[31] Russell Hunting (the American entrepreneur, cylinder company owner, and performing artist) was one of the 'stars' of these recordings. He arrived in Britain in the early 1900s having been charged with making obscene cylinder records in 1896, almost certainly one of the first record performers to achieve this status.[32] *The New York Times* described these records, made using pseudonyms such as Willy Fathand, as containing 'vile songs and stories'. On 'The Whores' Union', Hunting recites a list of acts and prices purporting to come from Union president, Ophelia Openhole: 'Common old-fashioned fuck, one dollar ... pudding jerking two dollars', and so on, for what seems much longer than the track's running time of two minutes and six seconds. On 'Gimlet's Soliloquy' (a satire on Hamlet's soliloquy), Hunting claims to be 'Manly Tempest' and intones 'To pee or not to pee, that is the question. Whether it is better in the flesh to suffer the stings and smarts of this outrageous clap or taking physic against a damned disease and with it a syringe'. James White's 'Dennis O'Reilly at Maggie Murphy's Home After Nine O'Clock' offers more obscene language and simulated sex (which does not sound consensual).[33] Hunting was found guilty of obscenity and sentenced to gaol; after this, the trade in obscene cylinder recordings almost ceased.[34]

There is no evidence that Hunting returned to his indecent activities when he arrived in Britain. Indeed, there does not appear to have been a British obscene records industry at this time. The demise of the cylinder may have something to do with this; Cumella believes that the major record companies held such strong control over disc production that it would have been extremely difficult for independent producers to make discs in the pre-electric era. Garth Cartwright reminded me of the adage that 'pornography leads technology' but also noted that no one he spoke to in his research mentioned any record shop trade in audio-pornography.

The British love of music hall and suggestive jokes and lyrics is clear from many surviving gramophone records. Overt obscenity may not have made it onto a disc, but the art of suggestion was part and parcel of many great music hall performers' talents. Harry Champion's 'A Little Bit of Cucumber', recorded around the end of 1914, is a personal favourite. Ostensibly, it is a rapid-fire song about Champion's favourite food, but his choice lends itself to different interpretations; the first chorus ends with a seemingly innocent 'Little bit of cucum, cucum, cucum, little bit of cucumber', but by the end, Champion has altered the line to 'Little bit of cucum, I cum, you cum'. Champion's discography shows his affinity with rude food; he also recorded 'I Was Holdin' Me Coconut' and sang of his wife's love for his 'Yorkshire Pudden'. A generation later, George Formby sang about his adventures 'With My Little Stick of Blackpool Rock' and the pleasure to be had 'With My Little Ukulele in my Hand', for major record labels Decca and Regal Zonophone.

Champion and Formby were part of a music hall tradition that relied on the audience's interpretations of lyrics rather than blatant obscenity. Generally, such songs generated little concern, even if the BBC might prefer to keep them off the wireless. The parliamentary debate that followed Mr Lipton's report on discs of indecent character was unusual. Previous parliamentary discussions had not mentioned specific records, but in this case Lloyd George named the discs that caused Mr Lipton such concern—'John and Martha' and 'Don't Touch Me Nylon'—although he failed to name the artists. 'John and Martha' seems to have been lost in time, but 'Don't Touch Me Nylon' exists in more than one version. The song was written by Al Timothy, a saxophonist and songwriter whose best-known song is probably 'Kiss Me, Honey Honey, Kiss Me'. In 1954, the short-lived London Calypso label released a version of 'Don't Touch Me Nylon' by Marie Bryant and Jackie Brown's Calypso Kings, as a 78-rpm 10-inch disc.[35] Over a jaunty calypso beat, Bryant (a black American singer and dancer who performed in Britain in the mid-50s) sings about her boyfriend, Johnny, whose hands are roaming all over her body. Despite the singer's insistence that he must stop this carry-on, Johnny continually grabs at her clothes—all nylon, it appears—eventually grabbing her bra. It is not clear exactly what Lipton was offended about, presumably the intimate contact between the man and woman being described so graphically. From a twenty-first-century perspective, the most offensive thing about the song is that it seems to describe and even celebrate a series of sexual assaults. Lipton may also have been upset by Bryant's anti-apartheid campaigning; her song, 'The Plea', upset South African Prime Minister Daniel F. Malan during his visit to Britain for the coronation of Queen Elizabeth II.[36]

Meet the Banned

The BBC's radio and TV services reached into almost every British home by the mid-50s. Music was a major feature of the corporation's programmes, especially on the wireless, but the BBC was keen to ensure that standards were maintained. The corporation could not stop people buying undesirable gramophone records, but it could identify unsuitable music on record or in live performances and keep it off the airwaves. From 1938–1954, the BBC banned 172 pieces of music, including 'What A Nice Lot of Nazis They Are', 'She Fell for My Twiddleybits', 'With a No That Sounds Like a Yes', and George Formby's 'In My Little Snapshot Album'.[37] In many cases, the titles alone make the reason for the ban clear, but others are now less obvious.

Take 'God Bless the Child', a song made famous by Billie Holiday, who co-wrote it with Arthur Hertzog Jr and first recorded it in 1941. Now acknowledged as a jazz standard, it has no sexual references, no obscene words or phrases, and no calls for violent revolution. What it does have is lyrics that could be construed as left-wing, or even anti-Christian—enough for the Beeb to keep it off the airwaves, but only from 13 April 1951 to 1 February 1952.

Popular singer Anne Shelton upset the BBC when she recorded 'Hank Janson Blues', which was banned in January 1954. Once again, there is little obvious cause for concern in the lyric as Shelton sings about the tough but kind guy she longs for but who gives her the brush-off. The problem lies with the titular hero. Hank Janson was the *nom de plume* of British author Stephen Frances, a prolific author of dozens of erotic pulp fiction books, such as *Broads Don't Scare Easy* and *The Filly Wore Red*; Shelton's song no doubt sought to cash in on Janson's infamy, but the BBC would have none of it.

The BBC did not always explain the reasons behind its record bans and the growing band of British teenagers viewed the bans as something to be derided. *New Musical Express* journalist Michael Winner reported that the BBC banned versions of 'Sixteen Tons' that referred to St Peter but was happy to broadcast those that referred to 'Brother' instead, that Johnnie Ray's recording of 'Such A Night' was banned because of the singer's suggestive grunting (grunt-free versions would be okay), and that the boisterous 'Oo Bang Jingly-Jang' was banned only from broadcast on the popular radio show *Music While You Work* because of concerns that workers would join in with the song so enthusiastically that they would damage machinery.[38] Winner's article may have struck a chord at the BBC. Less than a week after its publication, the corporation's Sound Publicity Officer warned staff that 'the word "banned" should not be used, despite its obvious suitability!' The preferred term was 'restricted'.[39]

The BBC's policy of 'restricting' certain records no doubt kept them from being accidentally heard by its listeners, but all of these discs were on open sale in shops across Britain and a ban could help sales. If Johnnie Ray, the 'Nabob of Sob', was rumoured to be grunting suggestively but couldn't be heard on radio, then the inquisitive teenager had no option but to buy a copy of the record. Even Mr Janson may have benefitted from the banning of Anne Shelton's disc. Could this man's books be that pornographic? There is one way to find out.

A Few Last Hurrahs

The age of the gramophone was coming to an end, but it staggered on for a few years more. There were plenty of parts of the world that were willing to give the instrument and its discs an afterlife of sorts and it still had the capacity to irritate the Establishment at home and abroad. The portable, clockwork gramophone was still available, priced at around £12 and selling in its thousands around the world.[40] It was the ideal instrument for those places still to benefit from mains electricity and in the mid-50s many such places existed. As Dr Barnett Stross explained, in a patronising and ill-informed fashion, the gramophone was a status symbol in many corners of the Empire:

I am advised, and I think that this is true, that so important is the gramophone record considered to be among the Negro population in places like Central Africa and South Africa that a person is not considered to have 'arrived' and is 'non-U' unless he has a gramophone and records. Once a person has a selection of records and a gramophone, then he is a very important person in the village or in the tribe.[41]

In the Gold Coast, the gramophone became a defender of democracy.[42] The British government, concerned that forthcoming elections in this colony would be prone to 'malpractices', sought ways of ensuring that only eligible citizens could vote and that they would understand exactly who and what they were voting for. David Gammans MP had little confidence in the citizens' grasp of the electoral process: 'Does the right hon. Gentleman realise that of every 10 people who go to the polling booths nine will not have the faintest idea of what is printed on the voting paper?' he asked James Griffiths, Secretary of State for the Colonies. Mr Griffiths clearly shared at least some of Mr Gammans's concerns. He was instituting a 'propaganda' campaign with the help of 'gramophone records in the vernacular to make clear to the electorate the procedure being adopted'. Gramophone records in the vernacular were fine when the British government was using them. In the wrong (i.e. non-British) hands, such records were dangerous, so the government prevented a shipment of gramophone records from being imported into British Guiana because the records were Russian and filled with communist propaganda.[43]

Vernacular discs and portable gramophones found another purpose in Kenya during the 'emergency' of 1952–1960; the spreading of subversion through the promotion of Mau Mau doctrines.[44] Although the British government attempted to ban these subversive records, including one that called for the killing of all Europeans and Masai, this proved impossible. According to the Nairobi correspondent of *The Times*, there were thousands of these records in circulation, many having been produced before the start of the insurgency. Newer recordings by singers such as Fred Kubayi could contain overt or covert messages: 'Even the stressing of certain words and syllables may give an apparently innocent song a harmful character.' Most of these records were Kenyan in origin, but some were being produced in Britain and South Africa, claimed the writer. 'Clearly, some steps will have to be taken to prevent so simple a medium as a gramophone record from being used to spread subversion', the correspondent continued.[45]

The portable gramophone's popularity extended into the '60s, drawing the venerable old instrument and its last few 78s into the dawn of contemporary pop. The HMV 102 portable, first on sale in 1931, stayed in production until mid-1960.[46] The entertainment market in countries such as India gave the gramophone its final moments of glory; huge populations, eager to hear music but lacking a regular electricity supply, sought out portable, wind-up gramophones and discs to play on them. Even the Beatles, that icon of modern pop music and recording innovations, have an extensive discography of 78-rpm recordings, with thirty releases on the Indian Parlophone label including a 1968 release of 'Lady Madonna' and 'The Inner Light'.[47]

On the Record: 'Move It', Cliff Richard and the Drifters (45 rpm and 78 rpm, Columbia, 1958)

Many people consider 'Move It' to be the first British rock 'n' roll record. It heralded a new youth scene as teenagers looked for their own unique music rather than rehashing the tunes of their parents' (and even their grandparents') generation, but it could still be bought as a 78.

Richard recorded the song in EMI's studios on 24 July 1958, when he was seventeen years old, and the disc was released on the Columbia label on 29 August. The label credit has Richard's name in large capital letters with 'and The Drifters' below in notably smaller text. Only two of the Drifters played on the track—the song's writer, guitarist Ian Samwell, and drummer Terry Smart. Session guitarist Ernie Shear and double bassist Frank Clarke completed the line-up. 'Schoolboy Crush' (originally recorded by American singer Bobby Helms) was intended to be the A-side but the record was flipped and 'Move It' became the lead track (possibly because TV producer Jack Good preferred it).

Sixty years after its release, 'Move It' still sounds fresh and exciting. The double bass and drums have a confident but relaxed feel, the rolling rhythm guitar gives it momentum, and the lead guitar is crisp and bright. Richard sings with less of a defiant sneer than Elvis, but he still has some swagger, although his slightly odd pronunciation of 'soul' and 'roll' towards the end of the song sounds incongruous. Whoever made the decision to flip the sides deserves a place in British pop history. 'Schoolboy Crush' is a close copy of Helms's recording, a doo-wop style song swamped by a bland chorus and whistling (courtesy of the Mike Sammes Singers), with Cliff trying to sound like a lovestruck American teen. The lyric speaks of 'graduating' from school, record hops, drive-ins, and candy shops—all alien to British life at the time. It is a poor imitation of American acts like Frankie Lymon or Danny and the Juniors. If 'Schoolboy Crush' had stayed on the A-side, the world might have heard little more of Cliff Richard.

'Move It' was released on a 10-inch 78 as Columbia DB 4178 (the 45-rpm version added a 45 prefix) and the song reached number two on the British charts. Soon after, a new Drifters line-up would change its name to The Shadows. Britain's teenagers had their own rock 'n' roll hero.

Shellac's Back!

It was late, damp, and dark, but the disused shoe factory was busy and buzzing, filled with artists, writers, musicians, and general hangers-on (including me). We were celebrating the launch of a fringe festival. There was plenty to see and eat or drink, and there was a DJ. Of course, there was always a DJ. In a far corner of an outlying room, the sound of music was barely audible, and there was no throbbing bass line to be felt through my shoes, but as we got closer to the centre of the factory, the music got louder. As we approached the stairwell, it got louder still, but it was not what you would expect—not techno, disco, rock, funk, or hip-hop. It was dance music from the 1920s or '30s, emerging from a disc spinning on one of two turntables. The turntables are not what you would expect either. Each one was contained in a black box, sat on its own small table, and had a winding handle in its side. Between them stood a dapper chap in tweeds. The turntables were HMV Model 102 portable gramophones. The dapper gentleman was DJ78 (a.k.a Dave Guttridge). He was giving me my first experience of the twenty-first-century shellac scene.[1]

78rpm: The Movie

The history of the gramophone and its discs is interwoven with the histories of other communication and entertainment technologies, from the phonautogram to the phonograph, the wireless, the tape recorder, TV, and the cinema, so it was not surprising that the instrument should attract the attention of a documentary film maker. Joel Schlemowitz's 2015 movie, *78rpm*, offers a rosy-hued but fascinating insight into the contemporary world of the gramophone, its discs and the people who love them. Filmed mostly in the USA, with a few scenes from the UK, *78rpm* is a part-fantasy, part-documentary movie that interweaves interviews with collectors, DJs, historians, and archivists with fantasy scenes filmed in grainy black and white.

The interviewees (including Guttridge and Oliver Berliner, grandson of Emile) are knowledgeable and enthusiastic. The black and white fantasy scenes are nostalgic visions of bygone lives, dance acts, burlesque titillation, steampunk drama, a bucolic scene of chickens being fed to the sound of Vess L. Ossman's banjo music, and a restful few minutes featuring DJ78 being punted down the River Wensum as he plays music on one of his 102s.

The film's focus on the USA means that the insights into the British scene are limited. DJ Foxtrot Fanny, one of the Shellac Sisters, explains that there is a big vintage scene in the UK but gets little time to expand on that comment. Guttridge is interviewed at greater length but mostly about his love of his HMV 'picnic gramophones' and records rather than the British scene. Foxtrot Fanny's comment merits exploration: does the current enthusiasm for shellac and gramophones have an independent existence, or is it part of the wider vintage scene where fashion, dance and nostalgia for a (real or imagined) simpler life are equally if not more important? Enjoyable though Schlemowitz's movie is, we will have to look elsewhere for the answer.

Frocks and Foxtrots: Britain's Vintage Scenes

Across Britain, lovers of all things vintage have a presence in almost every city and town of any size and in plenty of villages and hamlets as well. There are vintage festivals, dance clubs, dress shops, and fashion auctions. There are enthusiasts for vintage cameras, movies, cars, hairstyles, beards, moustaches, trains, musical instruments, teapots, teacups, and bicycles. People's interests, enthusiasms, and fascinations with all things vintage are so diverse that it would be wrong to speak of a British vintage scene as there are many scenes—'lots of different parts, which all come together from time to time' as Guttridge said.

When Schlemowitz came to Britain to film part of *78rpm*, he discovered a vintage-loving culture that contrasted with the scene in his home country. In the USA, he said, 'there's a very big vintage scene—vintage cars, vintage clothes, vintage cocktails, vintage music, burlesque'.[2] However, according to the director, this scene is fixated mainly on the 1920s—the age of prohibition, jazz, and speakeasies. In Britain, he found a scene that took a much broader view and he offered the theory that this might be due to the absence of prohibition and speakeasy culture. Without this brief but exciting period of history, the British vintage lover has less of a focus and can look to every decade from the 1900s to the 1950s for inspiration, whether such inspiration comes from clothes, objects, or dancing. One of the all-encompassing interests that bring these scenes together is a love of the gramophone, especially of the music it can still reproduce.

For those of us who only hear scratchy, indistinct noises pouring forth from elderly shellac discs, it can be hard to understand their attraction in an era of music as a stream of clean, compressed, faultless data (or should that be 'easy to understand'?). For those who love the discs and the gramophones that play them, the attraction is on a deeper level. Loren Schoenberg of the National Jazz Museum in Harlem, New York, emphasises this: 'The needle starts and all of a sudden ... you're in a world of 100 years ago ... In a sense you're breathing the air of 1904'.[3]

Peter Wilson, the Belfast-based musician better known as Duke Special, shares this sense of time (or space) travel. His first exposure to 78s was during his pre-teen years in Downpatrick when his father showed him an 'old orange crate of records ... a bunch of old, dusty records which played at this crazy speed and sounded like they came from a different world.'[4] Guttridge has a similar perspective: 'There's something about the sound of a 78 ... it's tangibly different. It still does something emotionally which other records on vinyl and CDs and MP3s don't do.'[5] Another musician, Lewis Durham of Kitty, Daisy and Lewis, first experienced the thrill of a 78 thanks to his maternal grandfather's wind-up gramophone. For Durham, however, it was the equipment, not the music, that intrigued him. He found the instrument 'absolutely fascinating, even more than the music that was being played. I can't even remember what that music was.'[6] A year or two later, Durham, now aged twelve or thirteen, became a fan of blues and R&B and began to search out the music on 78s, finding some at London record store Sounds That Swing. He stayed in love with the music but also developed a fascination for the discs themselves: 'I had a technical fascination with them: they were made from a different material and all this stuff. I don't know why, I just loved it.'

Durham took his fascination further than most. Still in his mid-teens, he acquired a Grampian cutting lathe: 'At the time, people didn't want this stuff ... no-one was into it.' Armed with this crucial instrument, he began cutting vinyl discs for his older sister's friends who were beginning to get into the UK garage scene as MCs and wanted the discs to use when performing. A combination of trial and error, self-education, and advice from his recording-engineer father enabled Durham to become proficient at producing discs—a talent he would use when producing his own records.

Click and Collect

Almost every enthusiasm has its troops of collectors and the gramophone scene is no different—but what to collect and why? Gramophones, discs, record label catalogues, needle tins, pictures, and models of Nipper all have their fans. Gramophones and discs lead the pack, but sub-groups of collectors exist even here. One group collects instruments and records as objects, prizing them for their appearance and their visual aesthetic, possibly refusing to play them under any circumstances. Another larger group collects instruments and records for what they allow us to do—their ability to release the content of the discs—so that twenty-first-century lovers of music, comedy, political speeches, or party records can hear the sounds within the grooves: can listen to, in most cases, the voices of the dead.

Both of these groups can specialise. A gramophone collector might only want HMV gramophones, or only HMV portable gramophones, or only HMV Model 102 portables. A record collector might concentrate on one record label, one genre, or one artist. Ethan Crenson, an American collector, refers to 'directed' and 'undirected' collecting.[7] An undirected collector may pick up anything that catches their eye, at a car boot or a record fair. The directed collector will search out only those objects that meet certain criteria (Crenson is directed, collecting songs about the atomic bomb).

Christopher Proudfoot, of the City of London Phonograph and Gramophone Society (CLPGS), has a long-standing fondness for obsolete machinery and a self-confessed failure to understand electronics, so he is attracted to the acoustic gramophone. A friend of Proudfoot's at Cambridge in the 1960s, the late Gavin Stamp ('Piloti' of *Private Eye* magazine) clearly explained the appeal of a gramophone, compared to an electric record player: 'A gramophone is a comprehensible mechanism.'[8] Proudfoot is a stalwart supporter of such comprehensible pre-electric instruments, but while some of his fellow CLPGS members share his love of the instruments, most, in Proudfoot's opinion, have an interest in records and usually specialise in a particular genre or type (such as those which were mechanically rather than electrically recorded). In Guttridge's experience, however, focused or directed collecting is not common in Britain; most people have broad tastes and while some collectors concentrate on specific time periods or subjects, 'they're quite a rarity.'[9]

DJ quartet the Shellac Sisters are fans of gramophone-era music generally, but each has their own interests—Latin, foxtrots, Charleston, and Balboa. Paul Buck, a collector who refers to himself as a ''78 rescue service', will happily buy job lots of shellac discs to get one or two rare discs. He is a self-described collector of the artefact rather than the content of a disc. He enjoys compiling the histories of the record labels and sharing those histories on the internet, studying the changes in label design, 'filling in the history of the 78 before it disappears into landfill'.[10]

With enthusiasm for vintage fashion, music, and technology increasing year on year, how does this affect collectors? The answer depends on what is being collected. Michael Cumella believes that the gramophone is an iconic antique, but such status does not necessarily mean that it is an expensive one. In Britain, HMV 102s finished in coloured fabric are on the market for around £250, the more usual black fabric machines costing less. In 2013, a Columbia Graphonola console grand attracted a winning auction bid of a mere £37.[11] Unloved gramophones, rescued from the back of a shed or garage and looking like they will never work again, can be had for a few pounds; Cumella is optimistic that many of them can be repaired relatively easily as they were originally so well made and robust. EMG gramophones—eulogised by serious audiophiles for many years—are attracting some of the highest prices at British auctions. An Expert Senior model sold for £3,800 in 2015, a Mark IX sold for £2,200 in 2016, and a mahogany-cased model (without a turntable) sold for £850 in the same year.[12]

Many shellac discs can be collected for very low prices, as little as 50p or £1. Cumella, Guttridge, and dealer Greg Butler all told me of being contacted by excited individuals who had unearthed boxes of discs from a dead relative's attic, expecting huge rewards for worn-out and almost unplayable Caruso or Melba records. In most cases, such discs are neither rare or desirable. They sold in their hundreds of thousands and many still survive so they are virtually worthless—'very common means very cheap', says Cumella. Disc jockey Jenny Hammerton finds that the increased interest in vintage dance music has not created a rise in prices at the bottom end of the market, probably because young people access their music digitally rather than buying their own gramophones and discs, so the Shellac Sisters are still able to acquire records relatively easily. Buck sees the days of the serious 78 collector as coming to an end: 'The collectors have dissipated and those that are left are greying. I'm the young 'un' (he is in his mid-50s).

Collectors may be on their way out, but at the top end of the disc market, a few vintage records can still sell for hundreds or even thousands of pounds. Buck finds that pre-1914 discs from music hall stars like Marie Lloyd have a strong commercial market, as do pre-revolution Russian opera records; few discs reach the market due to their age and even fewer will still be playable. A 12-inch first pressing of James Joyce reading 'Anna Livia Plurabelle', made for the Orthological Institute by the Gramophone Company in 1929, sold for £1,187 including premium at auction in 2015.[13] The top end of the international market bears out Buck's belief that 1920s and 30s blues is the strongest market. A Vocalion recording of bluesman Robert Johnson ('Me and the Devil Blues' backed by 'Little Queen of Spades') warranted a minimum bid of $20,000 on one specialist internet auction site.[14] Dave Guttridge believes that big money is to be had in 78s by major rock 'n' roll and pop stars that appeared in the 1950s or early 1960s. A quick search on the internet unearths some demands for extremely high prices, especially for Indian pressings of Beatles 78s, which are offered for prices ranging from $2,000 to $5,000; whether or not these prices are achieved is another matter.

Collectors of shellac discs face two perennial problems—storage and cleanliness. Dirty discs are dangerous; they will give poor sound and are prone to damage as the needle tracks dust and grit through the groove. Freshly discovered records, emerging from dusty garages or damp cellars after decades of neglect, offer a bigger challenge, requiring careful cleaning to remove dirt and even fungal mould before being played. Collectors have their own solutions to the cleaning problem as proprietary cleaning cloths and liquids, solutions of washing-up liquid, damp cotton cloths, and warm water all have their proponents. Paul Buck demonstrated his own preferred method on my dirt-encrusted and mould-ridden copy of the Cromer School Choir's disc—fragrance-free wipes to remove the worst of the filth (they leave no residue, unlike fragranced wipes), then quilted toilet tissue to dry the disc. Based on this single demonstration, the approach seems to work.

As for storage, the discs are heavy and even a small collection needs a strong floor to support it. Serious collectors, with thousands of discs, give over entire rooms to their collections and often need to devote their garages or outbuildings to their passion. They need space for their gramophones, too; most collectors or DJs I met owned more than one instrument. Although fragile, shellac discs appear to be resistant to the extremes of British weather, so they can survive without careful temperature control. One collection I visited was so large that much of it was stored under the collector's carport, sheltered from the worst of the rain and snow but exposed to high and low temperatures, wind, frost, and the idle gaze of passers-by.

Over 100 years after they first arrived, gramophone record societies such as the CLPGS have their own place on the contemporary scene. The Federation of Recorded Music Societies (FRMS), established at Abbey Road Studios in 1936, now has a membership of around 200 societies (including the CLPGS) and continues with its aim of promoting understanding of and enthusiasm for classical music, although it does not confine itself to 78 rpm records.[15] The CLPGS does concentrate on vintage gramophone and phonograph recordings, however. Christopher Proudfoot describes the CLPGS as 'untypical' of the FRMS as a whole: 'our membership is predominantly male, and predominantly grey-haired, and comes from all walks of life. Of the societies in the FRMS as a whole ... grey hair is equally prominent, but there are rather more women than we have.' It is also untypical, he says 'not least, ironically, in that classical music, apart from operatic arias, is probably the least popular kind within its membership!' The CLPGS has evolved from 'diehard aficionados for an already obsolescent technology' to an association with historical and educational activities (it is an educational charity), undertaking research as well as meeting to listen to records or discuss the technical details of gramophones and phonographs.

The CLPGS and the vintage scene rarely if ever meet, according to Proudfoot: 'I think that the CLPGS is probably outside the [vintage] trend you describe, since I am not aware of its having had much effect on our membership or activities.' Of course, it is not compulsory for lovers of vintage fashion, music or technology to join a scene or a society. Many 1950s teenagers are now in their seventies or eighties and retain a love of the music of their adolescence without taking an active part in any of the contemporary vintage scenes; they kept the records they bought in their youth, still have the record players they were given as presents or paid for with wages from Saturday jobs, and go to concerts by the rock 'n' rollers who still perform.

Let's Do the Show Right Here!

Some gramophone and 78 enthusiasts take things further than merely collecting. Carrying nothing more than a laptop, the twenty-first century disc jockey can travel the world with an entire record collection stored on their machine's hard drive. It is also possible to upload recordings from 78-rpm discs to a laptop, but the authentic gramophone DJ eschews such modern convenience. Armed with a couple of vintage gramophones and a few cases of fragile shellac discs, the gramophone DJ might need strong biceps, but travel is still possible and there is no danger of flat batteries or software crashes, although an evening's possible set list is far more limited.

Gramophone disc jockeys are at the heart of Britain's contemporary shellac scene. DJ78, Greg Butler, the Shellac Sisters, and others pride themselves on going the extra mile, playing original discs on original gramophones, dressed as fashionable (or not-so-fashionable) entertainers of the period. Michael Cumella performs using a pair of 1905 horned machines and has specially made flight cases to transport them by air when necessary. Britain's Shellac Sisters also use horned instruments; Shellac Sister Jenny Hammerton describes them as 'beautiful objects' and says that at gigs the gramophones are like 'magnets' to audience members.[16] Guttridge does not just put the records on the turntables of his HMV 102s; 'When I perform, I become DJ78,' he says. The look—for Guttridge, it is tweeds or dinner jacket, sideburns, and gold-rimmed glasses—is important, especially when he DJs for an audience of vintage dance or fashion fans: 'There's mutual respect: they recognise that I've gone to nearly as much trouble as them.' The Shellac Sisters agree that the look is important and adopt characters when they DJ; the quartet are known as Foxtrot Fanny, Lady Jane, Quickstep Queenie, and Miss V. The quartet share a passion for more than the music; as Jenny Hammerton (a.k.a. Foxtrot Fanny) put it, 'The Shellac Sisters are all passionate about the music, the clothes, the ephemera and everything in between of the gramophone era.'

Karla Richards, who performs as Ms Karla Chameleon, is another DJ for whom dressing up is part of the job. She already had a reputation for making costumes and outfits for parties before she began as a disc jockey so saw it as a natural thing to do. She told me, 'When I play [I] always make sure that I have my hair and makeup all done and lots of accessories—jewellery, handbags, etc.' Richards owns several HMV 102 picnic gramophones and, like Guttridge, she uses them when she DJs. She has her own piece of technology for some performances, a gramophone fitted to the base of a pram that she calls the 'Pramophone', which echoes the contraptions used by some of the gramophone-buskers of a century ago. It is a contraption that proves especially successful with younger audiences and gives her a chance to educate children and teenagers about the gramophone, its discs, and its history. In her experience, older teenagers know about vinyl records but are 'amazed' at the weight of shellac discs and the idea of steel needles. Younger children are equally amazed by the instruments' lack of batteries. She finds that most people, young or old, are not familiar with shellac discs: 'They get called "vinyls" a lot (eek … with the "s" too).' Jenny Hammerton finds that young people are becoming more interested in the music of the gramophone era, but it is the 'older folks' who get most enthusiastic, feeling nostalgic for the music and instruments of their own younger days.

Like Guttridge and the Shellac Sisters, Richards enjoys playing for dancers. She is pleased at the popularity of swing dance in Britain: 'there are some spectacular dancers out there. It's great to see the people decked out in vintage garb from head to toe.' This connection with the audience and other performers is clearly a key factor on the vintage gramophone scene. For Richards, the gramophone scene means 'a whole fantastic new group of friends, lots of festivals, parties and events…. I have done so many cool things since discovering 78s, it's really been a big surprise.'

Peter Wilson is another fan who enjoys the dance, fashion, and musical aspects of the vintage scene; as a musician and songwriter, it is not surprising that he feels a close affinity with the music, but for Wilson, this goes deeper than most:

> I do feel an affinity with the Shellac Collective and with [this] kind of music because I have never really wholly felt part of the contemporary music scene…. the music I write has been influenced by this pre-rock 'n' roll music … I am a musical magpie and I love floating around the edges and drawing inspiration from forgotten things, people and pathways.[17]

Playing old 78s is all well and good, but what about creating new 78s? It is not easy, but it is possible and a few musicians are willing and able to do it. Peter Wilson is one of those musicians. As Duke Special, he has released discs such as 2005's 'Freewheel', which played at 78 rpm with the 2-track second side playing at 45 rpm, and 2006's 'Portrait', which was coupled with a 4-track B-side that played at 33⅓ rpm. Wilson found it impossible to produce records on shellac, so he made the decision to release these discs on vinyl. He also acknowledges that it is difficult to make money on these specialist and limited-release discs. For him, the act of producing 78 rpm records is a labour of love.

Wilson has delved even further back into audio technology, producing the Duke Special album, *Look Out Machines*, as a limited-edition package of twelve individually boxed cylinders. He is not alone in his homage to wax and shellac. Lewis Durham's childhood love of 78s and gramophones meant that when Kitty, Daisy and Lewis began to record, he was eager to go beyond the CD, downloads and streaming. Using his own equipment, Durham produced 78-rpm albums of the band's first three releases. Like Wilson, he was forced to press the discs on vinyl. Unlike Wilson, he produced shellac-style albums, lavishly packaging five or six double-sided 78s together in the same way as the earliest record albums from the first decades of the twentieth century.

Legacy

In the hi-tech, interconnected twenty-first century world, the gramophone is redundant. In this, it shares the fate that eventually befalls all entertainment technologies. It has even been responsible for inflicting this fate itself. The gramophone made the cylinder-playing phonograph obsolete, then met the same fate at the hands of the record player. The vinyl record, the cassette, the 8-track cartridge, the digital compact cassette, the minidisc, the compact disc, and the instruments that played them are all consigned to history or on their way there (even though vinyl is undergoing a resurgence in popularity). Even the downloading of digital files to a hard drive seems quaint and old-fashioned as streaming services become the entertainment technology of choice, to be replaced on their own account at some point in the future, no doubt, as the robots take over and implant microchips in our brains that play a constant, monotonous, A-minor chord and yet persuade us that we are hearing Mozart, Duke Ellington, Led Zeppelin, Kendrick Lamar, or whoever takes our fancy (or the fancy of our robot masters).

It is tempting to focus on the instrument's obsolescence, to see the gramophone as a quaint old piece of brown wood furniture, sitting in the corner of a country gastropub or a barn conversion as an interior designer's idea of retro-chic, or gathering dust in the loft of a suburban '30s semi, forgotten by the current (or even the previous) owner. It is tempting, but to do so would be like ignoring the first ninety years of an elderly relative's life and remembering them only for their last few months of existence. After all, the gramophone was young once, and even in middle age, it was a vibrant and exciting part of Britain's social and cultural life.

For around sixty years, the gramophone was our primary source of recorded sound. It brought music into millions of homes, enabling us to hear our favourite singers, bands, orchestras, and songs even if the BBC was refusing to broadcast them. When the BBC did want to broadcast music, then for much of the time, it used gramophone records to do so. The gramophone brought other sounds into the home too—comedy, political speeches, drama, birdsong, trains, and even the sounds of war. The gramophone's pioneers were often the creators of fake news, keen to establish their own places in the development of the industry and not averse to an occasional economy with the truth; as one recent researcher puts it, 'These sometimes shaky recollections, often written decades after the events they describe, provide at best highly colourful and partisan accounts of the industry's early years.'[18] The discs hide their own secrets. Just how many takes did Melba require to produce a perfect performance? Without the skills of Fred Gaisberg, could Caruso have simply faded away after the 1902 Milan recordings? Did people really believe they were listening to a genuine gas bombardment?

Shellac discs are still with us in their millions, even if most of them are hidden away, unloved, scratched, cracked, getting mouldy, and already unplayable. Those discs that have been re-issued on vinyl or CD, or made available on streaming services, represent just a minority of the recordings that were made in the sixty or so years of the 78's supremacy. The Great 78 Project estimates that around 3 million recordings were released on 78s between the 1890s and 1960s and it aims to find, digitise, and archive as many of these recordings as possible, making them accessible on the internet. It has already gathered together over 200,000 discs and looks forward to collecting many more.[19]

Peter Wilson, like many others, connects with these records on a deep level, as an art and as a way of understanding something fundamental about people:

> Music isn't necessarily good just because it's old but there's so much to learn from these records of lives lived, incredible musicianship and early recording techniques where the goal was to capture something powerful and magical … and human.[20]

Much of this music is indeed magical, but for me, the magic extends beyond the content of those dusty and scratchy grooves. The gramophone is a survivor. Out of date, old-fashioned, and unfashionable, useless as a means of reproducing all but a tiny number of modern recordings, dull-looking and battered it may be, but it lives on, bringing the voices of the dead back to some sort of life amidst the crackles and pops.

On the Record: 'Me and the Devil Blues',
Robert Johnson (Vocalion 01408, 1938)

Robert Johnson travelled around the Mississippi delta (and occasionally further afield), playing his guitar and singing. He was not famous, he often played on the streets, and he never performed in major venues; however, in 1936 and 1937, he recorded a couple of dozen songs at two sessions in Texas. The songs tell eternal stories of this poor young black man's life in the American south of the early twentieth century: of women, drinking, travel, cars, guns, and sexual frustration. There is one about a phonograph: 'Phonograph Blues'; although as he sings about problems with his rusty needles and the machine's inability to play properly, it strikes me that it may not be about phonographs at all.

By the middle of August 1938, Johnson was dead—poisoned, so legend has it, by a jealous husband. His records, mostly released after his death on a number of different labels, sold in the low thousands at most; the American Record Corporation released just eleven of the recordings, on Vocalion, in his lifetime. Fame eluded him. He had little if any influence on rock 'n' roll or '50s pop. Then, in 1961, Columbia released a compilation of sixteen of his songs, *King of the Delta Blues Singers*. The album did not make the charts, but Eric Clapton, Bob Dylan, Jimi Hendrix, the Rolling Stones, and many other rock and blues musicians heard it and took inspiration from the obscure and long-dead bluesman. Within a few years, Johnson was a crucial influence on rock music.

'Me and the Devil Blues' appears on the Columbia album, but it is as a 78 that it has become one of the most expensive records in the world. One of the songs released on Vocalion during Johnson's lifetime, it is likely that only a handful of copies of the original pressing have survived. This is not a cheery, singalong, song; it is not ironic and it is not funny. It is a dark and mysterious song in which the Devil calls on Johnson, takes him for a walk, and somehow persuades him to beat up 'his woman'. In the closing verse, Johnson asks to be buried by the highway, so that his evil spirit can easily catch a bus and travel on. He sings the lyrics clearly, but while their meaning is at times opaque, Johnson's vocal and guitar make it obvious that he is a man in torment, his life out of control, and his evil spirit on its way to Hell. The song also lends credence to the legend that he sold his soul to the Devil in exchange for his talent as a guitarist.

So why choose the downbeat and initially obscure 'Me and the Devil Blues' as this book's closing gramophone record? Edison and Berliner can take the credit. Berliner saw the gramophone record as the next great entertainment medium, a repository for music that could be heard time and time again over many years. Both Berliner and Edison wanted to record the voices of the dead, famous or not, so that they could speak to future generations and remind us of past times. Without the gramophone record, an obscure young blues singer, dead at twenty-seven years of age, would have faded into oblivion as soon as the poisoned whiskey worked its dark magic. With the gramophone, Johnson's music was ready to be heard again whenever the time was right. When that time came, those elderly 78s were at hand, ready to transfer to the new medium of the long-playing record and give fresh life to his powerful, magical, and all-too-human songs.

Endnotes

Prologue

1 De Martinville, 'Fixation Graphique de la Voix' (1857) in Feaster, ed., *The Phonautographic Manuscripts of Édouard-Léon Scott de Martinville* (2010), p. 24.
2 Feaster, *Édouard-Léon Scott de Martinville: An Annotated Discography* (2010), pp. 43–82.
3 Berliner, *The Gramophone. Etching the Human Voice* (1909, originally published 1888), p. 4.
4 First Sounds has these recordings online at www.firstsounds.org

Chapter 1

1 De Martinville, 'Principes de Phonautography' (1857) in Feaster, ed., *The Phonautographic Manuscripts of Édouard-Léon Scott de Martinville* (2010), p. 5.
2 *Morning Chronicle* (19 September 1859), p. 6.
3 Berliner, *The Gramophone. Etching the Human Voice* (1909, originally published 1888), p. 4.
4 In 1948, L'Académie Charles Cros was established in France. It awards annual prizes for recorded music of different genres, including jazz, pop and classical.
5 Rutgers University, *Thomas A. Edison Papers* (undated)
6 Berliner, *The Gramophone. Etching the Human Voice* (1909, originally published 1888), p. 8.
7 Edison, *The Phonograph and its Future* (1878), pp. 527–537.
8 Hubert, 'The New Talking Machines', *The Atlantic* (February 1889), pp. 256–261.
9 *The Times* (9 January 1878), p. 6; (17 January 1878) p. 4; (22 January 1878) p. 4.
10 *The Times* (25 February 1878) p. 12; (19 March 1878) p. 8; (27 May 1878) p. 1.
11 *The Times* (21 May 1885), p. 10. Phonograph would race regularly across Britain, but never with any great success.
12 'The New Phonograph', *The Times* (21 January 1888), p. 15.
13 Martland, *Business History of the Gramophone Company Ltd 1897–1918* (1992), p. 61. A second recording of Gladstone may have been faked by an impersonator called Frank Lindo.
14 Gouraud (letter) *The Times* (27 June 1888), p. 12. It is not clear if the house was called Little Menlo before Gouraud took up residence or if he renamed it in tribute to Edison's headquarters.

15 'Mr Edison's Phonograph', *The Times* (30 June 1888), p. 5. The correspondent obviously saw the phonograph's recording function as more useful than its ability to reproduce sound.

16 'Mr Edison's Phonograph', *The Times* (15 August 1888), p. 9.

17 *Nature* (13 September 1888), p. 469.

18 Advertisement, *The Times* (26 December 1888), p. 1. The demonstration was timetabled for 8 p.m. The beautiful whistler was up against stiff competition from the Baldwin Monkey, who was set to drop 150 feet by parachute at the same time.

19 Advertisement, *The Times* (6 November 1888), p. 1.

20 Wile, *Etching the Human Voice: the Berliner Invention of the Gramophone* (1990), pp. 2–22.

21 Library of Congress online, *Emile Berliner and the Birth of the Recording Industry*. This website has an extensive collection of Berliner-related documents.

22 'The Berliner Gramophone', *The Electrical World* (12 November 1887), pp. 253–254.

23 Houston, *On the Gramophone* (1887), pp. 420-421.

24 The full text of Berliner's presentation can be found in Berliner, *The Gramophone. Etching the human voice* (1909, originally published 1888), pp. 2–19.

25 Berliner, *The Gramophone. Etching the human voice* (1909, originally published 1888), p. 18.

26 Berliner, *The Gramophone. Etching the human voice* (1909, originally published 1888), p. 19.

27 *Manchester Weekly Times* (3 December 1887), Supplement p. 8; *Leeds Mercury* (16 December 1887), p. 3; 'Science in 1887', *The Times* (13 January 1888), p. 12; T.C.H., 'Scientific Notes', *The Graphic* (9 August 1890), p. 160.

28 'By the Way', *The Globe* (16 December 1887), p. 5.

29 'The Gramophone', *Aberdeen Weekly Journal* (14 January 1891), p. 5.

30 Advertisement, *The Times* (8 December 1891), p. 3.

31 'The Gramophone in the Bank Buildings', *The Belfast News-Letter* (15 December 1891), p. 4.

32 Library of Congress online, 'The Gramophone, invented by E Berliner, "Reproducing the Human Voice"' (undated).

33 This was the first of many improvements which Johnson developed. He would become a partner in the Gramophone Company and the Victor Talking Machine Company. See Martland, *Business History of the Gramophone Company Ltd 1897–1918* (1992), p. 48.

34 *Midland Daily Telegraph* (11 April 1893), p. 2.

35 The album was released on Dawn Records in 1969. 'Record' and 'disc' were both commonly used to refer to the pre-recorded object that the gramophone played. Of course, the cylinder is also a 'record.'

36 Wile, *Etching the Human Voice: the Berliner invention of the gramophone* (1990), pp. 2–22. It's likely that the toy machine with 5-inch discs is the one promoted by Parkins and Gotto.

37 Berliner, *The Gramophone. Etching the Human Voice* (1909, originally published 1888), pp. 13ff.

38 Martland, *Since Records Began. EMI the first 100 years* (1997), p. 24.

39 Hobby, 'How Shellac is Manufactured', *The Mail: Adelaide* (18 December 1937), p. 31.

40 Museum of Obsolete Media, www.obsoletemedia.org/10-inch-78-rpm-record/.

41   'Pathé and Edison Hill and Dale Discs', pspatialaudio.com/pathe_discs.htm
42   Stoker, *Dracula* (1897), Chapter 24: 'Dr Seward's Phonograph Diary, spoken by Van Helsing'.
43   Martland, *Business History of the Gramophone Company Ltd 1897–1918* (1992), pp. 60ff. Lambert's machine used a circular keyboard rather than the industry-standard QWERTY setup.
44   *The Times* (25 October 1907), p. 5.
45   Edison-Bell Consolidated Phonograph Co., *List of Records* (1898), pp. 3–21.
46   Most of the titles mean nothing today: 'The Edison Polka,' a xylophone solo, for example. Martland (*Business History*, p. 227) refers to the cylinder list as 'designed for the musically uneducated,' which seems rather harsh.
47   *Talking Machine News* (May 1903), pp. 1 and 6.
48   Martland, *Business History of the Gramophone Company Ltd 1897–1918* (1992), pp. 266–7.
49   City of London Phonograph and Gramophone Society, www.clpgs.org.uk/ sterling.html. Martland (1992, p. 272) estimates total cylinder sales of around 5.4 million between 1904–1907.
50   'Comstock Arrests an Actor', *New York Times* (26 June 1896), p. 3.
51   *Talking Machine News* (November 1908), p. 370.
52   Jones, 'The Gramophone Company: An Anglo-American Multinational, 1898-1931', *The Business History Review* 59:1:76–100 (1985). Columbia was taken over by British owners in 1923.
53   Martland, *Business History of the Gramophone Company Ltd 1897–1918* (1992), p. 229.
54   'Berliner Left $1,527,573', *New York Times* (22 August 1929), p. 8.
55   Library of Congress online, 'Berliner's wishes for when he dies. Written 9 May 1928', *Emile Berliner and the Birth of the Recording Industry*, www.loc.gov/ item/berl0091/.
56   'Simple Rites Held for Emile Berliner', *Washington Evening Star* (6 August 1929), p. 9.
57   Featherstone, 'Chevalier, Albert Onésime Britannicus Gwathveoyd Louis', *Oxford Dictionary of National Biography online*, www. oxforddnb.com/view/10.1093/ref:odnb/9780198614128.001.0001/ odnb-9780198614128-e-32394.
58   *Encyclopedia Britannica online*, 'Albert Chevalier, British Actor', www. britannica.com/biography/Albert-Chevalier.
59   Gramophone Company, *Gramophone Record Catalogue* (1899) p. 11.

Chapter 2

1   Martland, *Business History of the Gramophone Company Ltd 1897–1918* (1992), pp. 79–83. Gaisberg's stay was intended to be temporary, but he made England his home and lived there until his death in 1951.
2   Strötbaum, ed., *The Fred Gaisberg Diaries: Part 1* (2010), p. 7. www. recordingpioneers.com/docs/GAISBERG_DIARIES_1.pdf. Gaisberg makes few references to these recording sessions in his diary and rarely mentions performers by name.
3   Baker, *British Music Hall* (2014), p. 258.
4   He was happy to socialise with his competitors. On 17 January 1899 he dined at the Savoy Hotel with Colonel Gouraud, the Edison company's agent in Britain. (Gaisberg Diaries, Part 1).
5   See Strötbaum, ed., *The Fred Gaisberg Diaries: Part 1* (2010).

6 See Martland, *Caruso's First Recordings: Myth and Reality* (1994), pp. 192–201, for a detailed discussion of the circumstances behind this recording session.

7 Owen, 11 November 1903. Cited in Martland, *Business History of the Gramophone Company Ltd 1897–1918* (1992), p. 103.

8 Gramophone Company, *Gramophone Record Catalogue* (1899) p. 32.

9 Begbie, 'Making the Gramophone Records', *The Times* (20 January 1905), p. 12.

10 Berry, 'How I Sing to make Records', *Talking Machine News*, p. 3.

11 Gramophone Company, *Gramophone Record Catalogue* (1899) p. 60. Hunting's command of an Irish accent is, at best, variable. Based on these sketches a 'typical Irishman' was a buffoon.

12 Columbia Records, *Columbia Records Catalogue 1916–17*, pp. 36–37.

13 Frank Seaman, originally a business partner of Berliner and Eldridge Johnson, established the Zonophone brand for his gramophones and records. In 1901 he founded the International Zonophone Company and began to compete with the Gramophone Company in Europe. See Martland, *Business History of the Gramophone Company Ltd 1897–1918* (1992), pp. 53–104.

14 Zonophone Records, *Zonophone Record Catalogue, Season 1913–14*, p. 11. The catalogue was 100 pages long.

15 Gramophone Company, *Gramophone Record Catalogue* (1899), pp. 26–28; Columbia Records, *Columbia Records Catalogue 1916–17*, p. 40. Williams and Robey had recorded for HMV previously. Many artists recorded for more than one label, even though each label advertised that the artists were 'exclusive'.

16 'Gramophone Records and Mme Melba', *The Times* (10 December 1904), p. 4.

17 Martland, *Business History of the Gramophone Company Ltd 1897–1918* (1992) pp. 230–251. Sydney Dixon described Lauder and Forde in 1905 as 'enormous sellers' (cited in Martland, *Business History*, p. 372).

18 Martland, *Business History of the Gramophone Company Ltd 1897–1918* (1992), pp. 373–397. This was still a decent income compared to average earnings of around £40–50 per year and was added to by concert fees.

19 Gramophone and Typewriter Ltd, *Catalogue of Gramophone 7-inch Records* (April 1903), pp. 2–14.

20 This approach was used on some of the Berliner records, predating the use of paper labels. For a detailed study of the Gramophone Company's labels see Friedman, *The Collector's Guide to Gramophone Company Record Labels, 1898–1925* (2013), www.musicweb-international.com/Friedman/index.htm.

21 Osborne, *Vinyl: A History of the Analogue Record* (2014), pp. 88–145. *Talking Machine News* (November 1908), p. 377. In the late 1920s, HMV re-released 'records of historical interest' some of which feature different performers on each side, with speeds varying by as much as 9 rpm between the sides.

22 Zonophone Records, *Zonophone Record Catalogue, Season 1913–14*, pp. 74–75.

23 Gramophone Company, *Gramophone Record Catalogue* (1899).

24 Opera Scotland, www.operascotland.org/person/3375/George-Snazelle.

25 Strötbaum, ed., *The Fred Gaisberg Diaries: Part 1* (2010), 30 September 1899.

26 Gramophone Company, *Gramophone Record Catalogue* (1899), p. 53.

27 Strötbaum, ed., *The Fred Gaisberg Diaries: Part 1* (2010), 8 September 1899.

28 Gramophone Company, *Gramophone Record Catalogue* (1899), p. 42.

29 Gramophone and Typewriter Ltd, *The Russo-Japanese War: supplement* (February 1904).

30 *The Times* (19 October 1905), p. 10.

31 Winner records were introduced by a syndicate including Edison-Bell. The label removed the racehorse image from its religious records. See *Early British Disc Record Labels*, 1898–1926, early78s.uk/w/.

32 Rust, *Jazz Journal* (November 1951), p. 19.

33 Columbia Records, *Columbia Records Catalogue 1916–17*, inside cover.

34 *Early British Disc Record Labels*, early78s.uk/

35 *The Times* (20 January 1905), pp. 11–12. Pius X was the lucky Pope.

36 Advertisement, *Wellington Journal & Shrewsbury News* (16 July 1898), p. 1.

37 'Entertainment at the Workhouse', *Exeter Flying Post* (16 July 1898), p. 6.

38 Cody, W. F., *Sentiments on the Cuban Question*. Berliner Recording 5014.

39 Advertisement. *The Times* (4 December 1906), p. 1. The Auxeto-Gramophone, or Auxetophone, was developed by two English inventors, Horace Short and Sir Charles Parsons. For more about the machine see Self, *The Auxetophone* (undated), www.douglas-self.com/MUSEUM/COMMS/auxetophone/auxetoph.htm.

40 Advertisement, *The Times* (30 November 1908), p. 1. Caruso and Melba in particular seem to have 'appeared' at every gramophone concert.

41 Edison-Bell Consolidated Phonograph Co., *List of Records* (1898), p. 2.

42 Pathé, *Complete Catalogue of Pathé 'Rooster' Double-Sided Discs* (1917).

43 Advertisement, *Eastern Daily Press* (6 January 1908), p. 1.

44 Cartwright, *Going for a Song: A Chronicle of the UK Record Shop* (2018), pp. 18–25.

45 Cartwright, *Going for a Song: A Chronicle of the UK Record Shop* (2018), p. 10.

46 Advertisement, *The Gramophone* (April 1944), inside cover.

47 Advertisement, *The Times* (20 January 1905), p. 12.

48 Wells, *The War in the Air* (1908), Chapter 2.

49 Sydney Dixon, May 1907. Cited in Martland, *Business History of the Gramophone Company Ltd 1897–1918* (1992) p. 235.

50 Edison Gold Moulded Records, *British and American List* (July 1907), front cover.

51 Zonophone was by this time owned by the Gramophone Company.

52 Pathé was involved in cinema as well as records from its earliest days. The rooster gained its greatest fame in Britain as the image of the company's newsreels.

53 Martland, *Business History of the Gramophone Company Ltd 1897–1918* (1992), p. 90. The Recording Angel was designed by Theodore B Birnbaum, a British businessman who became involved with the company soon after it was formed.

54 Gramophone Company, *New Gramophone Records* (November 1907) and *New Gramophone Records* (December 1909), front covers.

55 Francis James Barraud (1856–1924) is not to be confused with another English artist, Francis Philip Barraud (1824–1901). The trademark was also used by Victor in the USA. The painting was Barraud's only well-known work.

Chapter 3

1 Barnett, *Furniture Music: The Phonograph as Furniture, 1900–1930* (2006), p. 303.

2 *Sounds*, British Library online, sounds.bl.uk/Sound-recording-history/Equipment/029M-1XBIRSX1956X-0001V0.

3 Faire, *Making Home. Working-Class Perceptions of Space, Time and Material Culture in Family Life, 1900–1955* (1998), p. 128.

4 Oakley and Proudfoot, *His Master's Gramophone* (2011), p. 123. Jazz historian Francesco Martinelli first suggested to me that this may explain the popularity of arch-topped instruments, which were not at risk of this potentially damaging use. (Personal discussion, Siena, July 2017).

5 Gramophone and Typewriter Ltd, *Catalogue of 12-inch Monarch Records* (March 1904), front cover.

6 National Archives, *Events of 1901*, www.nationalarchives.gov.uk/pathways/census/events/polecon3.htm. This gives the average annual wage in 1900 as £42.7.0. Most working-class individuals would have earned less than this.

7 Gramophone Company, *New Gramophone Records* (December 1909), inside cover. The company supplied one to Queen Alexandra.

8 Gramophone and Typewriter Ltd, *Catalogue of Gramophone 7-inch Records* (April 1903), inside back cover. The cheapest model featured a single spring motor, the most expensive sported a triple spring version.

9 Gramophone and Typewriter Ltd, *To Meet Competition In Cheap Lines*, letter to dealers (October 1904).

10 Advertisement. *Penny Illustrated Paper* (18 January 1908), p. 47. The total cost of the instrument wasn't given.

11 *Sounds*, British Library online, sounds.bl.uk/Sound-recording-history/Equipment/029M-4XFROWX1988X-0001V0.

12 Cited in Barnett, *Furniture Music: The Phonograph as Furniture, 1900–1930* (2006), p. 315.

13 For a detailed exploration of record piracy, see Wile, *Record Piracy: the attempts of the sound recording industry to protect itself against unauthorised copying, 1890–1978* (1985), pp. 18–40. Also see the early chapters of Heylin, *Bootleg: the secret history of the other recording industry* (1995).

14 Heylin, *Bootleg: the secret history of the other recording industry* (1995), p. 24.

15 Sutton, *Black Swan Carusos and Other Pirate Tales (1898–1951)*, 78records.wordpress.com/2017/12/01/black-swan-carusos-and-other-pirate-tales-1898-1951/.

16 Martland, *Business History of the Gramophone Company Ltd 1897–1918* (1992), p. 155.

17 *Early British Disc Record Labels*, http://early78s.uk/. This site has a plethora of information about record labels of the mechanical recording period.

18 Gramophone and Typewriter Company, *New Gramophone Records* (November 1907), back cover.

19 'Gramophone Records and Mme Melba', *The Times* (10 December 1904), p. 4. Mme Melba was named with the company as bringing the prosecution, but there's no indication that she took any active role.

20 'The Merchandise Marks Act', *The Times* (28 November 1905), p. 4. The court dismissed the case.

21 'High Court of Justice', *The Times* (6 July 1910), p. 3.

22 Advertisement, *The Times* (19 October 1910), p. 6.

23 Gramophone and Typewriter, *Supplement to the Catalogue of Gramophone Records* (March 1904), pp. 1–5.

24 'A Gramophone Concert', *The Times* (2 March 1909), p. 12.

25 *The Times* (5 October 1909), p. 11.

26 'Notes from the Emerald Isle', *Talking Machine World* (15 September 1906), p. 39.

27 *Launceston Examiner* (1 January 1898), p. 7.

28 Gramophone and Typewriter Ltd, *Special Supplementary List of Gramophone Records Made by the Staff Band of the Salvation Army* (undated); Columbia Records, *Columbia Records Catalogue 1916–17*, p. 27. Booth died in 1912, so was presumably unaware of this competition.

29 *The Times* (24 January 1908), p. 13.

30 *Talking Machine World* (15 July 1905), p. 1.

31 Gramophone and Typewriter Ltd, *Health In Play for Children* (undated).

32 *Belfast Newsletter* (20 December 1900), p. 5.

33 'Political Notes', *The Times* (23 July 1909), p. 12.

34 HMV, *Catalogue of Records of Unique and Historical Interest, Series 2* (1925), p. 66.

35 'Wilful Damage', *The Times* (28 February 1907), p. 17. The Mutual Reform Party, established in 1906, was allied to the Conservatives. Mr Gardner was fined 10s and ordered to pay £2.10.0, an amount equal to the damage he caused.

36 *Hansard*, 6 March 1903, vol. 119 cc27-59.

37 *Hansard*, 24 April 1907, vol. 173 cc136-175.

38 Westphal, 'Paris Opera Unearths 100-year-old Recordings by Melba, Caruso, Others', *Playbill* (18 December 2007), www.playbill.com/article/paris-opera-unearths-100-year-old-recordings-by-melba-caruso-others. The recordings are available on the internet at expositions.bnf.fr/voix/index.htm.

39 'Melba's Stories of Herself', *The Times* (5 May 1921), p. 7.

40 Lucy Wright PhD, interview (27 June 2018).

41 Grainger made recordings on an Edison-Bell 'Standard' phonograph, beginning in the summer of 1906. See Grainger, *Collecting with the Phonograph* (1908), pp. 147–242.

42 Greig, *Joseph Taylor of Lincolnshire: a biography of a singer* (2004), pp. 386–392.

43 Greig states that Taylor recorded nine songs, in June and July of 1908. In his May 1908 article Grainger listed 12 songs which he claimed Taylor had already recorded for the Gramophone Company—see Grainger, *Collecting with the Phonograph* (1908), p. 153.

44 Harry Cox (1885–1971) would record dozens of songs and make many TV appearances. See Young, *Electric Eden: unearthing Britain's visionary music* (2011), p. 107.

45 *The Times* (28 October 1905), p. 6. The 'effects' weren't described.

46 'Walking Through A Wall', *The Times* (17 June 1914), p. 6.

47 'Wingman', 'Theatre Topics', *Burnley Express* (30 June 1923), p. 13: *Birmingham Daily Gazette* (8 February 1956), p. 4.

48 Wells, *Marriage* (1912).

49 Wodehouse, *Mike* (1909). The gramophone episode is in chapters 5 and 6.

50 Galsworthy, *The Inn of Tranquillity: Studies and Essays* (2016, originally published 1910) p. 1.

51 Federation of Recorded Music Societies, www.thefrms.co.uk/latesthistory.htm. The City of London Phonograph and Gramophone Society claims that the first such organisation began in 1911 (see www.clpgs.org.uk/about-us.html).

52 Gramophone and Typewriter Ltd, *A Constant Money-Earner: the latest Penny-In-The-Slot Gramophone* (undated). The instrument was supplied with a special sound box that enabled the horn to be turned in any direction and with a box of 400 needles, barely four days' supply if the machine was achieving its maximum financial potential.

53   Sousa, 'The Menace of Mechanical Music', *Appleton's Magazine* (September 1906), pp. 278–84.
54   'Legalised Peace Disturbers', *The Times* (17 December 1908), p. 15.
55   C.L.G., 'The Decline of Domestic Music', *The Spectator* (26 May 1906), pp. 830–831. According to C.L.G., 'so-called Hungarian' bands posed a particular threat to professional musicians as they were becoming popular at private musical parties even though such a band was '...more notable for the brilliance of its uniform than its playing.'
56   Advertisement, *Daily Mail* (10 October 1903), p. 1.

Chapter 4

1   *Hansard*, HC Deb 26 April 1911 vol. 24 cc1881-924.
2   Needles were made of fibre, thorn or steel and discs contained abrasive material. The intention was to wear down the needle as it played to ensure a close fit between needle and groove to maximise sound quality. The downside was that needles wore quickly into the groove and could cause damage if used to play other discs.
3   I'm indebted to Lewis Durham, of rock band Kitty, Daisy and Lewis, for this information.
4   'Woman's Realm', *Diss Express* (13 April 1928), p. 8.
5   Odeon Records, *Orange Label catalogue 26* (1912) p. 3.
6   Leech-Wilkinson, *The Changing Sound of Music: Approaches to studying recorded musical performances* (2009), Section 3.1.
7   *Sounds*, British Library online, sounds.bl.uk/Sound-recording-history/Equipment/029M-29XFROWX1988-0001V0.
8   Gramophone Company Catalogue (April 1903).
9   'Woman's Record Swim', Supplement to the *Poverty Bay Herald* (19 October 1912), p. 3. Smith broke the record in August 1912. A few days later she made an unsuccessful attempt to swim the English Channel.
10   'The Greatest Lady Swimmer in The World', Unidentified newspaper clipping (1912).
11   National Archives online, *Entertaining the Penguins*, discovery.nationalarchives.gov.uk/details/r/C14233827.
12   One of Scott's gramophones is now part of the EMI archive (see www.emiarchivetrust.org/captain-scotts-gramophone/).
13   Science Museum online, *Barnett Samuel and Sons Limited*, collection.sciencemuseum.org.uk/people/cp126679/barnett-samuel-and-sons-limited.
14   Samuel, *Decca Days: the career of Wilfred Sampson Samuel, 1886–1958* (1987–88), pp. 235–274. Edgar Samuel (Wilfred's son) gives a detailed history of the Samuel family and the business.
15   Advertisement. *The Times* (19 July 1889), p. 16. Challen and Son of Oxford Street sold (and claimed to have patented) the device, advertising regularly in the pages of *The Times* from 1886 to 1889.
16   'The Decca Story', *The Times* (12 March 1957), p. 14.
17   Advertisements, *The Times* (13 November 1917), p .11; (18 October 1918), p. 10. Barnett Samuels soon set up the Dulcephone Company to sell its portable, which it then named simply as the *Decca*.
18   Samuel, *Decca Days: the career of Wilfred Sampson Samuel, 1886–1958* (1987–88), p. 248. One of life's intriguing but ultimately unimportant coincidences?

19 HMV, *Catalogue of Records* (November 1914), p. 170. Each disc cost 5/6d. Lord Roberts died on 14 November 1914, shortly before the catalogue was printed. The catalogue refers to him as 'The Late.'

20 HMV, *His Master's Voice New Records* (February 1915), p. 17.

21 Pathé, *Pathé Rooster double-sided discs* (1917–18), pp. 19–20. At some point the song lost one of its *Long*'s, but by this time it was clearly associated with the armed forces.

22 Columbia Records, *Columbia Records Catalogue 1916–17*, pp. 5–14.

23 'He Wrote the Songs Britain Sang', *The Bulletin* (23 February 1953), p. 3. Blighty was a slang term for Britain.

24 Zonophone Records, *Zonophone Records Complete Catalogue* (1917), pp. 43–44.

25 Columbia Records, *Columbia Records Catalogue 1916–17*, p. 41.

26 HMV, 'His Master's Voice' New Records for December 1918, p. 13.

27 *Talking Machine World* (15 January 1919), p. 117.

28 Hoffmann, *Encyclopedia of Recorded Sound* (2005), p. 847. Hoffmann states that Will died on 5 November 1918.

29 *Talking Machine World* (15 January 1919), p.117.

30 Martland, *Business History of the Gramophone Company Ltd 1897–1918* (1992), pp. 420–21.

31 Sterling, 'Conditions in the Talking Machine Industry in Britain', *Talking Machine World* (15 April 1918), p. 55.

32 In the USA, songs such as 'I Didn't Raise My Boy to be a Soldier' did appear and possibly helped to stoke opposition to the country's entry into the war.

33 Advertisement, *The Times* (18 October 1918), p. 10.

34 HMV, 'His Master's Voice' *Catalogue of Records* (November 1914), pp. 165–70.

35 In Arras, *The Sketch* (16 October 1918), p. 91. The poem was credited to Ernest C. Crisp. Philip Gibbs was knighted at the end of the war.

36 Advertisement, *The Times* (28 May 1919), p. 7.

37 'First Gramophone Record', *The Times* (21 July 1921), p. 7.

38 Stone (writing as C. R. S.), 'A Decca Romance', *The Gramophone* (August 1923), p. 56.

39 *Talking Machine World* (15 January 1919), pp. 117–18.

40 This gramophone was sold at auction by Denhams of Sussex for £125 on an unspecified date (see denhams.com/lots/search/gramophone).

41 The case was designed by Corporal Crutchley, made by Cpl Boarder, possibly from wooden propellers. The instrument is now part of the Australian War Memorial collection, but none of the three men appear to have been in the Australian forces (see www.awm.gov.au/index.php/collection/C119201).

42 Johns, *Biggles In France* (1935). The story is told in Chapter 19, *Getting A Gramophone*. Johns was a bomber pilot during the final months of the Great War.

43 'The Cockney in Hospital', *The Spectator*, 30 June 1917, pp. 9–11.

44 *Talking Machine World* (15 January 1919), p. 118.

45 Sassoon, *Dead Musicians*, 1918. In his original manuscript Sassoon wrote 'smash,' not 'stop.' See the First World War Poetry Digital Archive, ww1lit.nsms.ox.ac.uk/ww1lit/collections/item/9789.

46 *Talking Machine World* (15 September 1918), p. 37.

47 Sterling, 'Conditions in the Talking Machine Industry in Britain', *Talking Machine World* (15 April 1918), p. 55.

48 See Martland, *Business History of the Gramophone Company Ltd 1897–1918* (1992), Chapter 9, for a detailed study of the impact of the Great War on the Gramophone Company.

49 *Hansard*, HC Deb 17 November 1914 vol. 68 cc323-4.

50 *Talking Machine World* (15 February 1919), p. 132.

51 *Talking Machine World* (15 July 1919), p. 158. The East-to-West crossing was the first by an airship.

52 Advertisement, *The Times* (19 July 1917), p. 3.

53 Cooper, *The Perfect Portable Gramophone* (2003), p. 21.

54 *Hansard*, HC Deb 31 May 1911 vol. 26 cc1136-55.

55 *Hansard*, HC Deb 15 February 1911 vol. 21 cc1067-179.

56 *Talking Machine World* (16 July 1919), p. 168.

57 HMV, *The Catalogue of Records* (1919), pp. 72–3.

58 Brinton, *Carpets* (1919), p. 30.

59 *Talking Machine World* (15 August 1914), p. 47. The *Linguaphone* system is still in use.

60 'Noise', *The Spectator* (12 November 1921), p. 9.

61 Joyce, *Ulysses* (1922), p. 109.

Chapter 5

1 HMV, *The Catalogue of Records* (1919), p. 78. Cohan wrote the song in 1917. See the Library of Congress article on the song at www.loc.gov/item/ihas.200000015/.

2 Brunn, *The Story of the Original Dixieland Jazz Band* (1963), pp. 64–65. LaRocca is not the most reliable source of information, but it's a good tale. Columbia released both tunes later in 1919, when it became clear that the ODJB was gathering a fan base.

3 Brunn, *The Story of the Original Dixieland Jazz Band*, pp. 66–68; pp. 120–26.

4 'Death of Lieut. James Europe', *Talking Machine World* (15 May 1919), p. 154. Europe died after returning to the USA, stabbed during what the magazine called 'an altercation with a member of this famous band.'

5 For more on the American military bands in Europe, see Vernhettes, *Commemoration of the Centenary of the arrival of the African-American military bands in France during World War I* (2017), pp. 3-54.

6 Advertisement, *The Times* (1 July 1919), p. 24.

7 Advertisement, *The Times* (5 July 1919), p. 22; 'Syncopation and Sentiment', *The Times* (9 December 1919), p. 12.

8 HMV, *The Catalogue of Records* (September 1919), pp. ix–li.

9 *Hullo America!* The Guide to Musical Theatre, www.guidetomusicaltheatre.com/shows_h/hulloamerica.htm. The revue featured Janis, Stanley Lupino and, for a time, Maurice Chevalier.

10 *Hansard*, HC Deb 08 April 1919 vol. 114 cc1889-956.

11 *Hansard*, HC Deb 06 November 1919 vol. 120 cc1707-94.

12 *Talking Machine World* (15 April 1919) p. 156.

13 HMV, *New Records of Dance Music*. The catalogue is undated but references to the Victory Ball suggest it was published later in 1919 or perhaps early 1920.

14 Irene Castle (named in the catalogue as 'Mrs Vernon Castle') was half of the famous dance pairing of Vernon and Irene Castle. Her husband Vernon was born in Norwich and died during a training flight towards the end of the Great War after serving with the RFC. Henri (or Henry) de Bray was a dancer who appeared in West End productions. The Tickle-Toe was a ragtime tune written by Louis Hirsch in around 1918.

15 Zonophone Records, *Complete Catalogue* 1922), p. 12.

16 Martinelli, email interview (16 June 2018).
17 Abravanel, *Americanizing Britain* (2012), p. 55.
18 Taylor, *Bright Young People* (2008), p. 113.
19 Décharné, *Vulgar Tongues. An alternative History of English Slang* (2016), pp. 220–223.
20 Jackson, *Rhythm Style, Series 2* (c. 1941–2), pp. 2–5 and 32.
21 Taylor, *Bright Young People* (2008), p. 135.
22 *Merchandising Survey of Great Britain* (1930): Volume VII Gramophones, p. 71. 15.3 per cent of respondents expressed no preference for any particular style.
23 HMV, 'His Master's Voice' Record Catalogue (1922), p. 14.
24 Aeolian Vocalion Records, *Vocalion Records Bulletin No. 20* (February 1923), p. 10
25 'Gramophone Notes', *The Times* (24 August 1925), p. 8.
26 Nicholson, *Among the Bohemians: Experiments in Living 1900–1939* (2003), p. 257.
27 Pereyra, *Jack Hylton Discography*, 2007, static1.squarespace. com/static/536c00ede4b09724c107b00b/t/536c0fdbe4b0c3c1 5ef04dd6/1399590875032/hylton_discog.pdf.
28 Information on the store is taken from 'New Gramophone House', *The Times* (15 July 1921), p. 8; 'First Gramophone Record', *The Times* (21 July 1921), p. 7; 'James', '363 Oxford Street', www.hmv.com/music/363-oxford-street-hmv-comes-home.
29 'First Gramophone Record', *The Times* (21 July 1921), p. 7.
30 'A New Violinist', *The Times* (6 May 1920), p. 14. The records were on the Victor label.
31 'The Gramophone Habit: popular records now unpopular', *The Times* (22 July 1921), p. 7.
32 'The Future of the Gramophone', *The Times* (23 July 1921), p. 8.
33 Aeolian Vocalion Records, *Catalogue* (December 1921), p. 30.
34 Aeolian Vocalion Records, *Catalogue* (December 1921), p. 56.
35 'Music of the Holidays', *The Times* (1 January 1921), p. 8.
36 Wright, interview (27 June 2018).
37 'The Gramophone in Education', *The Times* (20 April 1922), p. 10.
38 HMV, *His Master's Voice Records of Unique and Historical Interest* (Undated, probably 1927), p. 55.
39 *Merchandising Survey of Great Britain, 1930*, pp. 1 and 61.
40 Leech-Wilkinson, *The Changing Sound of Music: Approaches to Studying Recorded Musical Performances* (2009) Section 1.2.2. Leech-Wilkinson notes that the first gramophone magazine, Germany's *Phonographische Zeitschrift* began record reviews in 1905 or 1906.
41 'Gramophone Music', *The Times* (23 February 1922), p. 10.
42 *The Gramophone* (April 1923). The magazine is now known simply as *Gramophone*.
43 'Compton Mackenzie', *The Scotsman online* (11 April 2017), www.scotsman.com/200voices/literary-titans/compton-mackenzie-scots-nationalist-whisky-galore/.
44 'Gramophone Music', *The Times*, 23 February 1922, p. 10.
45 Cumella, interview (21 March 2018).
46 'Linguists and the Gramophone', *The Times* (28 February 1922), p. 10.
47 'Madrigals on the Gramophone', *The Times* (9 March 1922), p. 10.
48 'A Gramophone Concert', *The Times* (6 April 1922), p. 15. *The Times* articles often referenced HMV records.

49 'Gramophone Notes', *The Times* (12 August 1924), p. 10.

50 'Gramophone Notes', *The Times* (22 September 1925), p. 12.

51 Scholes, *The First Book of the Gramophone Record* (1924); *The Spectator* (22 August 1924), p. 23.

52 Jackson, *Rhythm Style Series No. 2* (undated), pp. 1–15.

53 Benson, *Queen Lucia* (2014, originally published 1920), pp. 131–132.

54 Benson, *Dodo Wonders* (1921), p. 260.

55 Conan Doyle, *The Adventure of the Mazarin Stone* (2009, originally published 1921), p. 1021.

56 'How Gourlay Died', *The Times* (20 June 1921), p. 10.

57 *Merchandising Survey of Great Britain, 1930*. Volume VII: Gramophones, p. 63.

58 Jones, *The Gramophone Company: An Anglo-American Multinational, 1898–1931* (1985), p. 98.

59 'Talking Pictures', *The Times* (20 January 1914), p. 8.

60 Advertisement, *The Times* (21 January 1914), p. 1.

61 Pereyra, *Jack Hylton Discography*, static1.squarespace.com/static/536c00ede4b09724c107b00b/t/536c0fdbe4b0c3c1 5ef04dd6/1399590875032/hylton_discog.pdf.

62 Hylton, 'Why I Play Jazz', *Radio Times* (27 November 1925), p. 438.

Chapter 6

1 *Merchandising Survey of Great Britain* (1930) Volume VII: Gramophones, pp. 8–11 and 63.

2 *Talking Machine World* (15 December 1921), p. 164.

3 Sturdy, *Talking Machine World* (15 August 1923), p. 158.

4 Advertisement, *The Times* (2 March 1921), p. 10.

5 *Talking Machine World* (15 December 1921), pp. 162–63.

6 *Talking Machine World* (15 January 1925), p. 186.

7 Advertisement, *The Gramophone* (June 1923), p. 42.

8 *Merchandising Survey of Great Britain* (1930) Volume VII: Gramophones, p. 63.

9 C. R. S., 'The Flame-Phone', *The Gramophone* (October 1923), p. 89.

10 HMV, *'His Master's Voice' Catalogue of Instruments* (1925), pp. 2–15.

11 'The Test of Endurance', *The Gramophone* (September 1923), p. 71.

12 'The Caxton Hall Tests', *The Gramophone* (August 1925), pp. 111–12.

13 Advertisement, *The Times* (6 June 1921), p. 9.

14 Callisthenes, 'The Lure of the 'Gadget', *The Times* (6 May 1924), p. 12. Callisthenes was the pseudonym of someone from Selfridge's marketing department or advertising agents, writing a daily column that promoted the store.

15 Advertisement, *The Gramophone* (July 1924), p. ix.

16 Callisthenes, 'Gramophone Records by Telephone', *The Times* (1 July 1924), p. 14.

17 Bouckley, *From Marconi and the Transistor Radio to DAB*, home.bt.com/tech-gadgets/from-marconi-and-the-transistor-radio-to-dab-the-history-of-radio-in-the-uk-11364015764901.

18 Engineering and Technology History Wiki. 'Milestones: First Wireless Radio Broadcast by Reginald A. Fessenden, 1906' (January 2016), ethw.org/Milestones:First_Wireless_Radio_Broadcast_by_Reginald_A._Fessenden,_1906.

19 Proudfoot, email (21 March 2018).

20 Bouckley, *From Marconi and the Transistor Radio to DAB*.
21 McCarthy, *Development of the BBC A.M. Transmitter Network* (May 2007), www.mds975.co.uk/Content/bbc_transmitter_development_clive_mccarthy.pdf. Accessed 20 December 2017.
22 BBC Genome, genome.ch.bbc.co.uk/page/ d58cef702a6a4b26adb3e9df7195cbd4.
23 Burrows, *Radio Times* (28 September 1923), p. 1. *Bradshaw* was the official railway timetable.
24 Sturdy, *Talking Machine World* (15 August 1923), p. 158; Sturdy, *Talking Machine World* (15 September 1923), p. 181.
25 *Radio Times* (2 October 1925), p. 51.
26 'Musical Resources: gramophone records', p. 1. BBC Archive C1/99. Archivist Kate O'Brien believes the author was David Price.
27 Price, *Gramophone Library History 1922–1992* (undated).
28 'Musical Resources: gramophone records', p. 6. BBC Archive C1/99.
29 Granville Soames, 'Letter', *The Times* (17 November 1925), p. 21.
30 *Merchandising Survey of Great Britain*, Volume VII: Gramophones (1930), p. 84.
31 *Hansard*, HC Deb 24 July 1933 vol. 280 cc2235-309.
32 *The Gramophone* (June 1924), p. 2.
33 *The Gramophone* (August 1927), p. 86.
34 Price, *Gramophone Library History 1922–1992* (undated), p. 8.
35 Decca K.714.
36 *The Times* (26 July 1929), p. 12.
37 BBC internal Memo dated 3 October 1928. Christopher Stone Talks File 1: 1928–1944. BBC Archive 910.
38 BBC internal memos, dated 7, 10 and 15 March 1932. BBC Archive, *Gramophone Library History: gramophone company agreements*, BBC Archive S333/2/1.
39 *The Times* (23 August 1933), p. 8.
40 *Hansard*, HC Deb 29 March 1923 vol. 162 cc743-4W.
41 *Hansard*, HC Deb 01 July 1924 vol. 175 cc1131-2.
42 *Hansard*, HC Deb 03 March 1925 vol. 181 c259W.
43 *Hansard*, HL Deb 13 July 1925 vol. 62 cc18-23.
44 *Hansard*, HC Deb 26 June 1925 vol. 185 cc1970-9.
45 *Hansard*, HC Deb 31 July 1925 vol. 187 cc867-9.
46 After the BBC began broadcasting, amateurs were restricted to frequencies below 100m while the BBC broadcast at above 220m: *Amateur Wireless*, 17 March 1934, p. 278.
47 *Hansard*, HC Deb 20 July 1925 vol. 186 cc1857-979.
48 'Unlicensed Broadcasting', *The Times* (14 January 1936), p. 16.
49 'Post Office and Amateur Transmitters', *The Times* (4 February 1927), p. 8.
50 'Private Radio Station Located', *The Times* (6 March 1934), p. 12.
51 'All About Britain's "Pirate" Broadcaster', *Amateur Wireless* (17 March 1934), p. 278.
52 'Unlicensed Broadcasting', *The Times* (5 November 1934), p. 9. This report named the older brother as George, not Gerald.
53 *Merchandising Survey of Great Britain* (1930) Volume VII: Gramophones, p. 6.
54 'Musical Resources: gramophone records', BBC Archive C1/99.
55 Symes, *A sound education: the gramophone and the classroom in the United Kingdom and the United States, 1920–1940* (2004), pp. 167–174.

56   *The Gramophone in School*, Special Educational Series No.4, Gramophone Company, April 1930.

57   Symes, *A sound education: the gramophone and the classroom in the United Kingdom and the United States, 1920–1940* (2004), p. 169.

58   'Education by Gramophone', *The Spectator* (1 December 1928), p. 27.

59   The IMDB website lists 43 film and TV credits for Sarony (See www.imdb.com/name/nm0765468/?ref_=ttfc_fc_cl_t37).

Chapter 7

1   Martland, *Business History of the Gramophone Company Ltd 1897–1918* (1992), p. 380.

2   Huffman, *Development of Electrical Recording*, www.stokowski.org/Development_of_Electrical_Recording.htm. It's doubtful if an acoustic recording of the service could have been made however, because of the size of the venue and the complexity of the task.

3   Maxfield and Harrison, *Methods of High Quality Recording and Reproducing of Music and Speech Based on Telephone Research* (1926).

4   Maxfield and Harrison, *Methods of High Quality Recording and Reproducing of Music and Speech Based on Telephone Research* (1926), pp. 6–7.

5   Advertisement, *The Sphere* (4 May 1929), no page number.

6   Leech-Wilkinson, *The Changing Sound of Music: Approaches to Studying Recorded Musical Performances* (2009), Section 1.2.2.65

7   Advertisement, *Punch* (23 November 1927), no page number.

8   Advertisement, *Punch* (30 November 1927), no page number.

9   *Hansard*, HC Deb 20 June 1932 vol. 267 cc848-66.

10   Advertisement, *Punch* (8 May 1929), no page number.

11   Taylor, email (31 May 2018). Of course, in 1943 there was no television service in Britain, which may explain the low value placed on the TV.

12   *Merchandising Survey of Great Britain* (1930) Volume VII: Gramophones, p. 25.

13   The discussion of speed setting is on the first record, serial number SH1E, in a series of four sides (on two discs) which Shaw recorded for Linguaphone.

14   *Hansard*, HC Deb 02 February 1932 vol. 261 cc39-122. Buchan's books include *The Thirty-Nine Steps*.

15   The gramophone is part of the National Trust's Felbrigg Hall collection.

16   'Clay Cross Goes to the Polls', *Nottingham Evening Post* (1 September 1933), p. 1. Henderson was Labour leader on three occasions and won the by-election. In 1934 he won the Nobel Peace Prize.

17   Melly, *Owning Up, The Trilogy* (2000), pp. 16–18.

18   Melly, *Owning Up, The Trilogy* (2000), p. 386 and p. 256.

19   Cutler, 'Plunderphonia' in Cox and Warner, eds., *Audio Culture: Reading in Modern Music* (2004) p. 145.

20   Langdon-Davies, 'Gramophone Notes', *The Spectator* (28 September 1929), p. 11.

21   *The Gramophone* (November 1936), p. 230.

22   The original postcard was first produced in 1918, so may have been discontinued by 1929. See *TuckDB Postcards* (tuckdb.org/) for a detailed history of the company.

23   Mackenzie, 'Our Symposium', *The Gramophone* (December 1926), pp. 262–265.

24   Ernest Lough Obituary, *The Guardian online* (24 February 2000), www.theguardian.com/news/2000/feb/24/guardianobituaries.

25 Mackenzie, 'Quarterly Review of Records', *The Gramophone* (July 1927), p. 43.

26 HMV, *'His Master's Voice' Records of Unique and Historical Interest*. Catalogue No. 2. Version 1 (Undated, probably 1927–8), p. 2.

27 The Gramophone Company and Columbia had merged by this time to become Electrical and Musical Industries Ltd (EMI) but the two familiar names continued to be used.

28 'Gramophone Company's New Studios', *The Times* (13 November 1931), p. 12.

29 It's likely that it was the writer and the actor. Shaw was notably interested in the gramophone. In 1934 Hardwicke (now Sir Cedric) recorded an appeal, to be shown in cinemas, for the Cinematograph Benevolent Fund urging people to buy a gramophone record specially recorded for the fund by 24 stars of stage and screen (See *British Pathé* www.britishpathe.com/video/introducing-sir-cedric-hardwicke/query/Benevolent).

30 The studios stand close to the junction of Abbey Road, Garden Road and Grove End Road. The crossing is slightly to the north of this junction, on Abbey Road itself.

31 Langdon-Davies, 'The Gramophone', *The Spectator* (31 August 1929), pp. 272–273.

32 Rubery, *From Shell Shock to Shellac: The Great War, Blindness and Britain's Talking Book Library* (2014), pp. 6–10. Fraser became the Chairman of St Dunstan's at the age of 24.

33 The gospel recording was sponsored by the British and Foreign Bible Society, which aimed to promote Christianity. See Rubery, *From Shell Shock to Shellac* (2014), p. 11.

34 Of the fifty-five, thirty-one were recorded in the USA, which had its own talking books service. See Rubery, *From Shell Shock to Shellac* (2014), p. 11.

35 Rubery, *Audiobook History*, audiobookhistory.wordpress.com/.

36 Rubery, *From Shell Shock to Shellac* (2014), p. 16.

37 Sayers, *The Second Omnibus of Crime* (1932) p. 9.

38 Langdon-Davies, 'Gramophone Notes', *The Spectator* (10 October 1931), p. 453.

39 Adorno, *The Curves of the Needle* (translated by Levin) (1990), pp. 50 and 54. Originally published as *Nadelkurven* in *Musikblätter des Anbruch* 10:47–50 (February 1928).

40 Langdon-Davies, 'The Gramophone', *The Spectator* (31 August 1929), p. 273. Lester's recording is on Homochord D1336.

41 Bankes, 'The Ordeal of Being Married to Augustus John', *The Spectator online* (6 May 2017), www.spectator.co.uk/2017/05/the-ordeal-of-being-married-to-augustus-john/.

42 The group was the house band for Durium Records, a label that produced cheap discs of durium resin coating on a cardboard base. The discs were brown in colour.

43 Harry Roy and his Bat Club Boys, *Pussy! (My Girl's Pussy)*, Oriole Record P104 (1931).

44 Bogan (1897–1948) also recorded as Bessie Jackson.

45 *Hansard*, HC Deb 15 May 1930 vol. 238 cc2072-3W2072W.

46 Nice, 'Elgar: Falstaff: Symphonic Study in C minor, Op. 68', BBC Radio 3 (8 October 2016), www.bbc.co.uk/programmes/p04bdt5t.

47 Encyclopedia Britannica online, *Sir Edward Elgar* (undated), www.britannica.com/biography/Edward-Elgar.

48   Martland, *Business History of the Gramophone Company Ltd 1897–1918*
      (1992), p. 371.
49   Advertisement for Elgar's Falstaff, *The Times* (8 June 1932), p. 12.
50   'The Musician's Gramophone: Elgar's "Falstaff"', *The Times* (28 June 1932),
      p. 12.
51   'The Musician's Gramophone', *The Times* (28 June 1932), p. 12.
52   Nice, BBC *Record Review* Podcast (undated), www.bbc.co.uk/programmes/
      p04bdq0w.

Chapter 8

1   Pallett, *Al Bowlly*. Memory Lane, www.memorylane.org.uk/al-bowlly.html.
      Bowlly was forty-three years old when he died.
 2   Rust and Debus, *The Complete Entertainment Discography, from the
      mid-1890s to 1942* (1973), p. 102. Bowlly and Mesene recorded the song in
      London on 2 April 1941. It was released as HMV BD-922, backed with 'Nicky
      The Greek'. Bowlly's list in this discography runs from pp. 65–102.
 3   'Battles by Broadcast', *The Times* (24 May 1938), p. 17.
 4   *Hansard*, HC Deb 04 April 1939 vol. 345 cc2633-752.
 5   'Advice on A.R.P.', *The Times* (2 September 1939), p. 11.
 6   HMV online, www.hmv.com/music/363-oxford-street-hmv-comes-home.
 7   *Hansard*, HC Deb 18 May 1939 vol. 347 cc1671-81.
 8   Advertisement, *The Times* (2 November 1939), p. 5.
 9   *Hansard*, HC Deb 11 October 1939 vol. 352 cc376-484. Mr Poole did not
      identify the performer.
10   *Radio Times* (4 September 1939), p. 3.
11   'Platterbug' (letter), *Radio Times* (8 September 1939), p. 9.
12   *Hansard*, HC Deb 28 May 1940 vol. 361 cc437-519.
13   *Radio Times* (1 March 1940), pp. 19–22 and 42–44. The Forces Service
      broadcast from 18 February 1940 to 26 February 1944: see *BBC Genome*,
      genome.ch.bbc.co.uk/schedules/forces/1940-03-09.
14   *Radio Times* (18 February 1940), p. 13.
15   Collins, *Souvenir of Oulton* (1995), p. 7. A copy can be viewed at the RAF
      Oulton museum at Blickling Hall.
16   Cutlack, *Tunnels, Colditz and Steve McQueen – Great Escapes at the IWM*
      (12 November 2004), www.culture24.org.uk/history-and-heritage/military-
      history/art24892.
17   *The Times* (2 November 1940), p. 6.
18   'Decca Record Company', *The Times* (30 October 1941), p. 9.
19   Pereyra, *Complete Jack Hylton Discography*, static1.squarespace.
      com/static/536c00ede4b09724c107b00b/t/536c0fdbe4b0c3c1
      5ef04dd6/1399590875032/hylton_discog.pdf.
20   Hylton became a successful theatre producer (See www.jackhylton.com/
      timeline/).
21   *The Times* (7 November 1939), p. 5: (24 January 1941), p. 6: (30 September
      1940), p. 2: (15 October 1940), p. 2.
22   BBC Internal Memo (30 May 1942), BBC Archives, R34/683.
23   '10,000,000 Gramophone Records Wanted', *The Times* (15 August 1942),
      p. 2. Presumably the stated labels were the only ones using an acceptable
      shellac mix.
24   Advertisement, *The Gramophone* (April 1944), inside cover.
25   Advertisement, *The Times* (3 November 1939), p. 7.

26   Advertisement, *The Times* (2 December 1939), p. 5. Piccaver was an operatic tenor, born in Long Sutton, Lincolnshire but brought up in the USA.

27   *Hansard*, HC Deb 11 December 1945 vol. 417 cc225-58.

28   Advertisement, *The Times* (7 June 1945), p. 3.

29   Advertisement, *The Times* (9 January 1940), p. 7.

30   Office for National Statistics, *Trends in births and deaths over the last century* (15 July 2015), visual.ons.gov.uk/birthsanddeaths/.

31   *Hansard*, HC Deb 13 May 1941 vol. 371 cc1067-8.

32   'Trading with the Enemy', *The Times* (28 January 1944), p. 2.

33   Troops stationed in Iceland received such an extensive package in 1940. *Hansard*, HC Deb 16 October 1940 vol. 365 c710W.

34   Stone (letter), *The Times* (1 September 1942), p. 5. The nightingale song was released in late 1942 as HMV BD-1016, the air battle in 1940 as Decca SP-35.

35   *The Times* (19 August 1942), p. 6.

36   Advertisement, *The Times* (1 October 1942), p. 2.

37   'The Two Ways in Tunisia', *The Times* (10 April 1943), p. 8.

38   Melly, *Owning Up, The Trilogy* (2000), p. 313.

39   'Voices Across the Sea', *The Times* (28 June 1943), p. 5.

40   Pennell, *Morocco Since 1830: A History* (2000), p. 258.

41   Foot, *SOE In France: An account of the work of the Special Operations Executive in France, 1940–44* (2004), p. 340.

42   'Work of the U.S. Red Cross', *The Times* (2 September 1943), p. 2.

43   Hogenboom, *How the GI influx shaped Britain's view of Americans*, BBC News Magazine online, 3 November 2012, www.bbc.co.uk/news/magazine-20160819.

44   Open University, *The V-Disc Programme*, www.open.edu/openlearn/history-the-arts/culture/music-and-its-media/content-section-4.1.

45   See archive.org/details/V-Discs1-991943-1944 for a complete V-Disc discography. Some discs came from radio broadcasts, others from studio sessions.

46   Martinelli, email (16 June 2018).

47   Spragg, *V-Discs* (2013), p. 5.

48   Rust and Debus, *The Complete Entertainment Discography, from the mid-1890s to 1942* (1973), p. 101.

49   Lasser, *America's Songs II: songs from the 1890s to the post-war years* (2014), p. 172.

Chapter 9

1   *Hansard*, HC Deb 09 April 1946 vol. 421 cc1803-68. Dalton included radiograms as well as standalone gramophones.

2   In August 1945 there were around 5,000,000 men and women in the British armed forces, by April 1946 there were 1,900,000. *Hansard*, HC Deb 30 April 1946 vol. 422 cc149-58.

3   *Hansard*, HL Deb 26 June 1946 vol. 141 cc1173-218.

4   Engineering and Technology Wiki, *Decca Records*, ethw.org/Decca_Records.

5   Buck, interview (12 April 2018).

6   Cartwright, *Going for a Song: A Chronicle of the UK Record Shop* (2018), p. 225.

7   Cartwright, *Going for a Song: A Chronicle of the UK Record Shop* (2018), pp. 32–3.

8   *Morpeth Herald & Reporter* (23 March 1951), p. 7. The reporter doesn't suggest that Mr Barnston was in any way dubious in his library activity, but neither is there any mention of his charges.

9   Cowley, *West Indian Gramophone Records in Britain, 1927–1950* (1985), pp. 1–2.

10 Pine, interview (17 May 2018).

11 Beardsley and Leech-Wilkinson, *A Brief History of Recording to ca. 1950*, www.charm.rhul.ac.uk/history/p20_4_1.html.

12 'New Broadcasting House', *The Times* (13 May 1932), p. 11.

13 Beardsley and Leech-Wilkinson, *A Brief History of Recording to ca. 1950*, www.charm.rhul.ac.uk/history/p20_4_1.html.

14 Phillips, *First Hand: Bing Crosby and the Recording Revolution*, ethw.org/First-Hand:Bing_Crosby_and_the_Recording_Revolution.

15 'Electrical & Musical Industries', *Times* (19 December 1949), p. 9.

16 'Vulcanite or Wire', *The Times* (20 October 1950), p. 6.

17 There were, of course, other options. Speech recordings could rotate at 16 rpm, 10-inch albums were produced and some 7-inch discs rotated at 33⅓ rpm, fitting two tracks on each side and becoming known as EPs (Extended Play).

18 *A Short History of Vinyl Records*, www.vinyland.com/index.php?main_page=vinyl&language=en.

19 Beardsley and Leech-Wilkinson, *A Brief History of Recording*, www.charm.rhul.ac.uk/history/p20_4_1.html.

20 *A Short History of Vinyl Records*, www.vinyland.com/index.php?main_page=vinyl&language=en.

21 The company made the announcement on the cover of *The Gramophone*, October 1952. Decca's MP discs were superseded by the EP (extended play) 7-inch, 33⅓rpm, discs.

22 Advertisement, *The Times* (24 February 1953), p. 7.

23 'Three Speed Music', *The Times* (7 August 1953), p. 2. The 'huge holes' enabled 45s to be played in jukeboxes: plastic or card inserts reduced the holes to the size needed to play on home gramophones.

24 '... and what of Decca?', *The Gramophone* (January 1954), inside cover; 'Announcing 45rpm records', *The Gramophone* (November 1954), inside cover.

25 The debate can be found at *Hansard*, HC Deb 15 June 1948 vol. 452 cc353-8. The Bill passed into law during 1948.

26 By the time the service closed in 1939 there were only about 20,000 sets, all in London and the home counties. *The Story of BBC Television*, www.bbc.co.uk/historyofthebbc/research/general/tvstory9.

27 'National Radio Exhibition', *The Times* (24 August 1938), p. 8. The Model 900's price was not given. The cheapest HMV television was 31 guineas, while the most expensive TV, the Scophony 24-inch, was £175.

28 *Radio Times* (7 June 1946), p. 4.

29 BBC online, *The Story of BBC Television*, www.bbc.co.uk/historyofthebbc/research/general/tvstory9.

30 Advertisement, *Punch* (28 September 1949, no page number).

31 'Lower Priced Television', *The Times* (7 September 1950), p. 2. The article did point out that TVs could be had for as little as £40.

32 BBC online, *The Story of BBC Television*. The UK population was around 52 million.

33 Mann, *September 22, 1955: Commercial television comes to Britain as ITV goes on air* (2017), home.bt.com/news/on-this-day/september-

22-1955-commercial-television-comes-to-britain-as-itv-starts-broadcasting-11364005683860. The first advertisement was for Gibbs SR toothpaste.

34 'Electrical & Musical Industries Ltd', *The Times* (12 December 1955), p. 15.

35 P. G., 'Mr F. W. Gaisberg', *The Times* (13 September 1951), p. 6. P. G. remains anonymous but claimed to have assisted Gaisberg in writing *Music on Record*.

36 Vacher, 'Ottilie Patterson Obituary', *Guardian Online* (8 July 2011), www.theguardian.com/music/2011/jul/08/otillie-patterson-blues-singer-obituary. Anne-Ottilie Patterson died in 2011, aged seventy-nine. At the time of writing, Barber is still performing.

Chapter 10

1 Advertisement, *The Times* (28 October 1948), p. 7. McGregor was a successful children's author.

2 Advertisement, *The Times* (26 March 1929), p. 9.

3 Advertisement, *The Times* (16 September 1931), p. 7.

4 Advertisement, *The Times* (4 November 1937), p. 10.

5 Lambert, *History of the Dansette*, www.dansettes.co.uk/history.htm (undated, accessed 8 March 2018).

6 Stanley, *Yeah, Yeah, Yeah: the story of modern pop* (2013), Prologue.

7 Lambert, *History of the Dansette*, www.dansettes.co.uk/history.htm (undated, accessed 8 March 2018).

8 Stanley, *Yeah, Yeah, Yeah: the story of modern pop* (2013), Chapter 1.

9 Lumley, 'Joanna Lumley's Diary', *The Times* (13 July 1983), p. 9.

10 Brophy, 'How Dansette failed in the big time', *The Times* (23 October 1969), p. 24.

11 'Adult "Spending Monopoly" Over', *The Times* (28 November 1958), p. 5.

12 Advertisement, *The Times* (16 March 1960), p. ix. 'Rhythm rock' seems to have been an invention of the advertising agency.

13 *Hansard*, HC Deb 25 June 1952 vol. 502 cc2374-91.

14 *Hansard*, HC Deb 22 May 1952 vol. 501 cc678-715.

15 'Report on the EMI Annual General Meeting', *The Times* (12 December 1955), p. 15.

16 Decca advertisement, *The Times* (13 March 1952), p. 7.

17 IM Needles advertisement, *The Gramophone*, November 1942, inside cover.

18 Dare (letter), *Jazz Journal* (April 1952), p. 22.

19 The November 1952 issue of *Jazz Journal* reviewed twenty-six 78's but only three LPs.

20 Delf, interview (14 May 2018).

21 'When Jazz Tries to Get Away from Itself', *The Times* (10 September 1960), p. 9.

22 Britten, V., BBC Gramophone Library Report (13 December 1963), BBC Archive S333/6/1.

23 Britten, V., BBC Internal Memo (12 May 1961), BBC Archive S333/5.

24 Britten, V., BBC Internal Memo (12 May 1961). BBC Archive S333/5.

25 Humphries, *Handling Edna: the unauthorised biography* (2010), p. 26.

26 See Cartwright, *Going for a Song: A Chronicle of the UK Record Shop* (2018) for discussion about many of these shops.

27 The Radio Norfolk show was broadcast live on 16 August 2018. Mrs Clarke phoned in, then we spoke on the telephone the following day.

28 The Cromer School discs, plus a few others on the Cromer Recording label, are listed at www.45worlds.com/78rpm/label/a-cromer-recording.

29   Advertisement. *Rugby Advertiser* (27 March 1951), p. 1.

30   *Hansard*, HC Deb 21 June 1956 vol. 554 cc1609-10; *Hansard*, HC Deb 02 August 1956 vol. 557 cc1571-2.

31   These examples, along with around forty others, can be found on *Actionable Offenses: Indecent Phonograph Recordings from the 1890s* (Archeophone Records, 2007).

32   'Comstock Arrests an Actor', *New York Times* (26 June 1896), p. 3.

33   The title reflects the name of White's Irish comedy character and the title of a saccharine waltz of a few years earlier, *Maggie Murphy's Home*.

34   National Public Radio, *Old, Lewd, Recordings Released on CD*, www.npr. org/templates/story/story.php?storyId=11131880. This broadcast states that Hunting was imprisoned, other sources state that he received a suspended sentence.

35   The London Calypso label was a subsidiary of London Records. The disc is CAY105.

36   'Marie Bryant's Song Riles So. African Minister; British Censors Laugh It Off', *The Afro-American* (13 June 1953), p. 6.

37   'List of banned music, 1938–1954'. BBC Archive, R19/940. This list of songs does not identify any artists, nor does it give reasons for most of the bans. For further discussion of the BBC and its record bans, see Leigh, S., 'Unfit for Auntie's airwaves: the artists censored by the BBC', *Independent Online*, www. independent.co.uk/arts-entertainment/music/features/unfit-for-aunties-airwaves-the-artists-censored-by-the-bbc-765106.html.

38   Winner, 'Focus on BBC Song-Banning', *New Musical Express* (24 February 1956), p. 3. Winner went on to be a famed film director and restaurant critic.

39   Sound Publicity Officer, 'Restricted Songs and Records', BBC Internal Memo (29 February 1956), BBC Archives, R44/840/1.

40   'Radio Price Battle with Television', *The Times* (August 25 1954), p. 3. The article did not identify the gramophone, but it could have been the HMV 102, which was still in production.

41   *Hansard*, HC Deb 28 April 1959 vol. 604 cc1106-231.

42   *Hansard*, HC Deb 25 October 1950 vol. 478 cc2766-8. The colony gained independence in 1957 and is now Ghana.

43   *Hansard*, HC Deb 28 January 1953 vol. 510 c116W.

44   National Army Museum, *Kenya Emergency* (undated), www.nam.ac.uk/ explore/Kenya-Emergency.

45   'Gramophones Used for Subversion', *The Times* (19 August 1955), p. 5.

46   Cooper, *The Perfect Portable Gramophone* (2003), p. 69. The final two years of production made use of the stock of parts held by EMI. Presumably production ceased when these parts were used up.

47   For a complete list of Beatles 78s see www.45worlds.com/78rpm/artist/ the-beatles.

Chapter 11

1   The event took place in Norwich. If memory serves me right, the year was around 2006 but I have no evidence to back this up.

2   Schlemowitz, interview (12 May 2018).

3   In *78 rpm*.

4   Wilson, interview (23 March 2018).

5   In *78rpm*.

6   Durham, interview (23 May 2018).

7 In *78rpm*.

8 Proudfoot, email (21 March 2018).

9 Guttridge, interview (19 March 2018).

10 Buck, interview (12 April 2018).

11 Bonham's Auctioneers—all prices include buyers' premiums of 25 per cent, www.bonhams.com/.

12 Derbyshire, 'Gramophones and early records could be sound investments' (25 May 2017), www.antiquestradegazette.com/news/2017/gramophones-and-early-records-could-be-sound-investments/.

13 Bonham's Auctioneers, www.bonhams.com/.

14 Nauck's Vintage Record Auction 63 (April 2018), www.78rpm.com/. In 2010 an example of this disc sold for $12,000: Sliwiki, *The blues lead to some serious green in online auctions* (16 November 2010), www.goldminemag.com/collector-resources/the-blues-lead-to-some-serious-green-in-online-auctions.

15 Federation of Recorded Music Societies, http://www.thefrms.co.uk/.

16 Hammerton, email (10 April 2018).

17 Wilson, interview (23 March 2018)

18 Martland, *Caruso's First Recordings: Myth and Reality* (1994), pp. 192–201.

19 The Great 78 Project can be found at great78.archive.org/.

20 Wilson, interview (23 March 2018)

[All websites were accessed on 14 October 2018 unless otherwise noted.]

Bibliography

Abravanel, G., *Americanizing Britain* (Oxford: Oxford University Press, 2012)

Adorno, T., *The Curves of the Needle* translated by Levin, T. Y. (October Magazine, 1990)

Baker, R. A., *British Music Hall* (Barnsley: Pen and Sword, 2014)

Bankes, A., 'The Ordeal of Being Married to Augustus John' (*The Spectator*, 31 August 1929)

Barnett, K. S., 'Furniture Music: The Phonograph as Furniture, 1900–1930' (*Journal of Popular Music Studies*, 18:3: 2006)

Beardsley, R, and Leech-Wilkinson, D., 'A Brief History of Recording to *ca.* 1950' (charm.rhul.ac.uk, undated)

Begbie, H., 'Making the Gramophone Records' (*The Times*, 20 January 1905)

Berry, W. H., *How I Sing to make Records* (Talking Machine News, May 1903)

Benson, E. F., *Mapp and Lucia: Queen Lucia* (London: BBC Books, 2014)

Benson, E. F., *Dodo Wonders* (New York: George H. Doran and Company, 1921)

Berliner, E., *The Gramophone. Etching the Human Voice* (Philadelphia: Franklin Institute, 1888)

Brinton, R. S., *Carpets* (London: Sir Isaac Pitman Ltd, 1919)

Brophy, W., 'How Dansette failed in the big time' (*The Times*, 23 October 1969)

Brunn, H., *The Story of the Original Dixieland Jazz Band* (London: Jazz Book Club / Sidgwick and Jackson, 1963)

Bouckley, H., 'From Marconi and the Transistor Radio to DAB' (bt.com, undated)

Burrows, A. R., Untitled (*Radio Times*, 28 September 1923)

C. L. G., 'The Decline of Domestic Music' (*The Spectator*, 1906)

Cartwright, G., *Going for a Song: A Chronicle of the UK Record Shop* (London: Flood Gallery Publishing, 2018)

Collins, D., *Souvenir of Oulton* (Blickling: Privately published, 1995)

Conan-Doyle, A., *The Complete Sherlock Holmes: The Adventure of the Mazarin Stone* (London: Vintage Books, 2009)

Cooper, D., *The Perfect Portable Gramophone* (London: New Cavendish Books, 2003)

Cowley, J., *West Indian Gramophone Records in Britain, 1927–1950. Occasional Papers in Ethnic Relations, No. 1* (Coventry: Centre for Research in Ethnic Relations, 1985)

Cox, C. and Warner, D., eds., *Audio Culture: Reading in Modern Music* (London: Continuum, 2004)

Cutlack, D., 'Tunnels, Colditz and Steve McQueen—Great Escapes at the IWM' (culture24.org, 2005)

Dare, D. A., Letter (*Jazz Journal*, April 1952)

Décharné, M., *Vulgar Tongues. An Alternative History of English Slang* (London: Serpent's Tail, 2016)

Derbyshire, T., 'Gramophones and early records could be sound investments' (antiquestradegazette.com, 2017)

Edison, T. A., 'The Phonograph and its Future' (*The North American Review*, May–June 1878)

Faire, L., *Making Home. Working-Class Perceptions of Space, Time and Material Culture in Family Life, 1900–1955.* Unpublished PhD thesis (Leicester: University of Leicester, 1998)

Feaster, P., 'Édouard-Léon Scott de Martinville: An Annotated Discography' (*ASRC Journal XLI*: i, 2010)

Feaster, P., ed., 'The Phonautographic Manuscripts of Édouard-Léon Scott de Martinville' (FirstSounds.org, 2010)

Featherstone, S., 'Chevalier, Albert Onésime Britannicus Gwathveoyd Louis' (oxforddnb.com, undated)

Foot, M. R. D., *SOE In France: An account of the work of the Special Operations Executive in France, 1940–44* (Abingdon: Frank Cass Publishers, 2004)

Friedman, H., *The Collector's Guide to Gramophone Company Record Labels, 1898–1925* (Music Web International e-book, 2013)

Galsworthy J., *The Inn of Tranquillity: Studies and Essays* (University of Adelaide e-books edition, 2016)

Gouraud, G. E., Letter (*The Times*, 27 June 1888)

Grainger, P., 'Collecting with the Phonograph' (*Journal of the Folk Song Society*, 1908)

Granville Soames, A., Letter (*The Times*, 17 November 1925)

Greig, R., 'Joseph Taylor of Lincolnshire: a biography of a singer: Folk Song Tradition, Revival and Re-Creation', *Occasional Publications* (3) (Aberdeen: Elphinstone Institute, University of Aberdeen, 2004)

Heylin, C., *Bootleg: the secret history of the other recording industry* (New York: St Martin's Press, 1995)

Hoffmann F., ed., *Encyclopedia of Recorded Sound* (Abingdon: Routledge, 2005)

Hogenboom, M., 'How the GI influx shaped Britain's views of Americans' (*BBC News Magazine*, 3 November 2012)

Houston, E. A., 'On the Gramophone' (*Proceedings of the American Philosophical Society*: 24:126: 420–421, 18 November 1887)

Hubert, P. G., 'The New Talking Machines' (*The Atlantic*, 63:2: February 1889)

Huffman, L., 'Development of Electrical Recording' (Stokowski.org, undated)

Humphries B., *Handling Edna: the unauthorised biography* (London: Orion Books, 2010)

Hylton, J., 'Why I Play Jazz' (*Radio Times*, 1925)

Jackson, E., *Rhythm Style, Series 2* (London: Parlophone Company, undated, probably 1941–2)

'James', '363 Oxford Street' (HMV.com, undated)

Johns, W. E., *Biggles In France* (London: The Boy's Friend Library No. 501, 1935)

Jones, G., 'The Gramophone Company: An Anglo-American Multinational, 1898–1931' (*Business History Review*, 1985) 59:1:76–100

Joyce, J., *Ulysses* (Paris: Shakespeare and Company, 1922)

Kruse, H., *Early Audio Technology and Domestic Space* (Stanford Humanities Review 3:2: 1993)

Lambert, J., 'History of the Dansette' (Dansettes.co.uk, undated)

Langdon-Davies, J., 'Gramophone Notes' (*The Spectator*, 28 September 1929)

Langdon-Davies, J., 'The Gramophone' (*The Spectator*, 31 August 1929)

Langdon-Davies, J., 'Gramophone Notes' (*The Spectator*, 10 October 1931)

Lasser, M., *America's Songs II: songs from the 1890s to the post-war years* (Abingdon: Routledge, 2014)

Leech-Wilkinson D., *The Changing Sound of Music: Approaches to studying recorded musical performances* (London: Centre for the History and Analysis of Recorded Music, 2009)

Library of Congress online, 'Emile Berliner and the Birth of the Recording Industry' (loc.gov, undated)

Library of Congress online, 'The Gramophone, invented by E Berliner, "Reproducing the Human Voice"' (loc.gov, undated)

Library of Congress online, 'Berliner's wishes for when he dies' (loc.gov, undated)

Lumley, J., 'Joanna Lumley's Diary' (*The Times*, 13 July 1983)

Mackenzie, C., 'Our Symposium' (*The Gramophone*, December 1926)

Mackenzie, C., 'Quarterly Review of Records' (*The Gramophone*, July 1927)

Mann, A., 'September 22, 1955: Commercial television comes to Britain as ITV goes on air' (bt.com, 2017)

Martland, P., *Since Records Began. EMI the first 100 years* (London: B. T. Batsford, 1997)

Martland, S. P., *Business History of the Gramophone Company Ltd 1897–1918*. Unpublished PhD thesis (Cambridge: University of Cambridge, 1992)

Martland, S. P., 'Caruso's First Recordings: myth and reality' (*ARSC Journal*, 25:2, 1994)

Maxfield, J. P. and Harrison, H. C., 'Methods of High Quality Recording and Reproducing of Music and Speech Based on Telephone Research' (*Bell System Technical Journal*, 1926)

McCarthy, C., 'Development of the BBC A.M. Transmitter Network' (mds975.com, May 2007)

Melly, G., *Owning Up, The Trilogy* (London: Penguin Books, 2000)

Merchandising Survey of Great Britain: Volume VII Gramophones (London: Lord and Thomas Logan Ltd, 1930)

Mitchell, O., *The Talking Machine Industry* (London: Sir Isaac Pitman and Sons, 1924)

Musical Resources: gramophone records (BBC Archive C1/99, undated)

National Public Radio, 'Old, Lewd, Recordings Released on CD' (npr.org, undated)

Nice, D., 'Elgar: Falstaff—Symphonic Study in C Minor, Op. 68' (bbc.co.uk, 2016)

Nice, D., *BBC Record Review podcast* (bbc.co.uk, undated)

Nicholson, V., *Among the Bohemians: Experiments in Living 1900–1939* (London: Penguin Books, 2003)

Notes from the Emerald Isle (Talking Machine World, 1906)

Oakley, B., and Proudfoot, C., *His Master's Gramophone* (London: self-published, 2011)

Osborne, R., *Vinyl: A history of the analogue record* (Farnham: Ashgate Publishing, 2014)

Pallett, R., 'Al Bowlly' (memorylane.org.uk, undated)

Pennell C. R., *Morocco Since 1830: A History* (London: C. Hurst and Co., 2000)

Pereyra, D., 'Jack Hylton Discography' (static1.squarespace.com, 2007)

Phillips R. R., 'First Hand: Bing Crosby and the Recording Revolution' (ethw.org, undated)

Price, D., *Gramophone Library History 1922–1992* (unpublished and undated, BBC Archive S333/3/1)

Rubery, M., *From Shell Shock to Shellac: The Great War, Blindness and Britain's Talking Book Library* (Twentieth Century British History, May 2014)

Rubery, M., 'Audiobook History' (audiobookhistory.wordpress.com, undated)

Rust, B., Untitled (*Jazz Journal*, November 1951)

Rust, B. and Debus, A. G., *The Complete Entertainment Discography, from the mid-1890s to 1942* (London: Arlington House, 1973)

Rutgers University, *Thomas A. Edison Papers* (edison.rutgers.edu, undated)

Samuel, E., 'Decca Days—the career of Wilfred Sampson Samuel, 1886–1958' (*Jewish Historical Studies*, 1987–88)

Sassoon, S., 'Dead Musicians' (ww1lit.nsms.ox.ac.uk, originally published 1918)

Sayers, D. L., *The Second Omnibus of Crime* (New York: Blue Ribbon Books, 1932)

Scholes, P. A., *The First Book of the Gramophone* (Oxford: Oxford University Press, 1924)

Self, D., 'The Auxetophone' (douglas-self.com)

Silver, P. and Silver, H., *The Education of the Poor: the History of a National School, 1824–1974* (London: Routledge, 1974)

Sliwiki, S., 'The blues lead to some serious green in online auctions' (goldminemag.com, 2010)

Sousa, J. P., 'The Menace of Mechanical Music' (*Appleton's Magazine*, September 1906)

Spragg, D. M., *V-Discs* (Boulder: Glenn Miller Archive, University of California Boulder, 2013)

Stanley, B., *Yeah, Yeah, Yeah: the story of modern pop* (London: Faber and Faber, 2013)

Sterling, L., 'Conditions In the Talking Machine Industry In Britain' (*Talking Machine World*, 15 April 1918)

Stoker, B., *Dracula* (London: Archibald Constable and Co., 1897)

Stone, C. R., 'A Decca Romance' (*The Gramophone*, August1923)

Stone, C., Letter (*The Times*, 1 September 1942)

Strötbaum, H., ed., 'The Fred Gaisberg Diaries, Parts 1 and 2' (recordingpioneers.com, 2010)

Sturdy, W. L., Untitled (*Talking Machine World*, 15 August 1923)

Sturdy, W. L., Untitled (*Talking Machine World*, 15 September 1923)

Sutton, A., 'Black Swan Carusos and Other Pirate Tales (1898–1951)' (78records.wordpress.com, 2017)

Symes, C., 'A sound education: the gramophone and the classroom in the United Kingdom and the United States, 1920–1940' (*British Journal of Music Education*, June 2004)

Taylor, D. J., *Bright Young People* (London: Vintage Books, 2008)

'The Story of BBC Television' (bbc.co.uk, undated)

Vacher, P., 'Ottilie Patterson obituary' (guardian.com, 8 July 2011)

Vernhettes, D., *Commemoration of the Centenary of the arrival of the African-American military bands in France during World War I* (Ivry-sur-Seine: Jazzedit, 2017)

Waugh, E., *Decline and Fall* (London: Chapman and Hall, 1928)

Wells, H. G., *The War in the Air* (Wikisource e-book, 2015. Originally published 1908)

Wells, H. G., *Marriage* (London: Macmillan, 1912)

Westphal, M., 'Paris Opera Unearths 100-year-old Recordings by Melba, Caruso, Others' (*Playbill*, 18 December 2007)

Wile, R. R., 'Record Piracy: the attempts of the sound recording industry to protect itself against unauthorised copying' (*ARSC Journal*, 17: 1: 1985)

Wile, R. R., 'Etching the Human Voice: the Berliner Invention of the Gramophone' (*ARSC Journal*, 21: 1: 1990)

Winner, M., 'Focus on BBC Song-Banning' (*New Musical Express*, 24 February 1956)

Wodehouse P. G., *Mike* (Wikisource e-book, 2012. Originally published 1909)

Young, R., *Electric Eden: unearthing Britain's visionary music* (London: Faber and Faber, 2011)